I0799869

IMAGES
of America

EAST BRONX

EAST OF THE BRONX RIVER

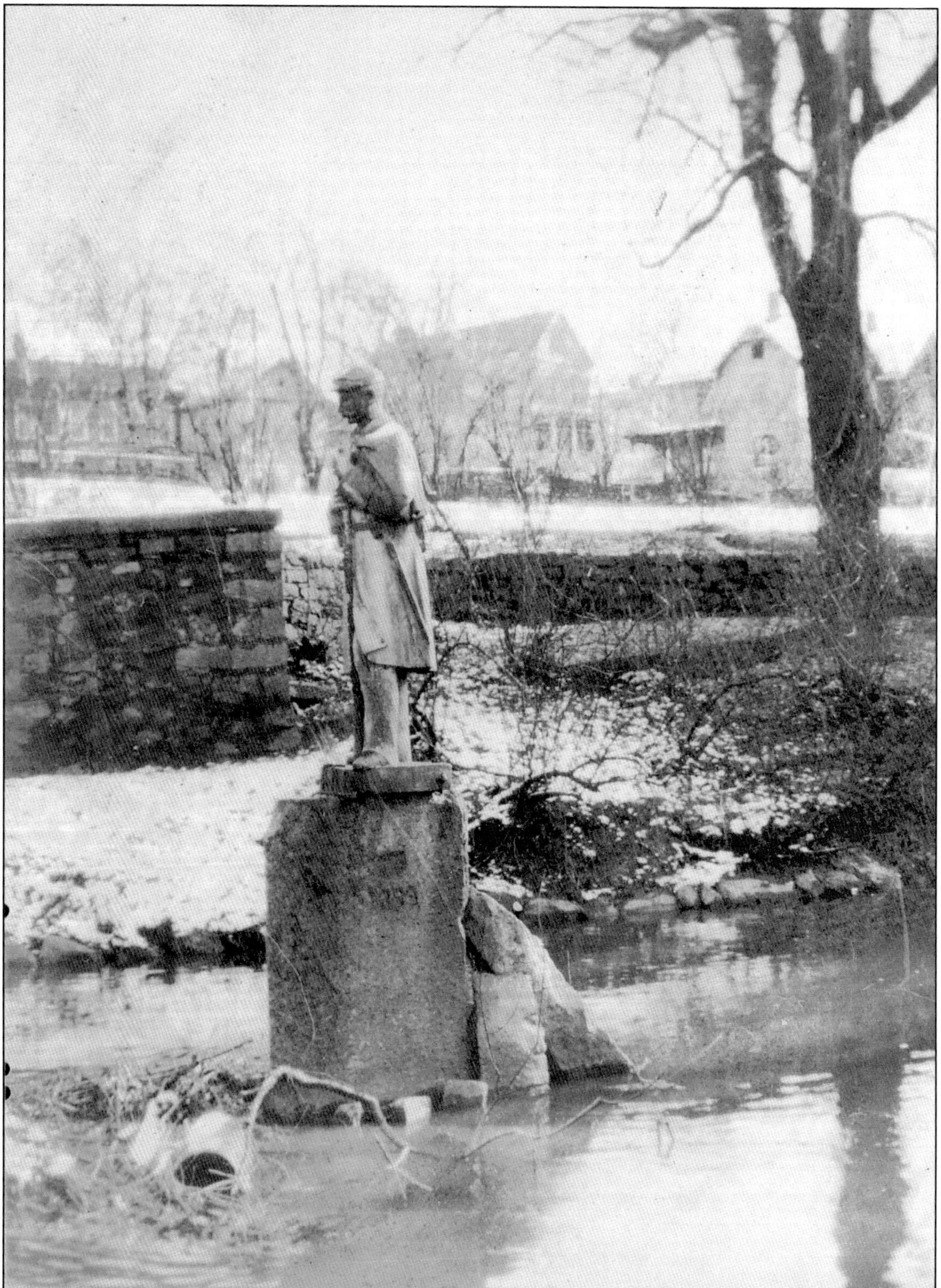

This statue of a Civil War soldier was sculptured by John Grignola. It stood on a pedestal in the Bronx River, south of Gun Hill Road, from 1898 to 1964. After it fell off its pedestal into the river, it was removed to the Parks Department facility at 173rd Street and Amsterdam Avenue. It was restored and moved to the grounds of the Valentine-Varian House in August of 1970. This 1932 photograph was supplied by John McNamara.

IMAGES
of America

EAST BRONX

EAST OF THE BRONX RIVER

Bill Twomey

ARCADIA
PUBLISHING

ISBN 978-0-7385-0301-1

Published by Arcadia Publishing
Charleston, South Carolina

Printed in the United States of America

For all general information contact Arcadia Publishing at:
Telephone 843-853-2070
Fax 843-853-0044
E-mail sales@arcadiapublishing.com
For customer service and orders:
Toll-Free 1-888-313-2665

Visit us on the Internet at www.arcadiapublishing.com

Dedicated to my wife and friend
Carol Twomey

CONTENTS

ACKNOWLEDGMENTS

This book would not have been possible without the help from some great friends. Ron Schliessman, John McNamara, Arthur Seifert, and the *Bronx Times Reporter* have supplied a number of the photographs presented here, and they have my heartfelt thanks. John McNamara also drew the area sketches. Gratitude is also extended to the Chippewa Democratic Club, Preston High School, the Bronx County Historical Society, Ken Roberts, John V. Riche, Jack McCarrick, Carol Gross, May Mastrarrigo, Skippy Lane, Italo Mazzella, Peter Macchia, John Pye, Frank Twomey Jr., Catherine Converso, Edward Wolf, the Scolaro and Slattery families, Ted Goodfleisch, Bob Barrett, Larry Haskell, John Carraher, Greta Zarookian, May Doherty, Edna Abraham, and Jim McSwigin.

INTRODUCTION

The area currently known as the Bronx was once part of Westchester County. That section west of the Bronx River was annexed to New York City in 1874. The area east of the river became part of the city in 1895; it is this area that the book seeks to detail.

Much of the development had to do with the arrival of mass transit; between 1910 and 1940, the population of the Bronx increased by over 300 percent. This growth coincides with the extension of the subway system into the borough. The White Plains Road Line of the Interborough Rapid Transit (IRT) swerved to the east side of the Bronx River at West Farms Square to the East 180th Street Station in 1920. The line had been scheduled to continue north at West Farms, but authorities at the Bronx Zoo objected to the potential adverse effect both the construction and subsequent noise would have on the animals. Thus, the line crossed the river and proceeded north to East 241st Street at White Plains Road, where the final station was opened on December 13, 1920. The Pelham Bay subway line rose above ground beyond Hunts Point Avenue to the first elevated station at Whitlock Avenue. It then crossed the Bronx River in 1920 and continued above ground along Westchester Avenue to Pelham Bay Park, where this last station on the line opened on December 20, 1920.

The erection of both elevated lines opened up suburbia to the masses seeking a more rural atmosphere in which to raise their families while retaining ready access to the city. Property values rose considerably, and soon, the vast estates and farms began to fall under the auctioneer's gavel. Waterfront areas from Pelham Bay south to Throggs Neck and west to Clason Point were soon spotted with summer bungalow colonies; when the Depression arrived, many of these summer homes became permanent residences. This coincided with the advent of the automobile industry. The Triborough Bridge opened on July 11, 1936, followed by the construction of the Hutchinson River Parkway and the opening of the Whitestone Bridge on April 29, 1939. They both had a great effect on the East Bronx in that the former facilitated vehicular travel to Manhattan and the latter brought motorists through previously rural and beautiful areas of the borough showcasing its appeal. The continued opening of the new roadways and the arrival of the Dyre Avenue line of the IRT in 1941 also helped expand the population. Even then, few people had ever heard of Throggs Neck, and its final development followed the opening of the Throgs Neck Bridge on January 11, 1961.

Since this work is limited to 128 pages, every aspect of life in the East Bronx cannot be shown, but it is hoped that the photographs available to me and presented here will offer an appealing view of the development of the Bronx east of the river. It is also my hope that it will give some insight into the lives and activities of the populace.

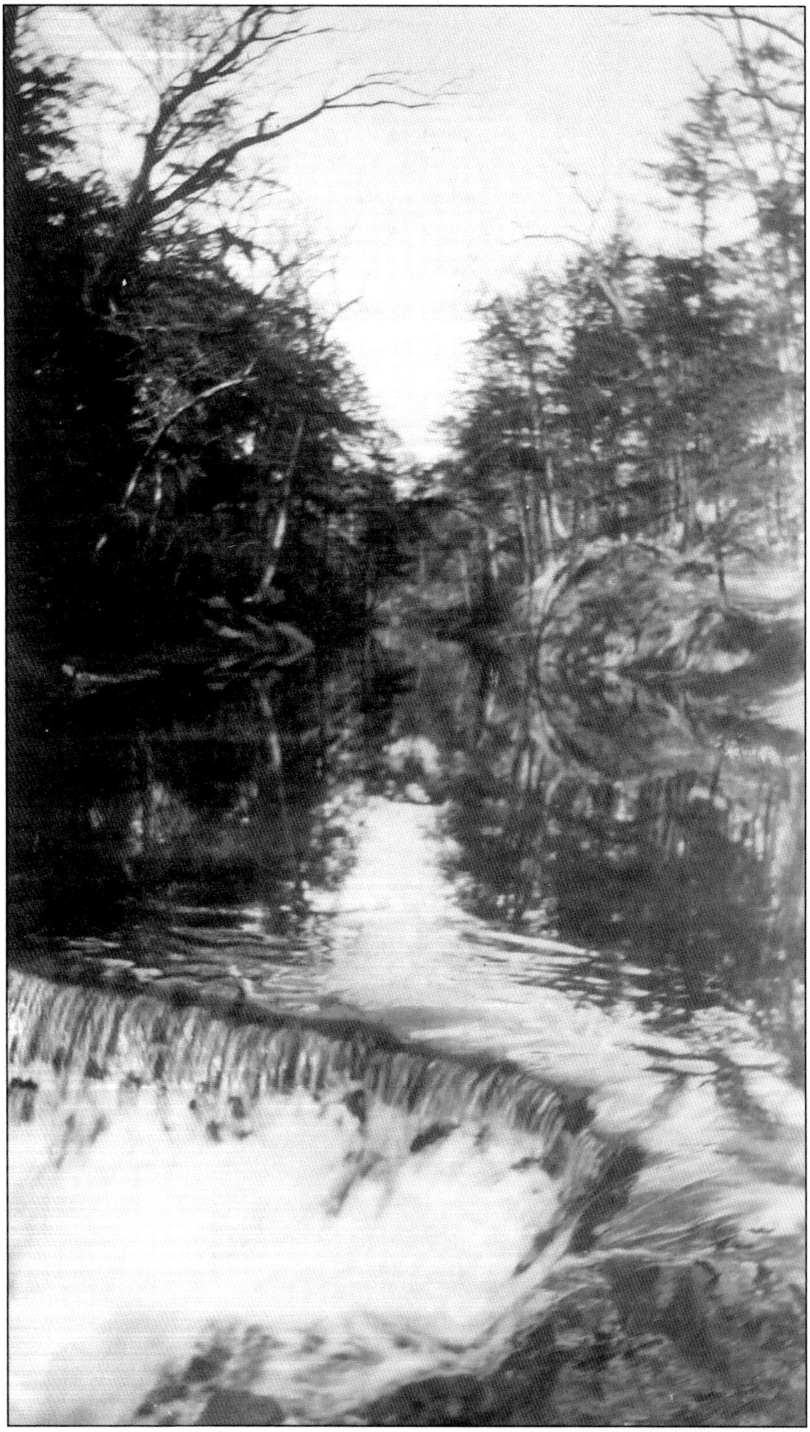

The Bronx River was the eastern boundary of the 1874 annexation and the western boundary of the 1895 annexation of the area we know as the Bronx from Westchester County to New York City. Supplied by John McNamara, this 1930 photograph was taken looking north toward the falls.

One

TRANSPORTATION

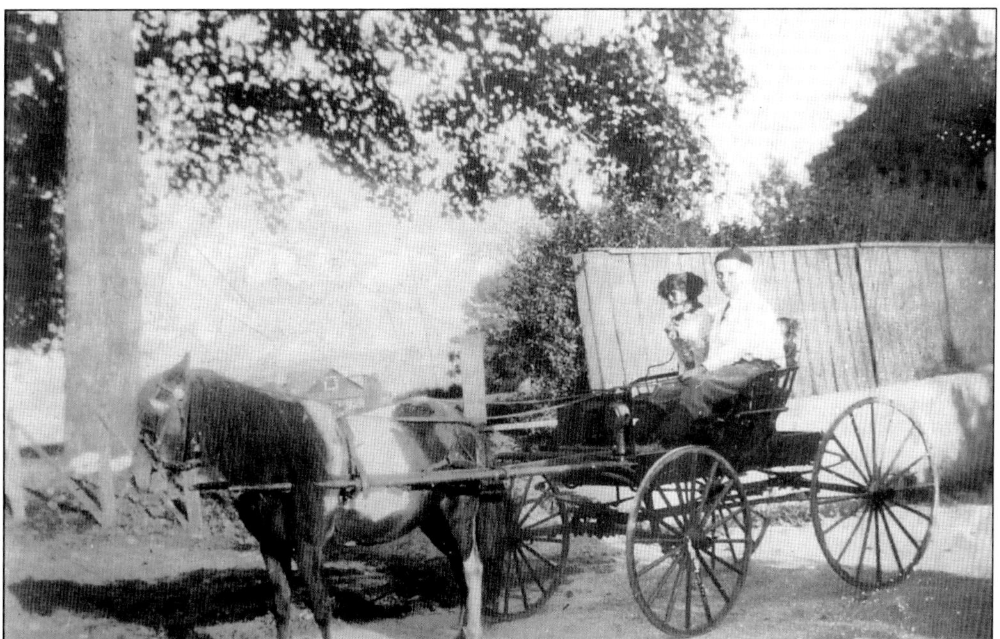

George Engeldrum was proud of his pony and cart; he can be seen driving on Longstreet Avenue, c. 1920. The dog seated next to him belonged to Gus Oppelt, a Viennese neighbor. John McNamara provided the photograph.

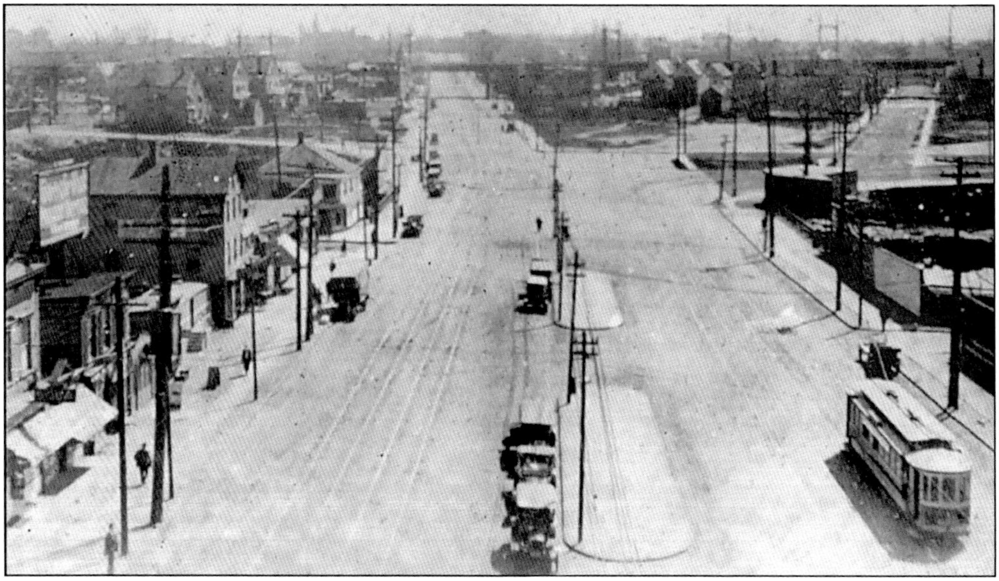

Ron Schliessman provided this view of West Farms Square, taken in 1918. Looking up Walker Avenue (now E. Tremont Avenue), the roadway angling in at the right is East 177th Street. The Bronx River runs north/south under Tremont Avenue where E. 177th Street starts. Starlight Park was once located at the right, on the east side of the river.

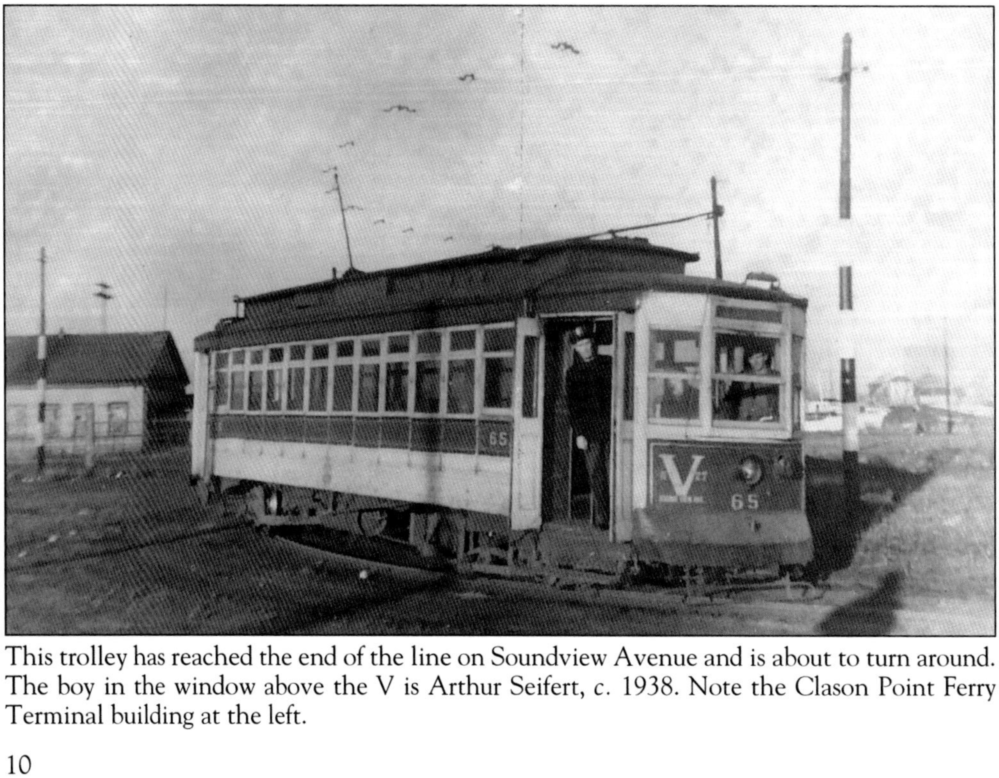

This trolley has reached the end of the line on Soundview Avenue and is about to turn around. The boy in the window above the V is Arthur Seifert, c. 1938. Note the Clason Point Ferry Terminal building at the left.

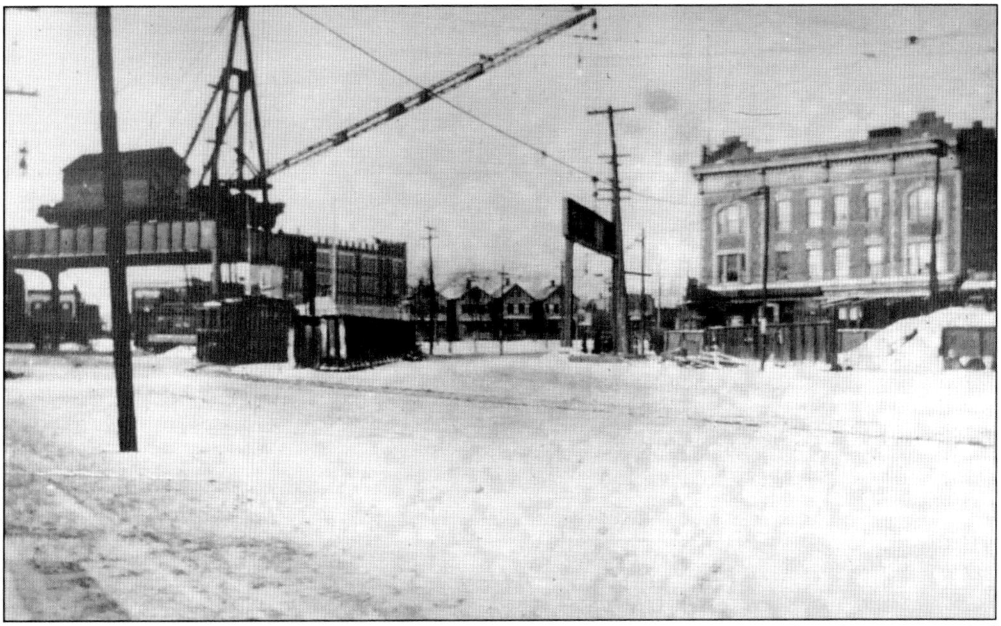

Ron Schliessman provided this photograph of the Westchester Avenue IRT line being extended beyond Westchester Square. A snow-laden East Tremont Avenue is in the foreground. The building at the right is still there; Councilman Michael DeMarco had his offices there until he became a judge. This photograph was taken shortly after the Westchester Square station opened on October 24, 1920.

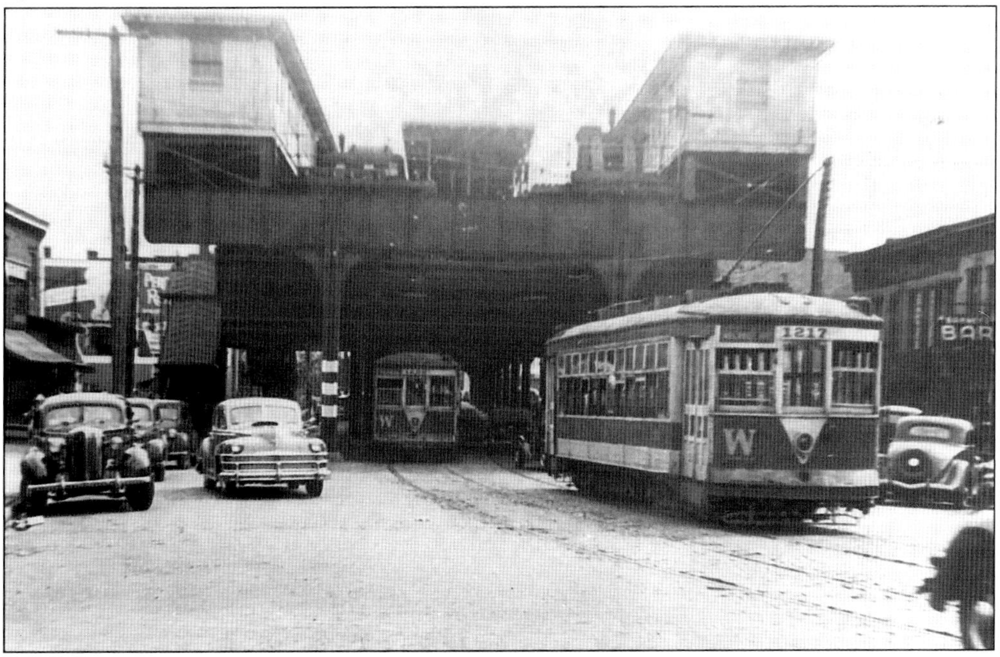

The White Plains Road elevated line was allowed to be extended as a result of the Rapid Transit Dual Contracts of 1913, and this final station on the line was opened on December 13, 1920. Ron Schliessman provided this 1947 photograph taken at White Plains Road and East 241st Street. The view looks to the south.

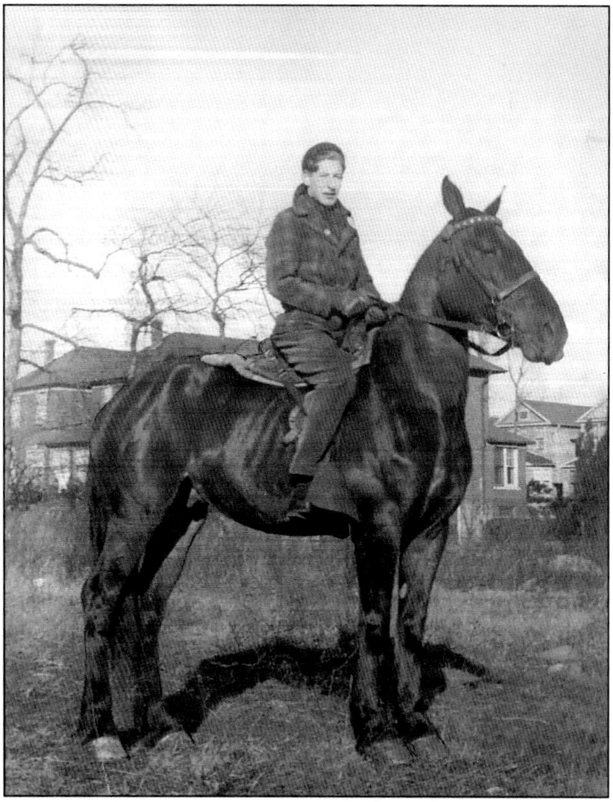

Walter Rohr was using a viable form of transportation in this 1940 photograph taken at Beach and Lacombe Avenues. He rented the steed for the day for $2; I'm not sure who provided the McClellan Army saddle. The photograph is from the Seifert Collection.

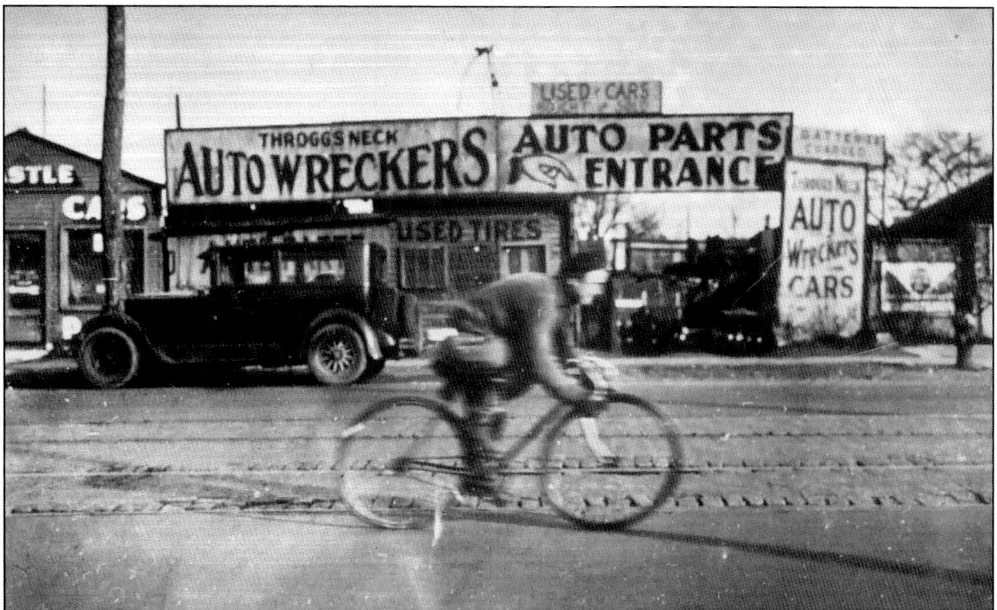

Ted Schliessman is riding his bicycle on E. Tremont Avenue in this 1920s photograph taken near Westchester Square. Throggs Neck Auto Wreckers can be seen in the background.

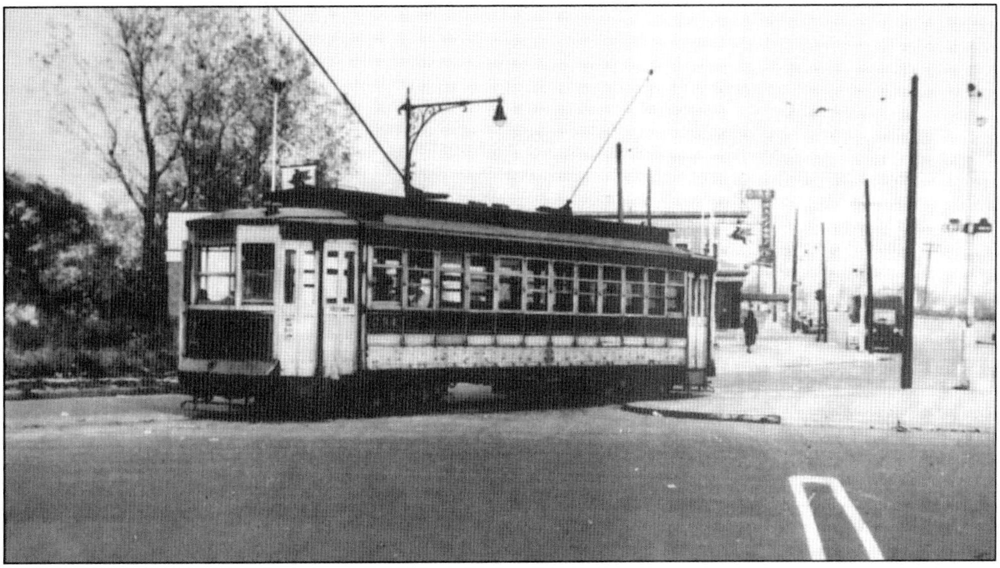

Ron Schliessman provided this photograph of the trolley at East 177th Street and Ludlow Avenue (now Bruckner Boulevard). The trolley traveled northwest along East 177th Street to West Farms. Ludlow Avenue is at the right, and Zerega Avenue crosses it just beyond the truck parked at the right. The sign between the trolley and the truck advertises Kaisers, which was popular for dining and dancing. The eatery also had a dock for access from Westchester Creek for those arriving by boat. Both East 177th Street and Ludlow Avenue lead to Unionport Bridge, which was just southeast of Kaisers. The photographer was facing east when he snapped this picture.

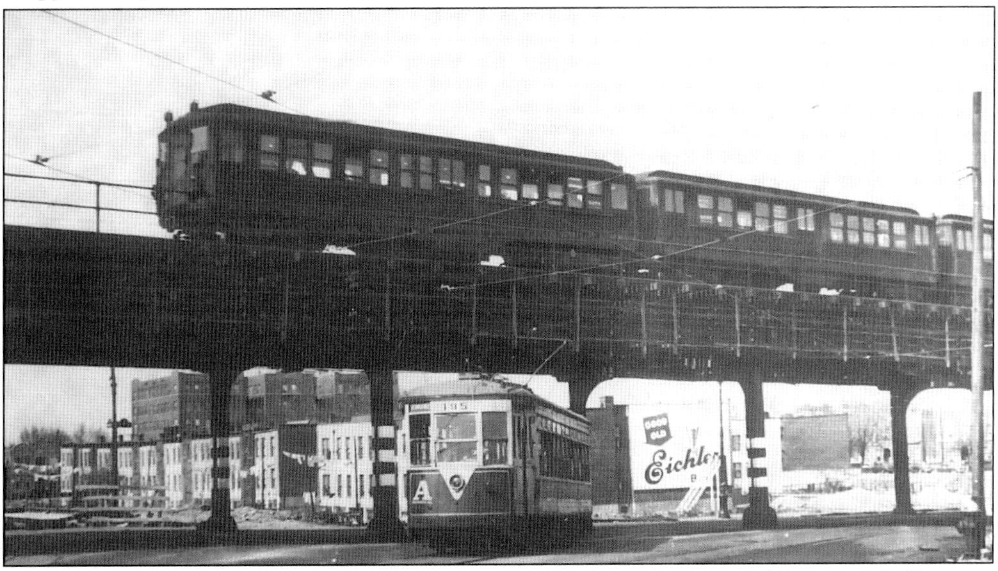

This photograph of the Westchester Avenue El came from the Ron Schliessman Collection. The train, traveling north, is the old type Gibbs with a single unit door; it is pulling the older style deck roof IRT cars on the #6 line. The A trolley (car #195) is facing forward below the elevated railway. Note the Eichler beer advertisement to the right and the construction activity to the left. Work was progressing on the extension of the Bronx River Parkway at Harrod Avenue. This view looks eastward.

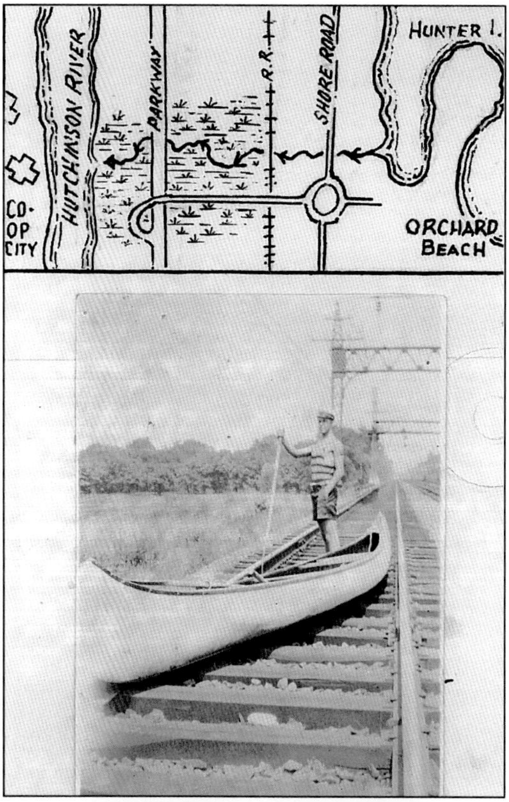

Ed McNamara portages his canoe over the NY, NH, & H railroad tracks below the Split Rock Golf Course in 1931. This old American Indian escape route is shown on the accompanying map as the winding waterway from Hunter Island.

Arthur Seifert took this photograph of Fred Fuellner, the farmer, in a 1915 Model T Ford in 1953. The farmhouse was located at Lafayette and St. Lawrence Avenues in Clason Point, and Arthur was looking east when he took this picture. Note the smokestacks in the far distance at the right. They are the only things in the picture that have not changed and are still located on Westchester Creek, beyond Zerega Avenue.

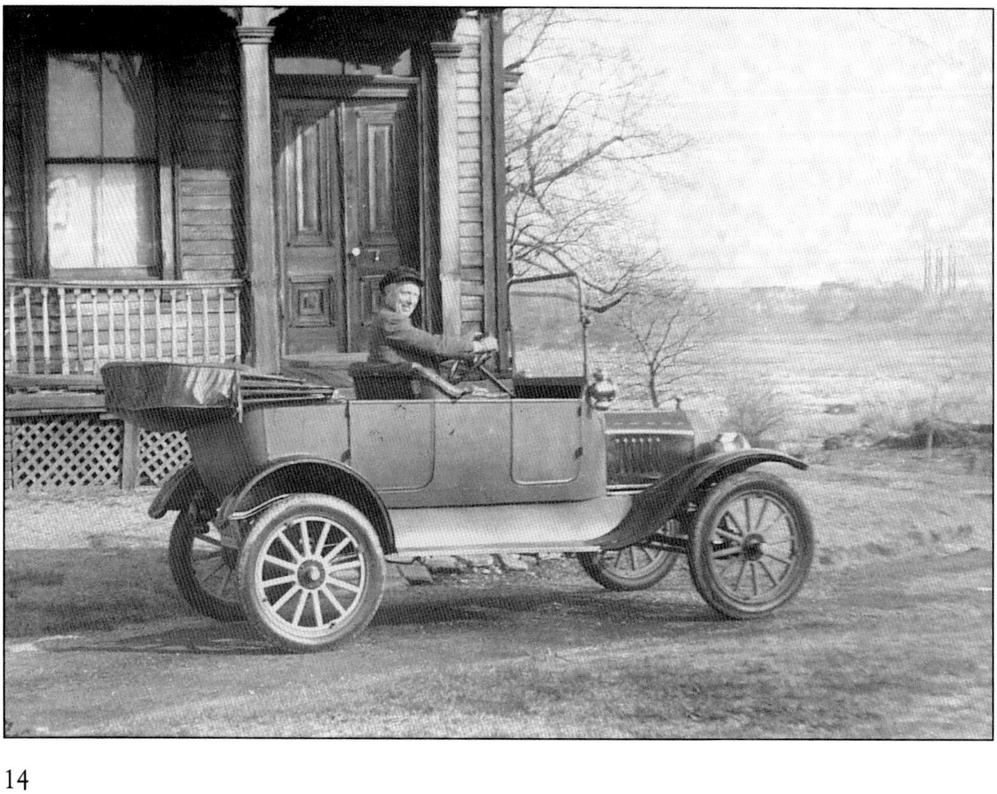

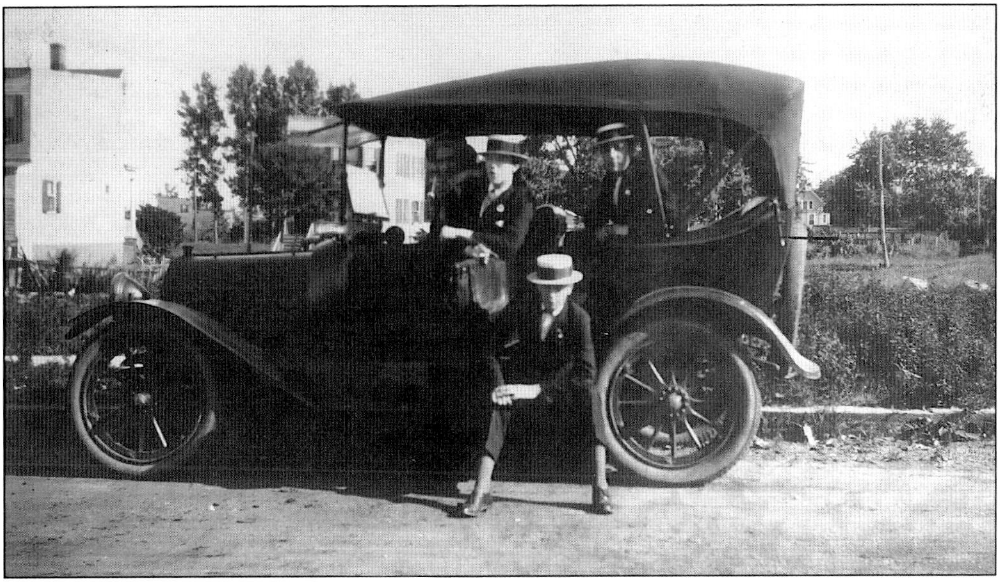

John McNamara provided this Donald Braithwaite image, photographed in June 1921. It was taken on Ludlow Avenue (now Bruckner Boulevard) in Clason Point. Braithwaite took quite a few pictures of the Unionport Walking Club, and this is one of the rare scenes where they are riding.

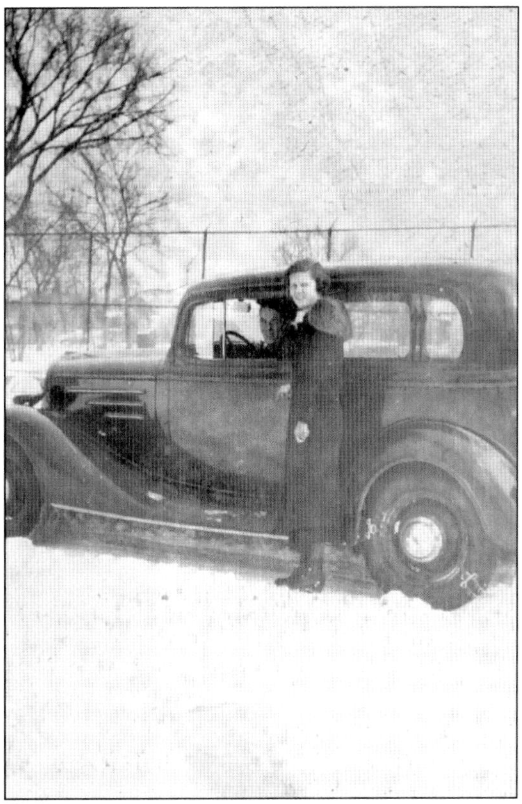

A young lady poses with a 1936 Dodge on Crosby Avenue at Eastern Boulevard (now Bruckner). The James Monroe High School Annex at the old P.S. 14 is in the background.

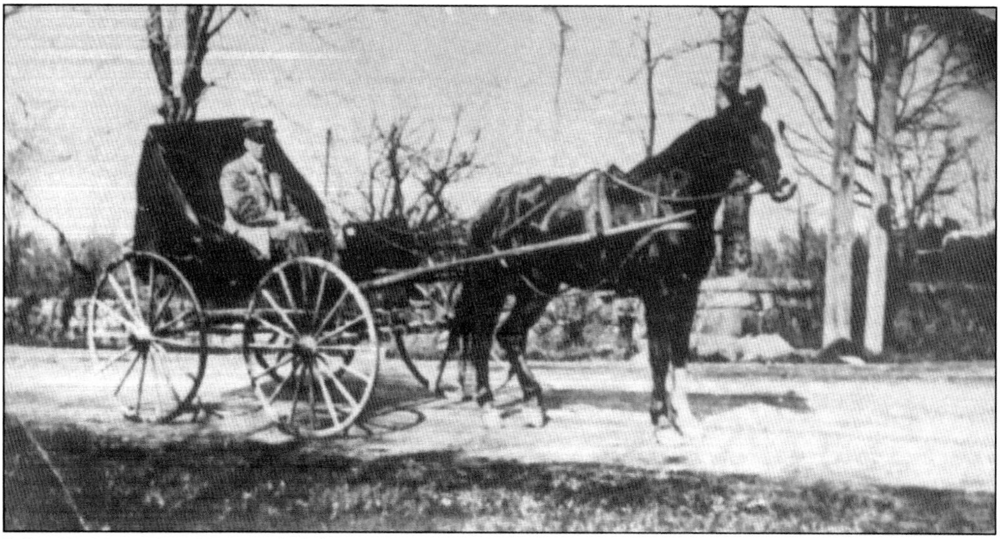

John T. Hunt (1869–1920) delivered mail in the northeast Bronx by horse and wagon in good weather and by horse and sled when snow conditions warranted.

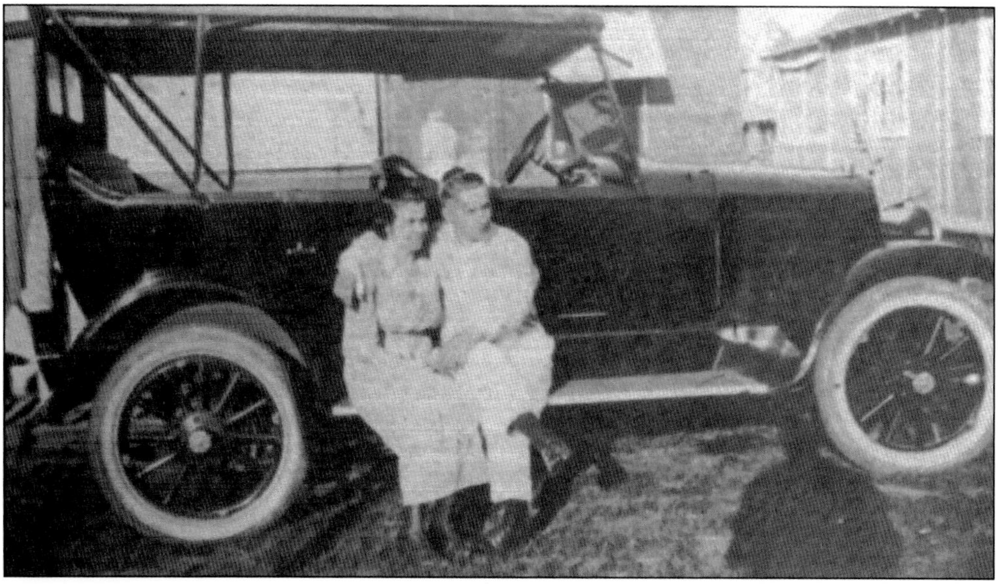

Marie and George Schultz of Edgewater Park enjoy the running board of this touring car. Note the work progressing on the bungalow in the right background during the Roaring Twenties.

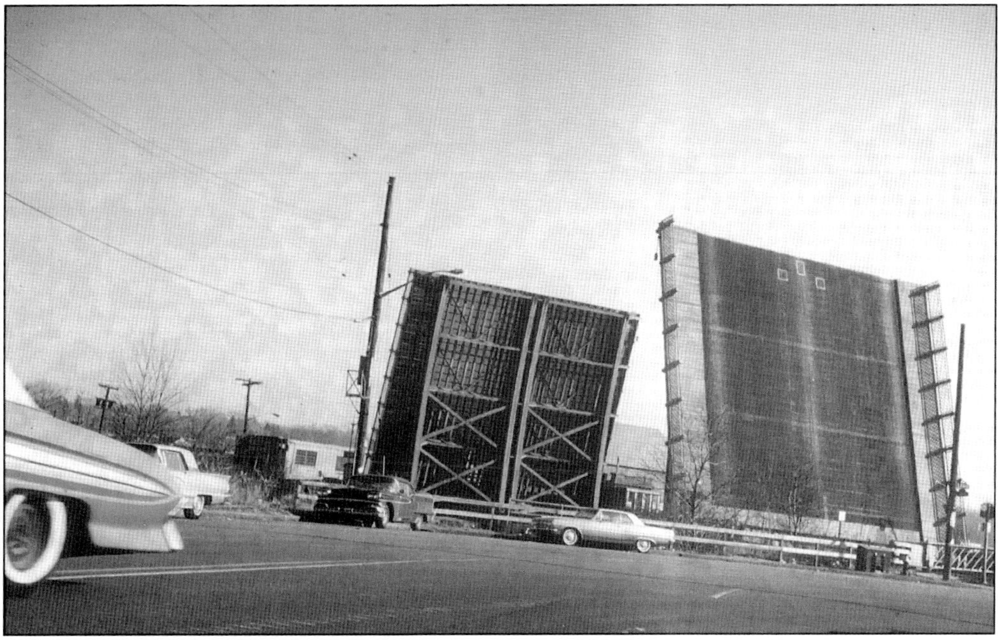

This great photograph of the Boston Road drawbridge in an open position was taken in December of 1965 by Ted Schliessman. The view is along East 233rd Street looking toward Boston Road.

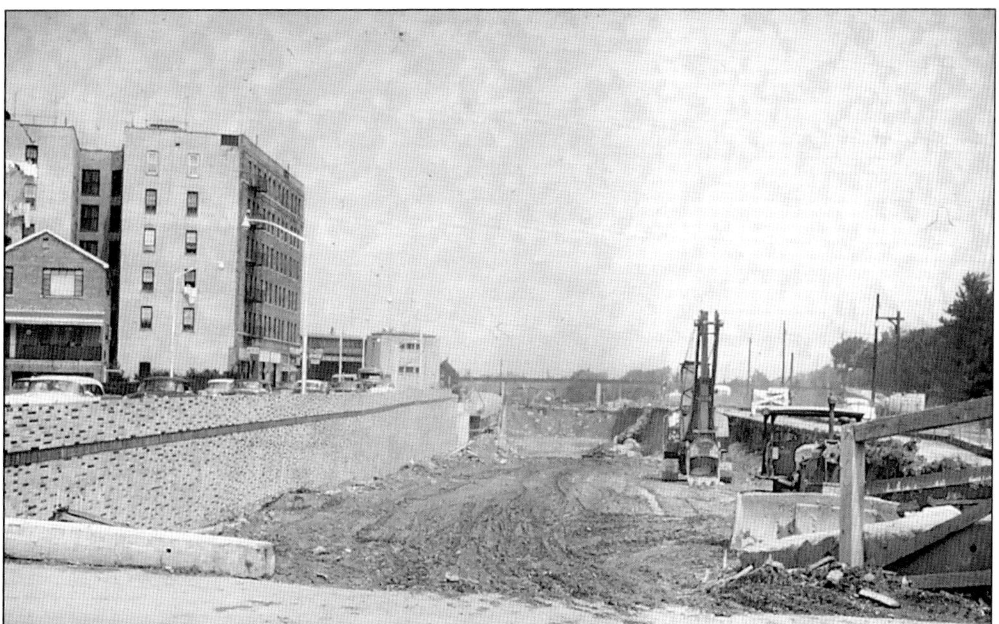

The Bruckner Expressway was under construction when Ted Schliessman took this photograph, c. October 1960. The view looks to the north toward the Pelham Bay Station of the IRT, which is seen to the left of the cut out roadbed.

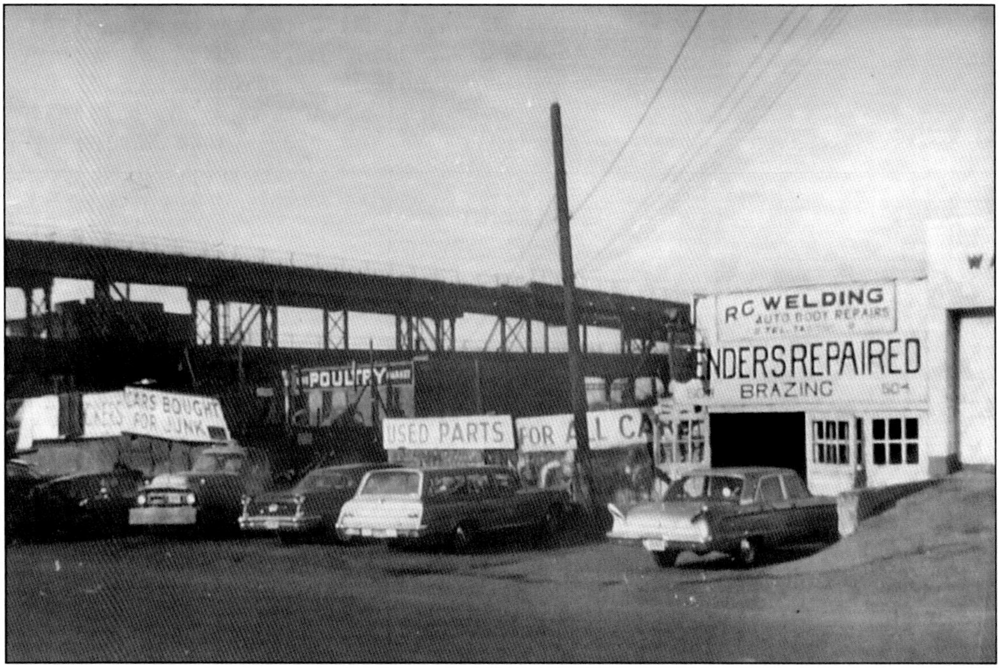

Tan place during the 1960s was still a popular spot for car parts or repairs as well as for the live poultry market seen in the background of this Ron Schliessman photograph. The Westchester Avenue El is in the background of this northward view.

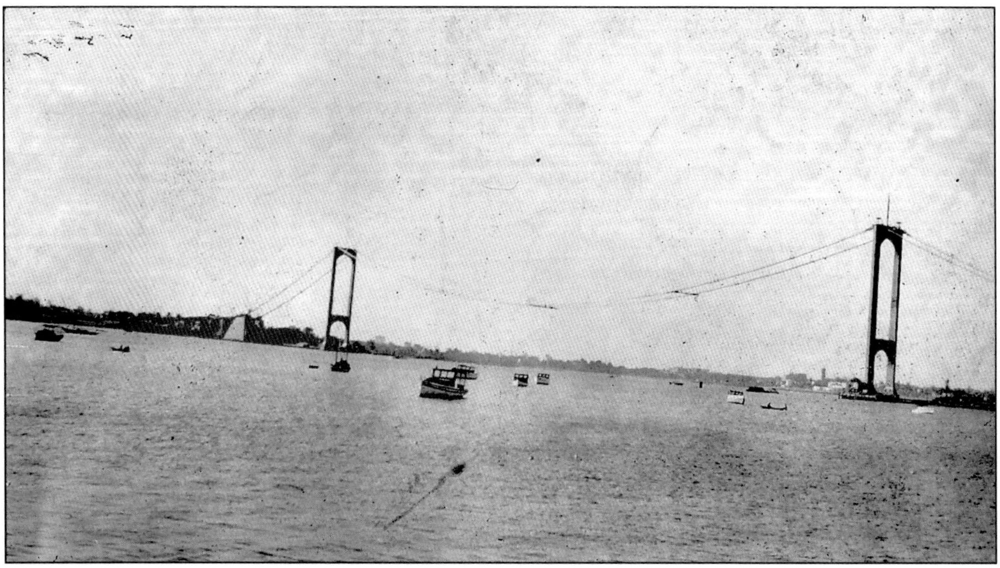

The Bronx-Whitestone Bridge was officially opened on April 29, 1939, and replaced the ferry that plied the waters between Clason Point and College Point. This photograph was taken in October of 1938, when the bridge was still under construction.

Two

Prayerful People and Places

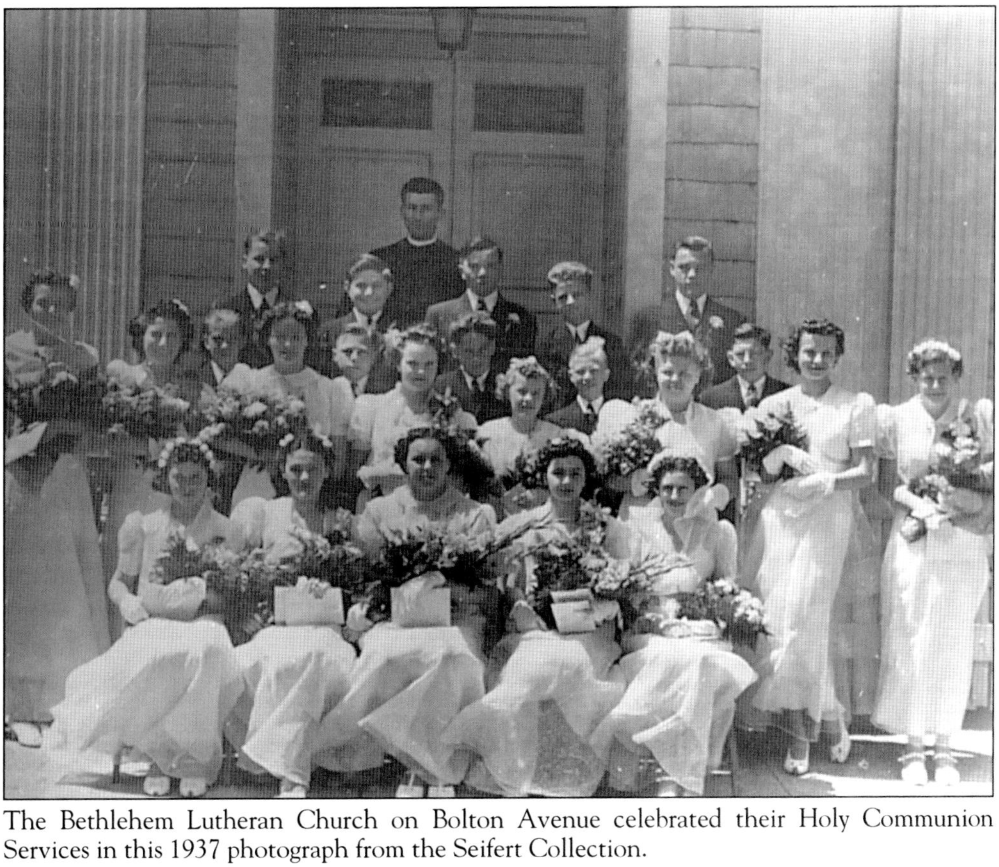

The Bethlehem Lutheran Church on Bolton Avenue celebrated their Holy Communion Services in this 1937 photograph from the Seifert Collection.

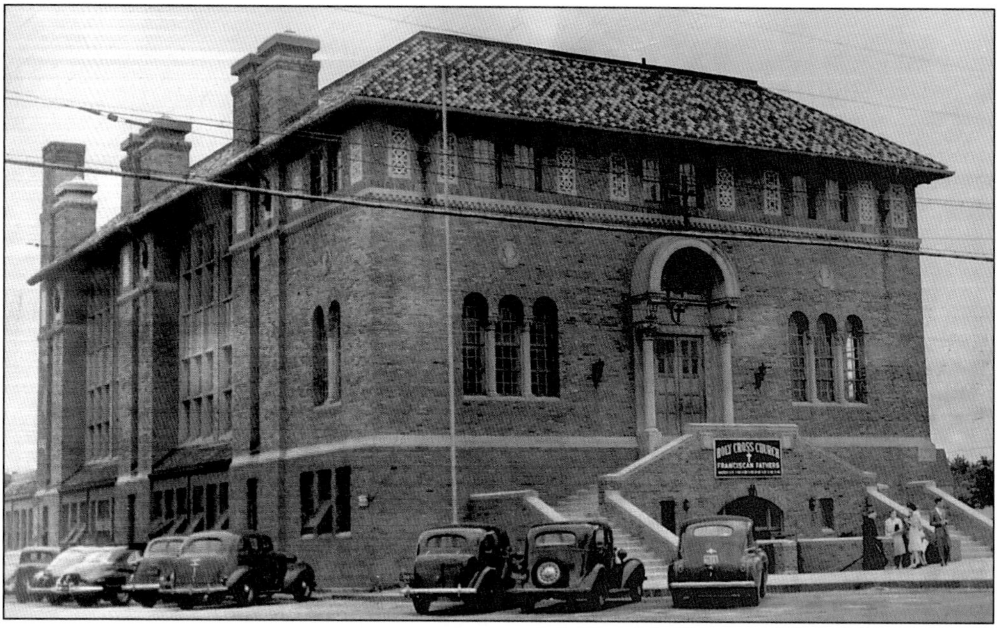

This photograph of Holy Cross Church and School at Soundview and Randall Avenues was taken *c.* 1949 and provided by Arthur Seifert. The property was part of Schmidt's Farms and was purchased in 1922 to establish a parish for the Catholics of Clason Point. They had previously celebrated Mass at Kane's Casino.

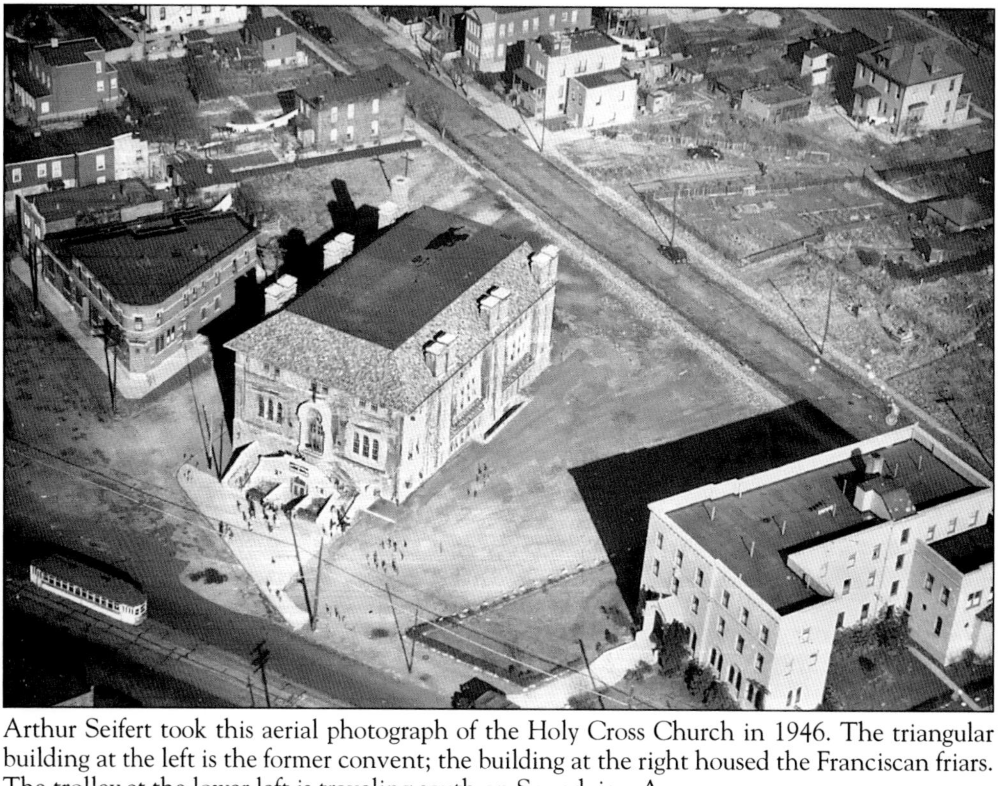

Arthur Seifert took this aerial photograph of the Holy Cross Church in 1946. The triangular building at the left is the former convent; the building at the right housed the Franciscan friars. The trolley at the lower left is traveling south on Soundview Avenue.

The honor guard for Cardinal Hayes at the dedication of St. Frances de Chantal Church and School is on the steps in the foreground of this picture taken in May 1930 on Harding Avenue. Note the now vintage vehicles on Throggs Neck Boulevard in the background.

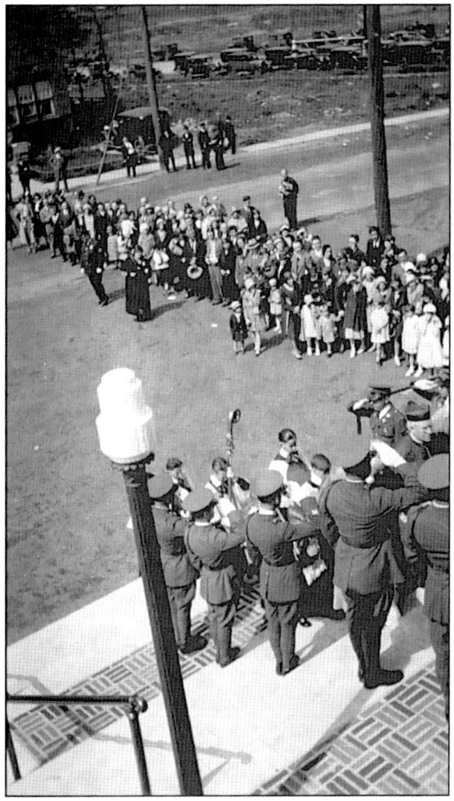

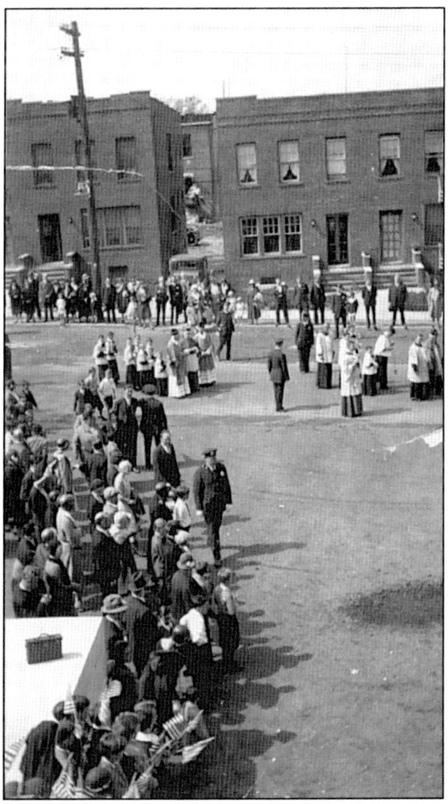

The dedication of St. Frances de Chantal Church and School on Harding Avenue took place in May of 1930; this photograph shows a part of the festivities. Note the American flags on the building in the right background and in the hands of the children in the foreground.

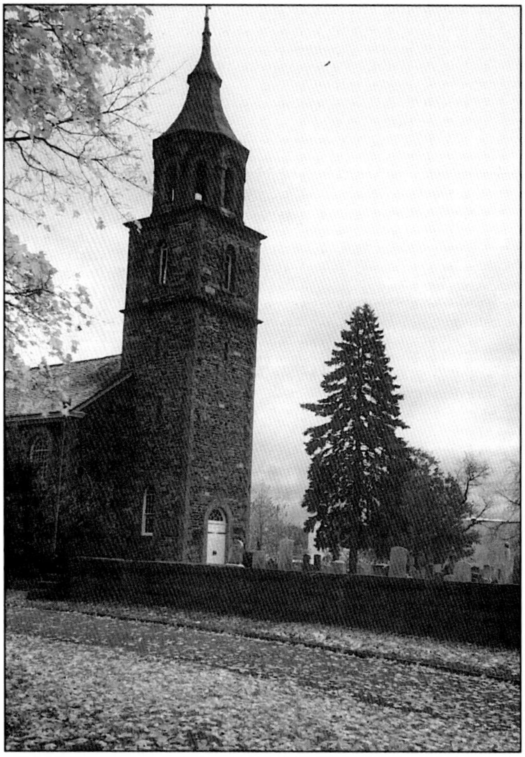

Construction of St. Paul's Church at the end of Provost Avenue, just over the Bronx line in Mount Vernon, was begun in 1765 to replace the old wooden structure that dated from 1700. The church played a part in the American Revolution and is one of the most historic sites in the area.

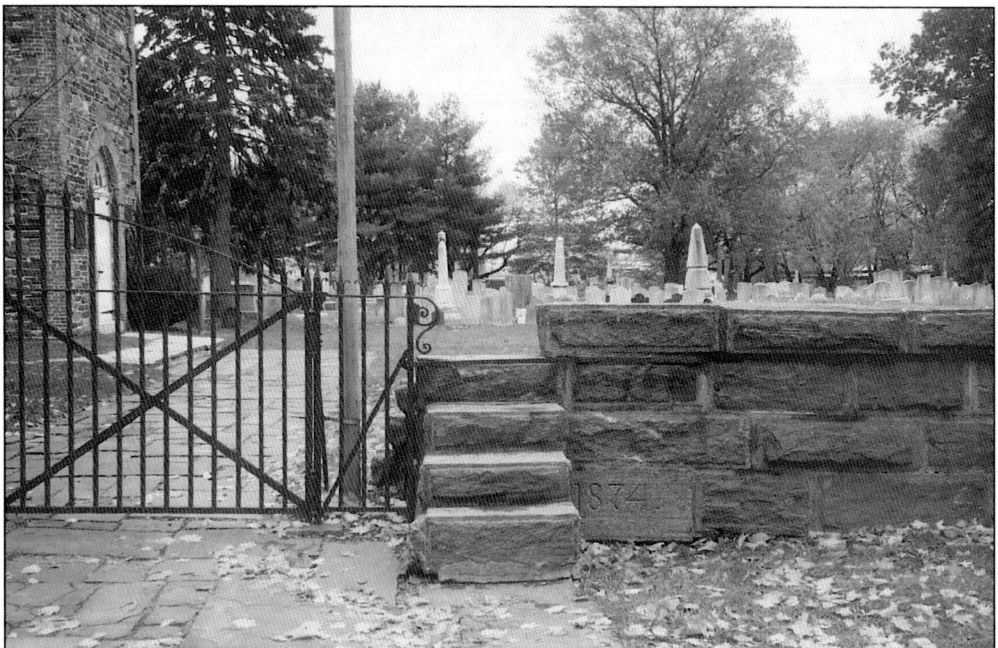

This stile at St. Paul's Church allowed the parishioners to easily walk over the wall for access to the churchyard and cemetery while keeping out the cattle and horses.

St. Helena's Church at Benedict and Olmstead Avenues was built by the George Fuller Company. The cornerstone was laid on June 8, 1941, by Monsignor Scanlon, who was joined by his assistants, Reverend C. Giblin and Rev. Francis Murphy. Trustees John Burke and Patrick Byrne also took part in the ceremonies.

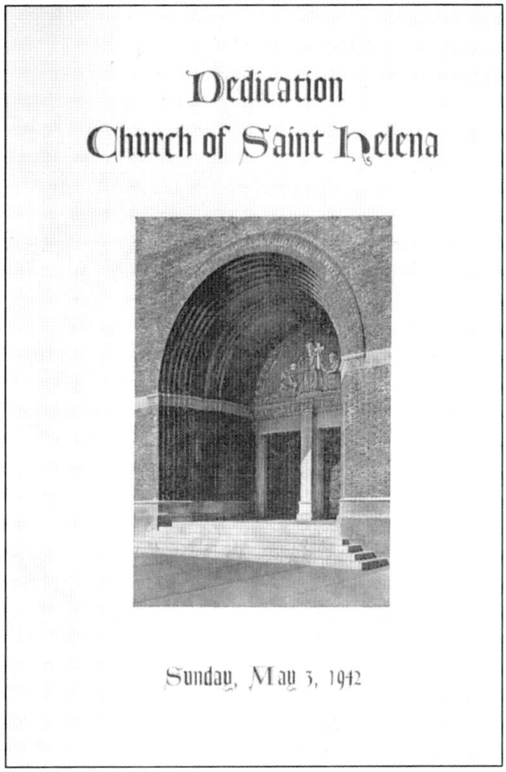

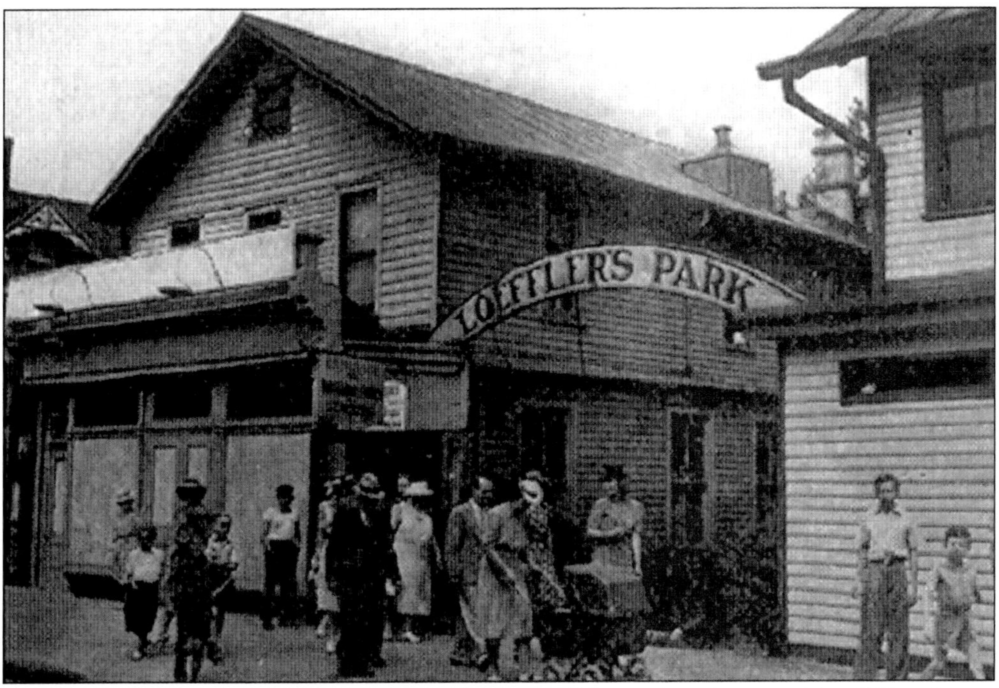

Loeffler's Park was a popular beer garden and dance hall located on the west side of Westchester Avenue, south of Olmstead Avenue. When St. Helena's Church was established prior to 1925, it became their temporary home while awaiting construction of a formal church and school.

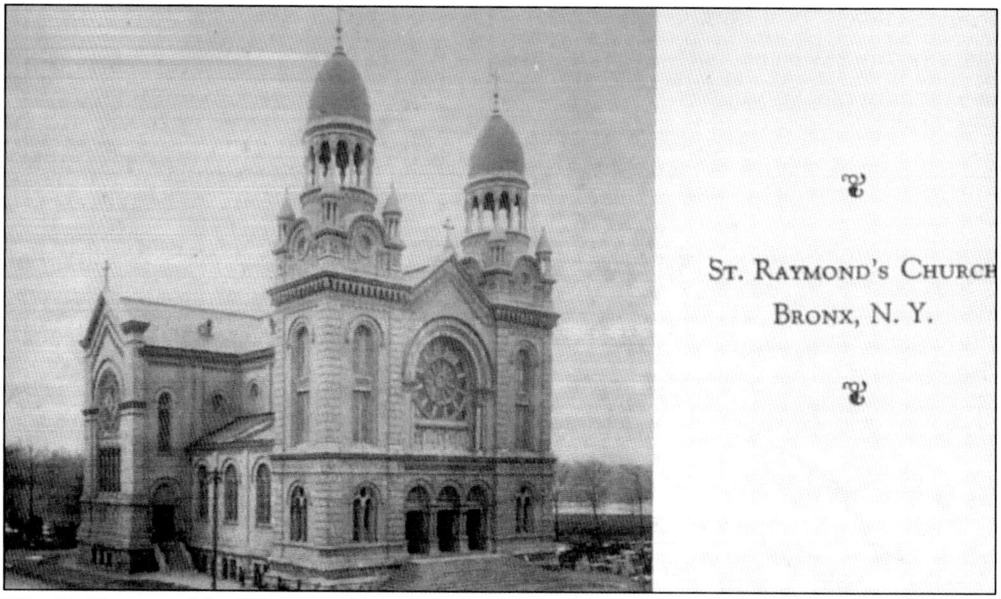

This 1900 view of St. Raymond Church on East Tremont and Castle Hill Avenues is unusual because there is nothing in the background. The parish was established in 1842, and the original church was dedicated in 1845. The cornerstone of this edifice was laid on October 10, 1897; the dedication took place on October 23, 1898.

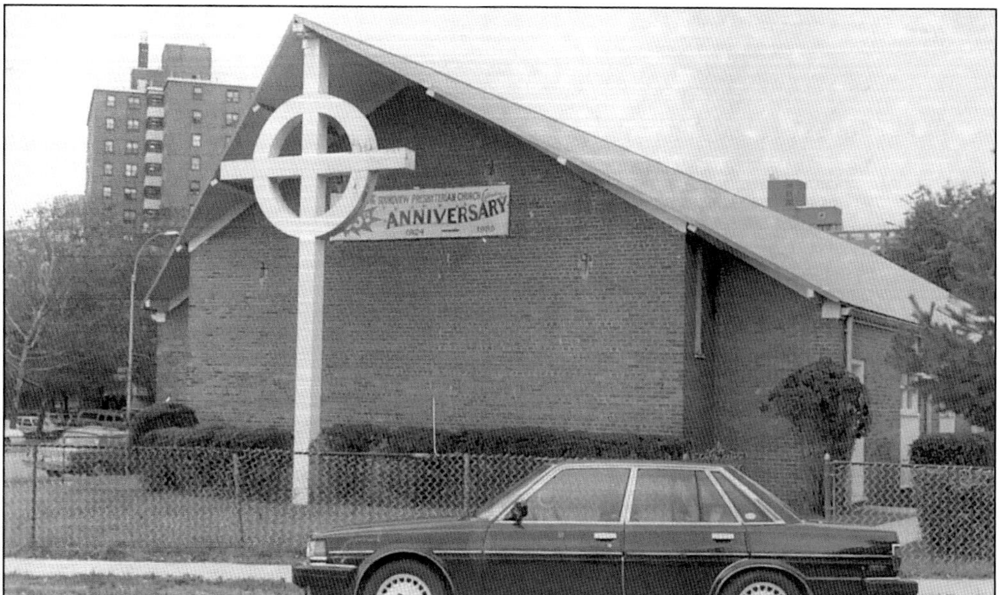

This photograph of the Soundview Presbyterian Church at 760 Soundview Avenue was taken in 1989, at which time it was celebrating its 65th anniversary. The church was established in 1924.

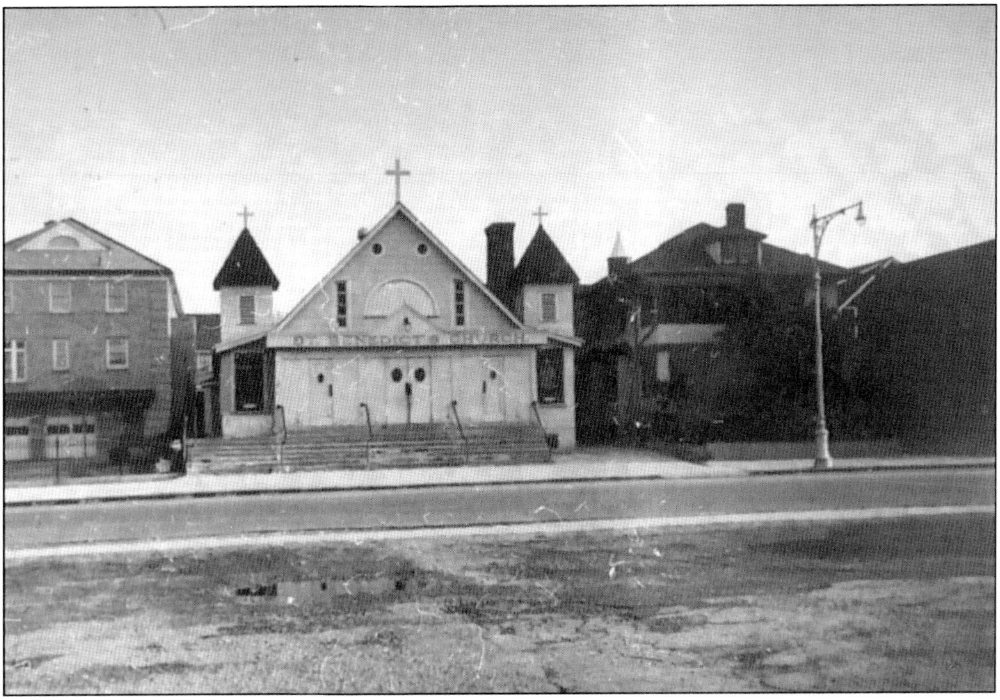

Ron Schliessman provided this 1956 photograph of the old St. Benedict's Church on Bruckner Boulevard. The parish dates from 1923.

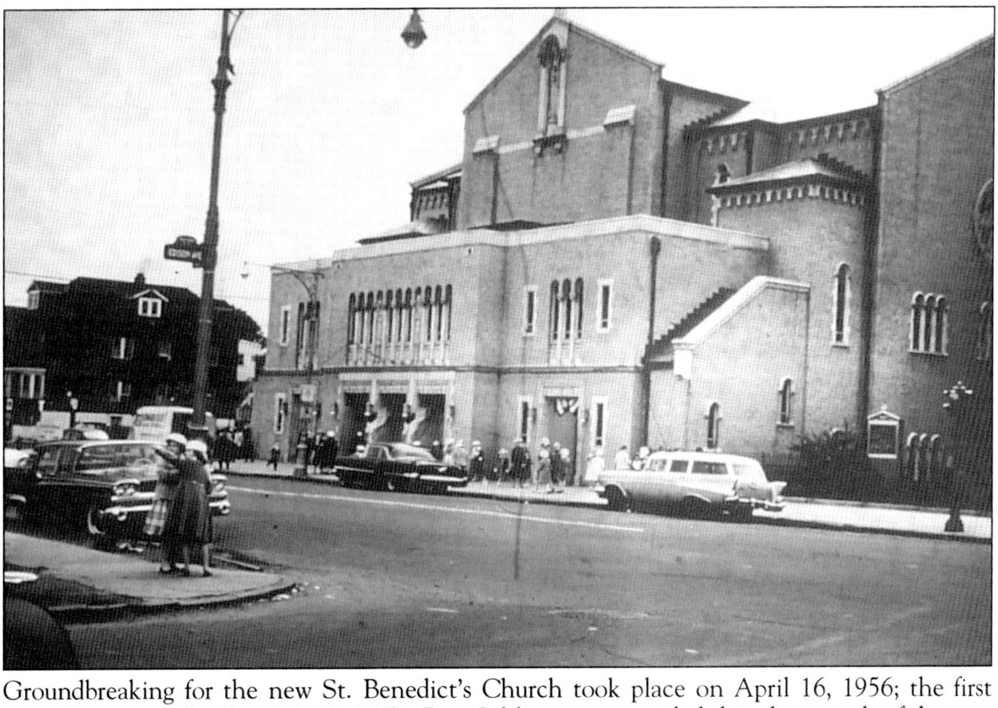

Groundbreaking for the new St. Benedict's Church took place on April 16, 1956; the first mass there was offered on May 8, 1958. Ron Schliessman provided this photograph of the new church taken on May 15, 1960.

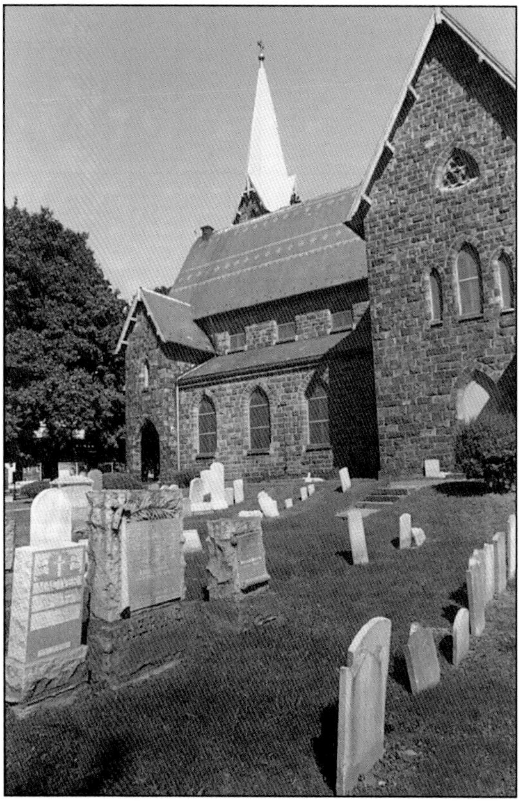

St. Peter's Episcopal Church was established in 1693 on today's Westchester Avenue, south of Commerce Street. The structure seen in this northward view dates from 1871. John McNamara provided the photograph, which also shows some of the historic headstones in the parish cemetery. A walk through the cemetery will reveal numerous names that also appear on local street signs.

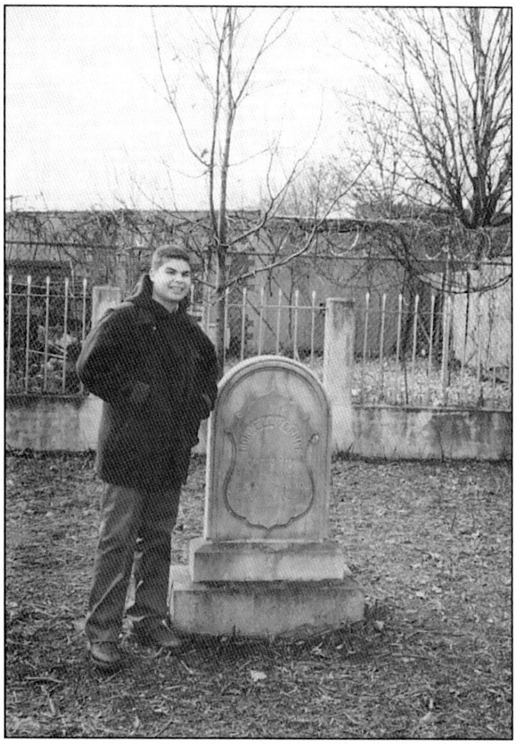

The Ferris family presence at the Westchester Square area goes back to the 17th century, as does their old family cemetery on the south side of Commerce Street east of Westchester Avenue. It gets overgrown every few years, and, fortunately, boy scouts occasionally choose it as an Eagle Scout project. Michael Ligouri did just that and is shown here on January 22, 1995, smiling after being congratulated on a job well done.

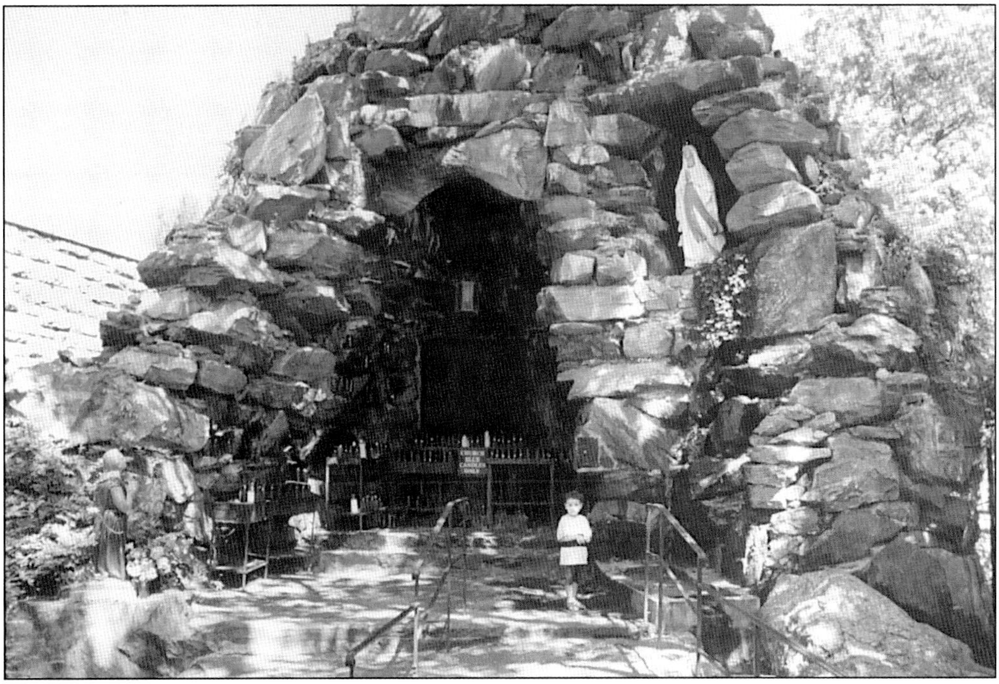

The Hitchcock Farm once stood where this shrine now stands. The grotto is referred to as the Lourdes of America and was dedicated on Memorial Day, 1939, by Monsignor Gaetano Arcese. It was attached to St. Lucy's Church at Bronxwood and Mace Avenues.

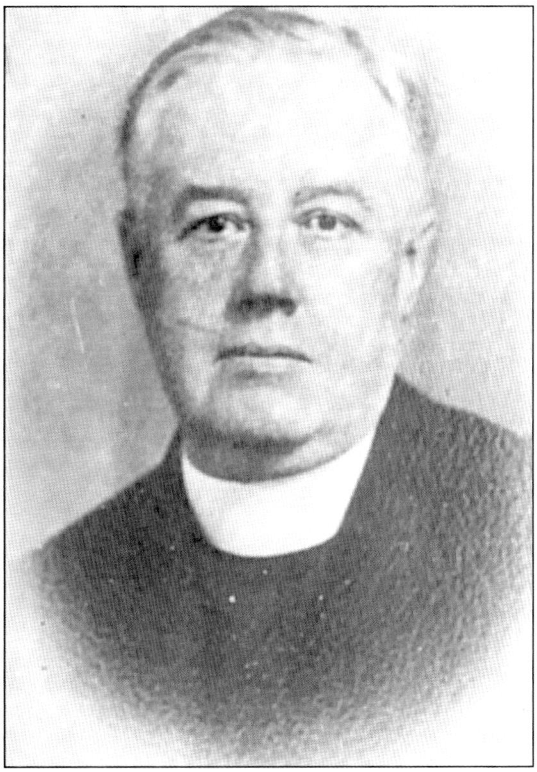

Father James M. Kilroe was born on June 19, 1878, and was ordained a Catholic priest on June 7, 1905. He was later assigned to St. Mary Star of the Sea Church on City Island and established their elementary school in 1926. Nearby Kilroe Street was named in his honor.

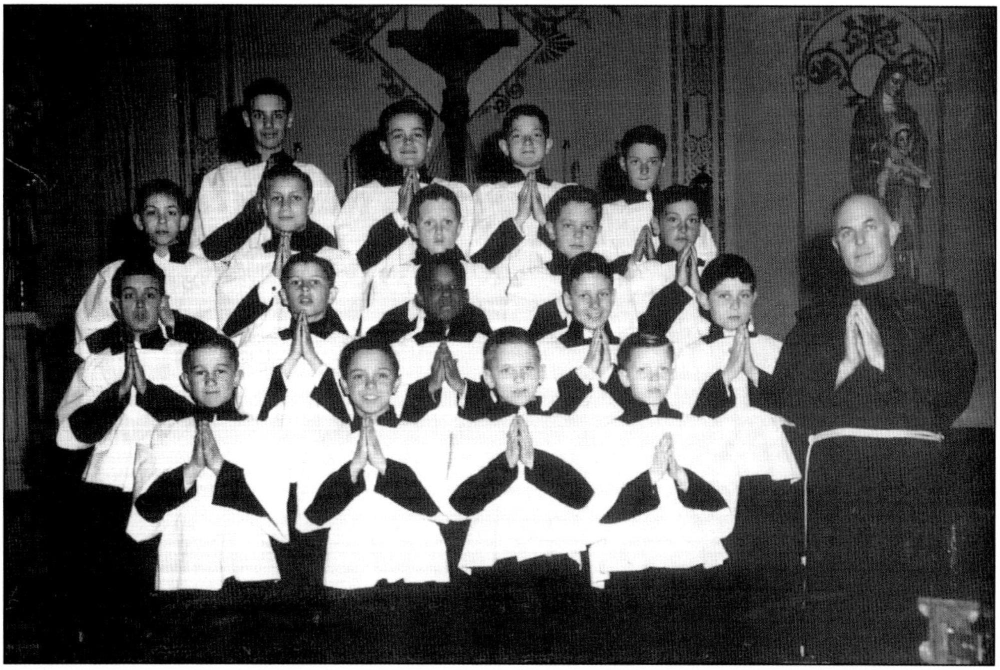

Arthur Seifert supplied this 1953 photograph of the boys choir of Holy Cross Church.

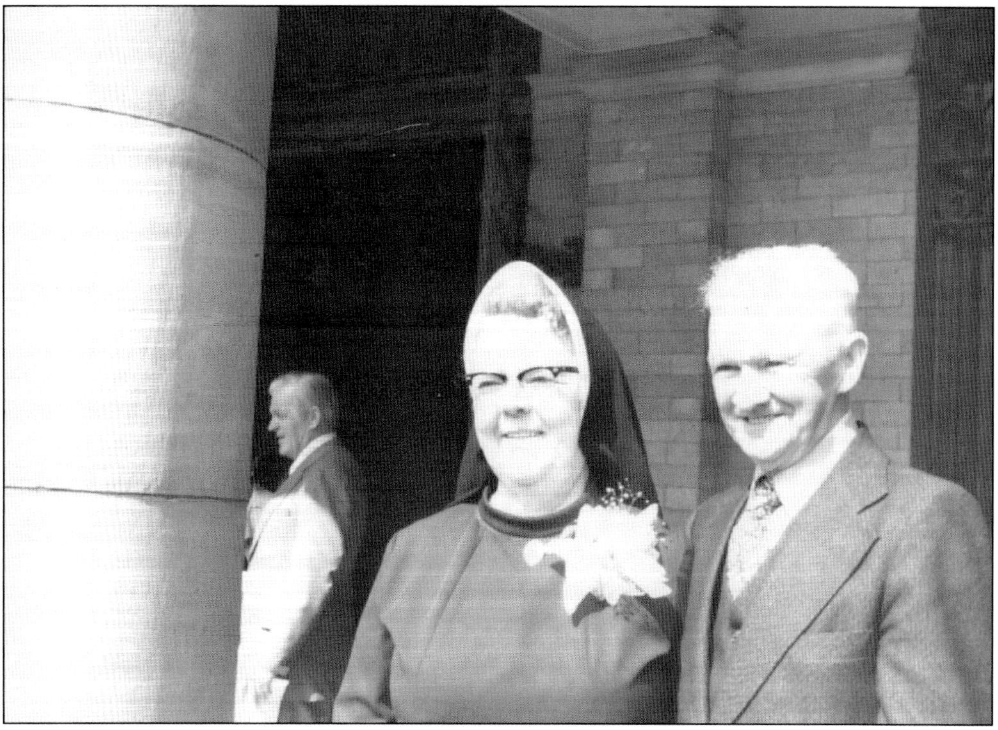

Sister Mary Stanislaus, R.D.C., poses in the Sisters of Divine Compassion modified habit in this 1979 photograph. Frank Twomey Sr. is standing by her side.

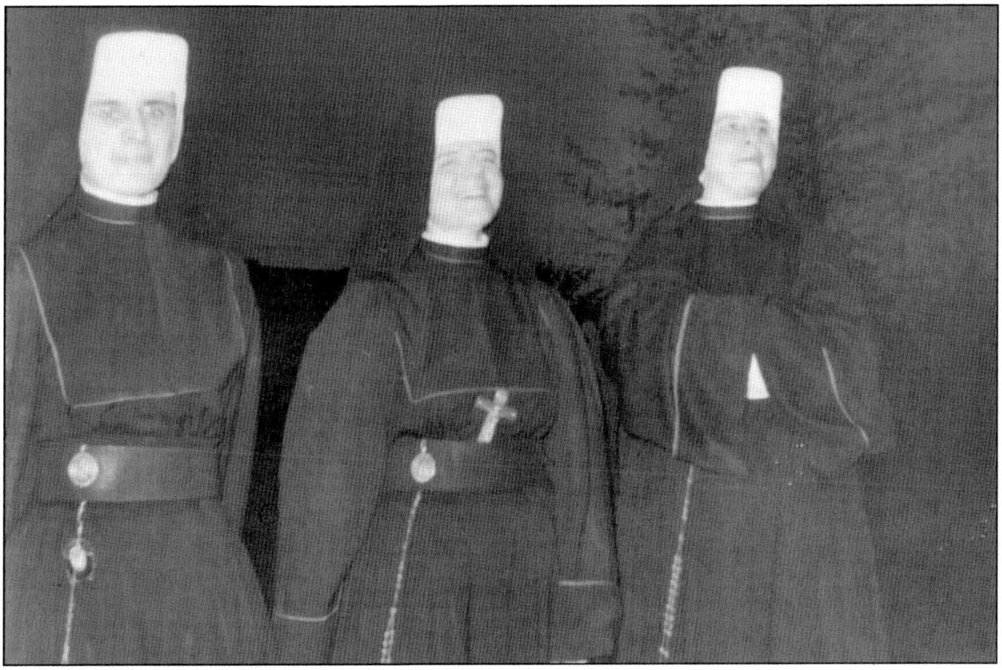

John V. Riche provided this snapshot of three Sisters of Divine Compassion with their former traditional habits at St. Frances de Chantal School. This image, taken in June of 1966, shows, from left to right, Sister Mary Gertrude, Sister Mary Clare, and Sister Mary Hyacinth.

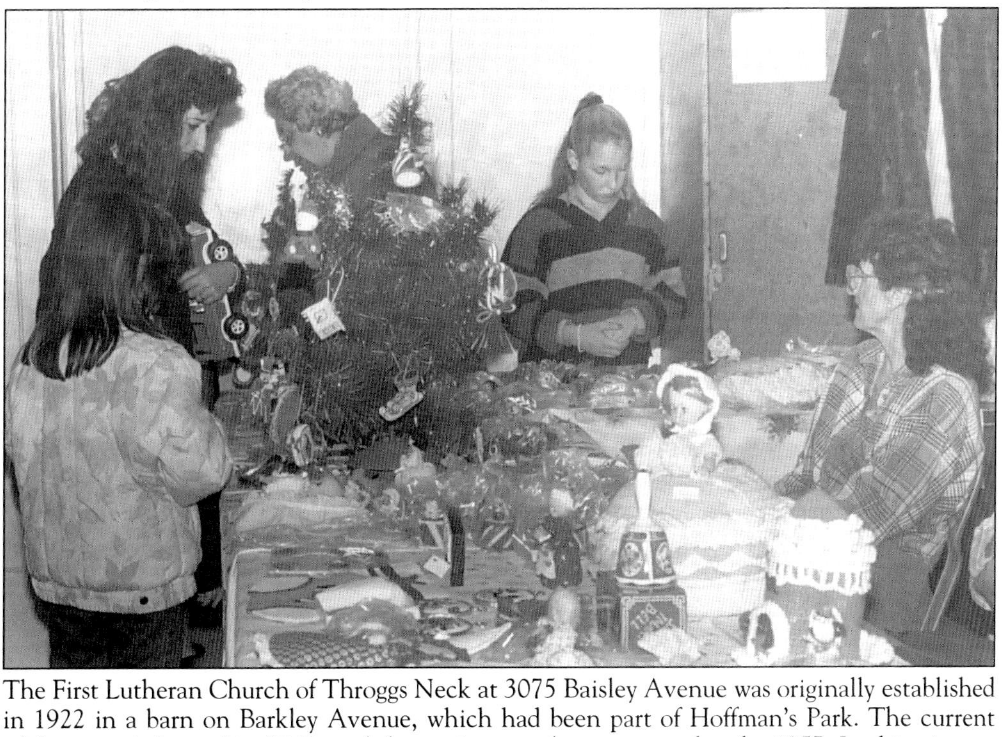

The First Lutheran Church of Throggs Neck at 3075 Baisley Avenue was originally established in 1922 in a barn on Barkley Avenue, which had been part of Hoffman's Park. The current edifice was dedicated in 1942, and the entire complex was complete by 1957. In this picture, Delores McKay is covering a booth at one of their church flea markets.

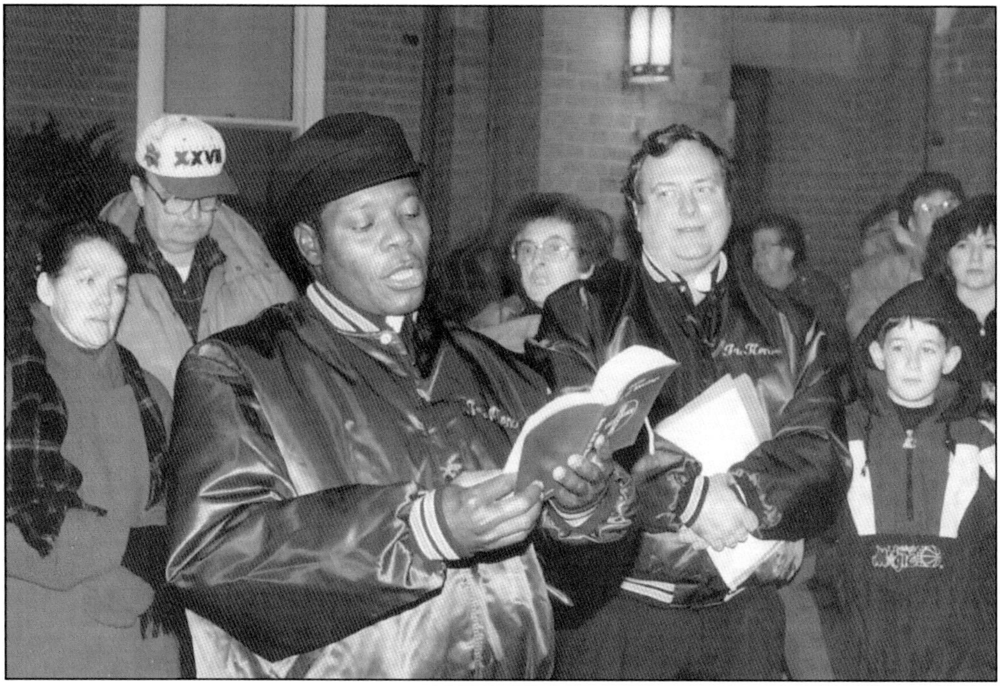

This recent snapshot portrays the annual Christmas tree lighting and caroling at St. Benedict Church on Otis Avenue. Father Kenneth Marks, the pastor, is toward the right.

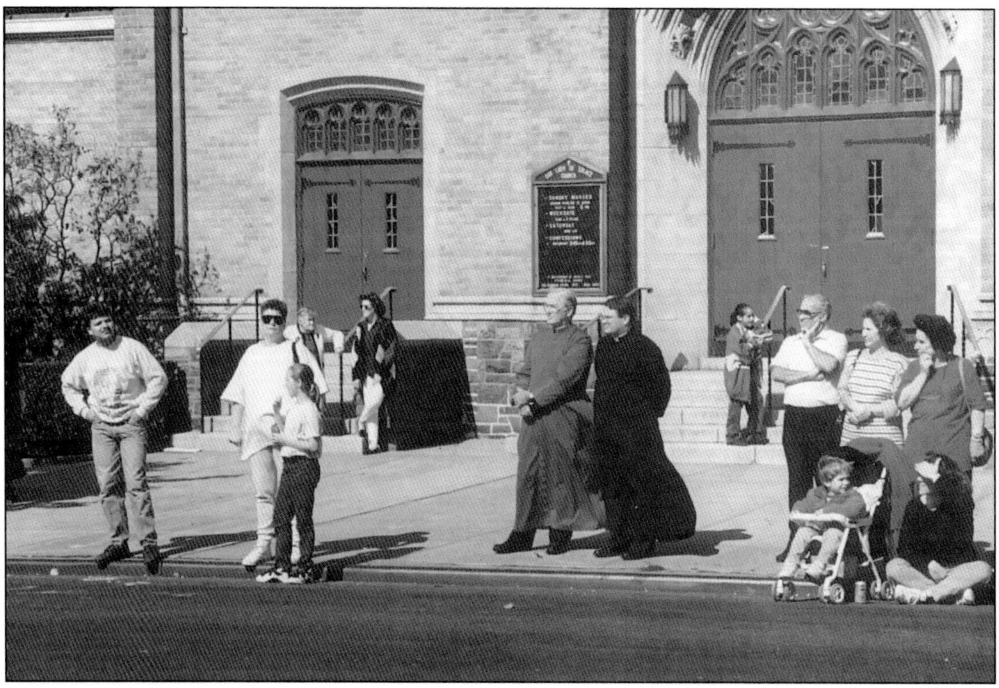

Father John Knapp chats with the pastor outside of Our Lady of Solace Church on Morris Park Avenue as they view a passing Columbus Day Parade in the 1990s.

Three

BY THE SEA

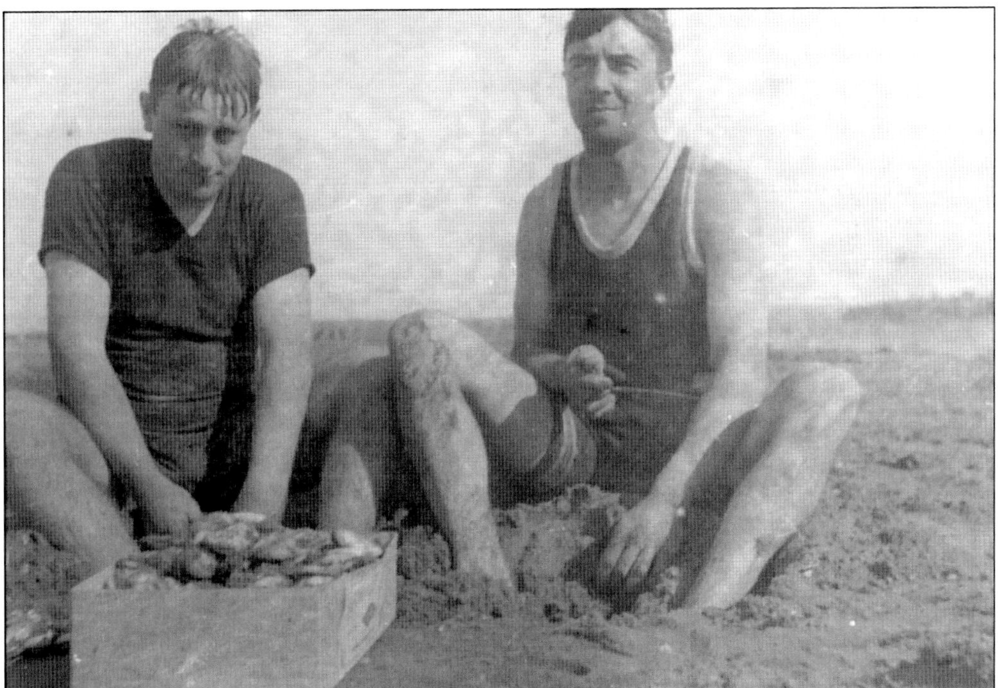

Cuban Ledge is an outcropping of sand and rock located in Eastchester Bay between Rodman's Neck and Country Club. It is visible only at low tide. Jack McCaffrey and John McNamara were clamming there, *c.* 1912, when this picture was snapped.

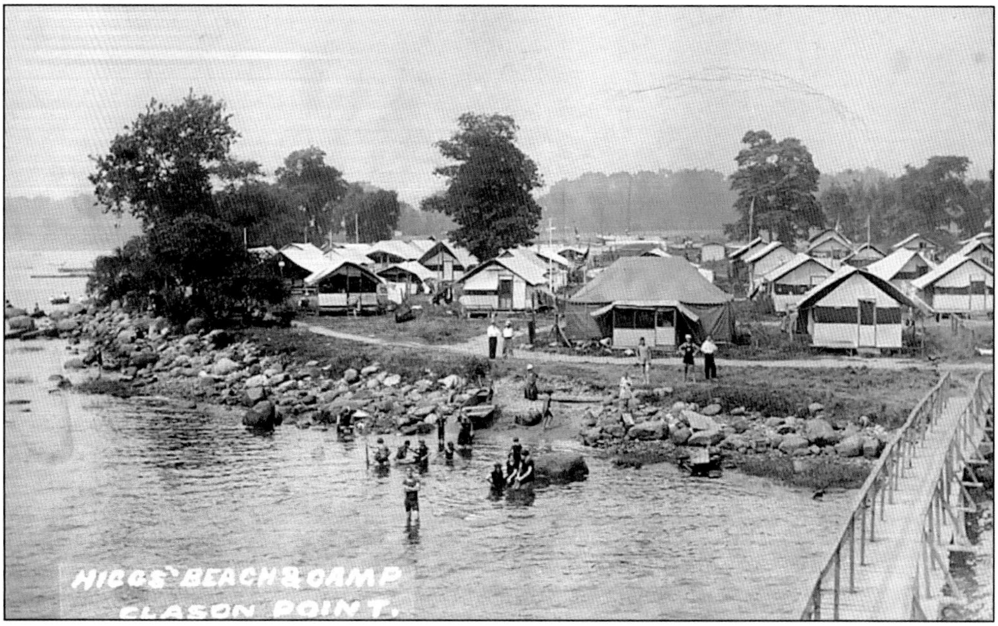

Harding Park is bounded on the east by White Plains Road and on the south by the East River. The Bronx River is to the west. Originally a campground for tents, it soon evolved into a bungalow colony. Until 1924, it was known as Higgs Beach. This postcard view was taken during that period. Art Seifert supplied this northward-looking picture.

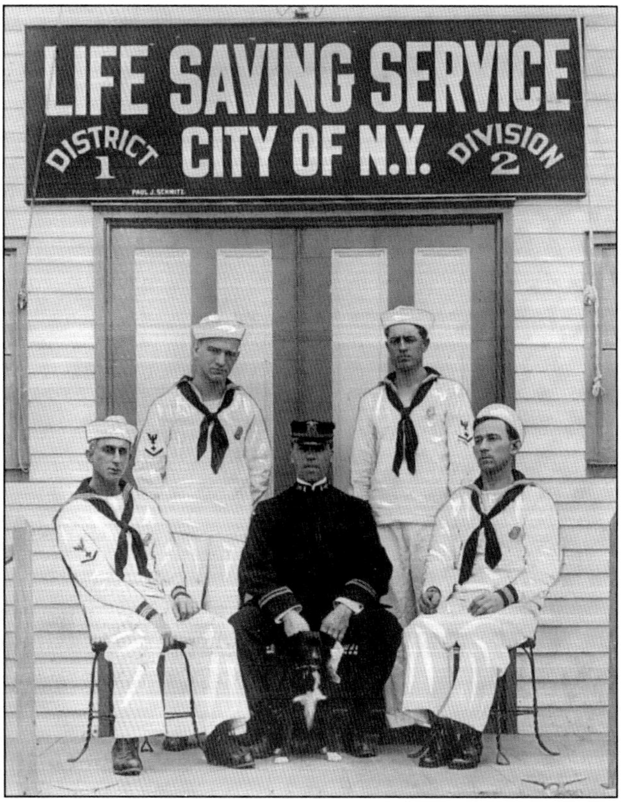

Lifesaving stations were dotted along the Bronx shoreline during the 1920s, 1930s, and 1940s. This one, from District 1, Division 2, was located on Clason Point and boasted 30 volunteers. (Courtesy of the Seifert Collection.)

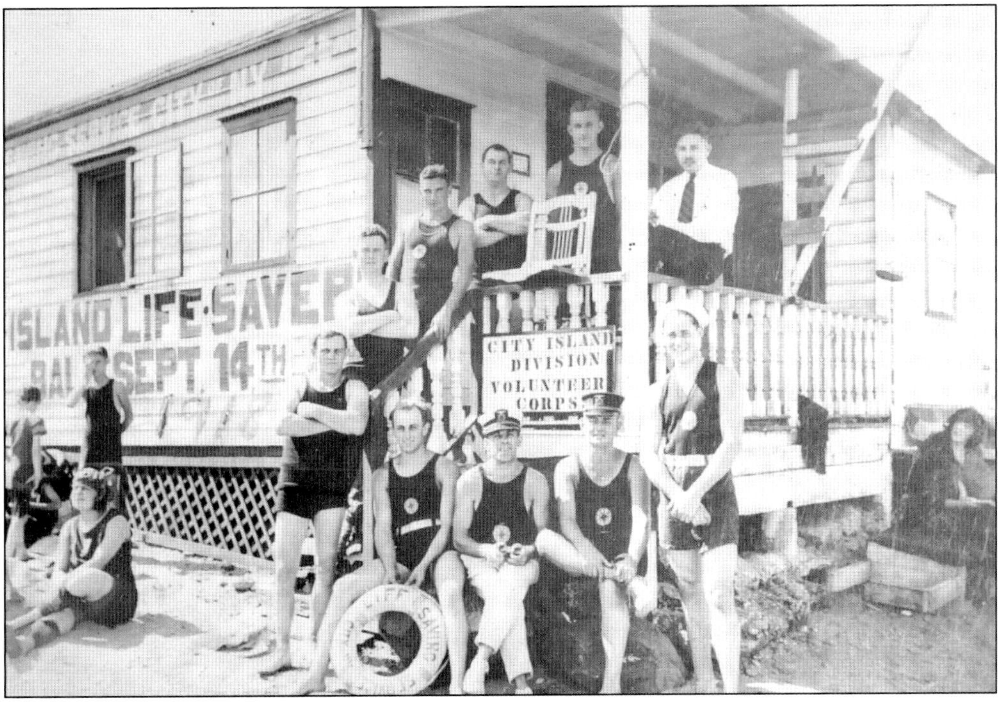

The sign in the center behind the young men at the City Island Life Guard Station reads "City Island Division Volunteer Corps." The sign at the left on the side of the building dates the picture. It advertises the City Island Life Savers Ball to be held on September 14, 1918.

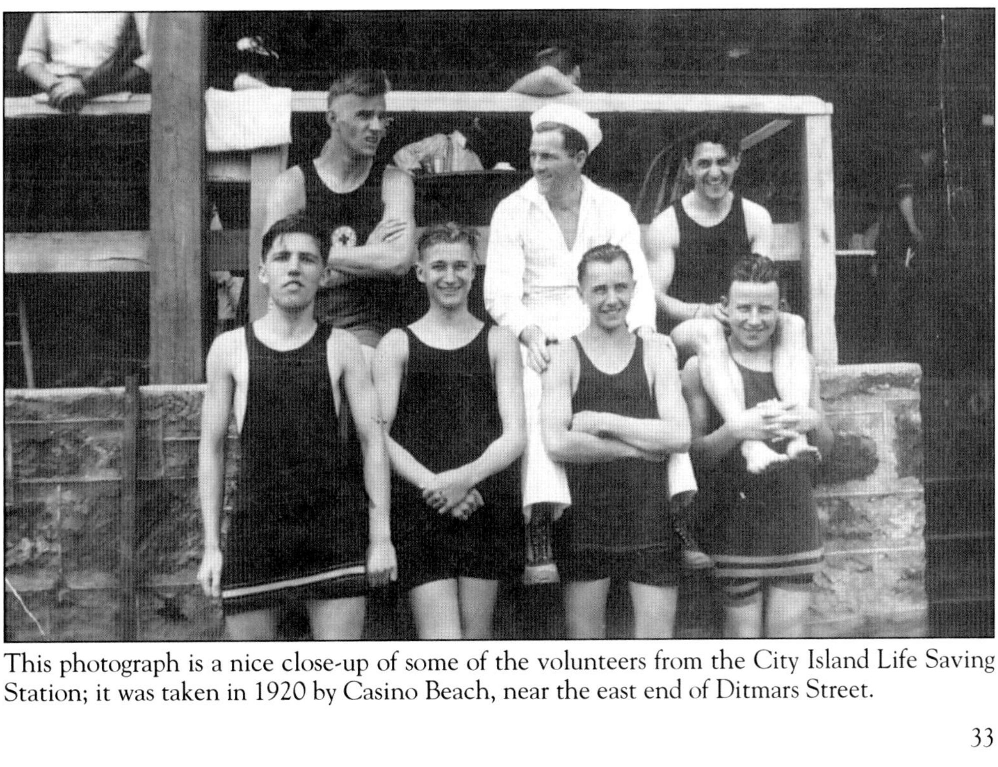

This photograph is a nice close-up of some of the volunteers from the City Island Life Saving Station; it was taken in 1920 by Casino Beach, near the east end of Ditmars Street.

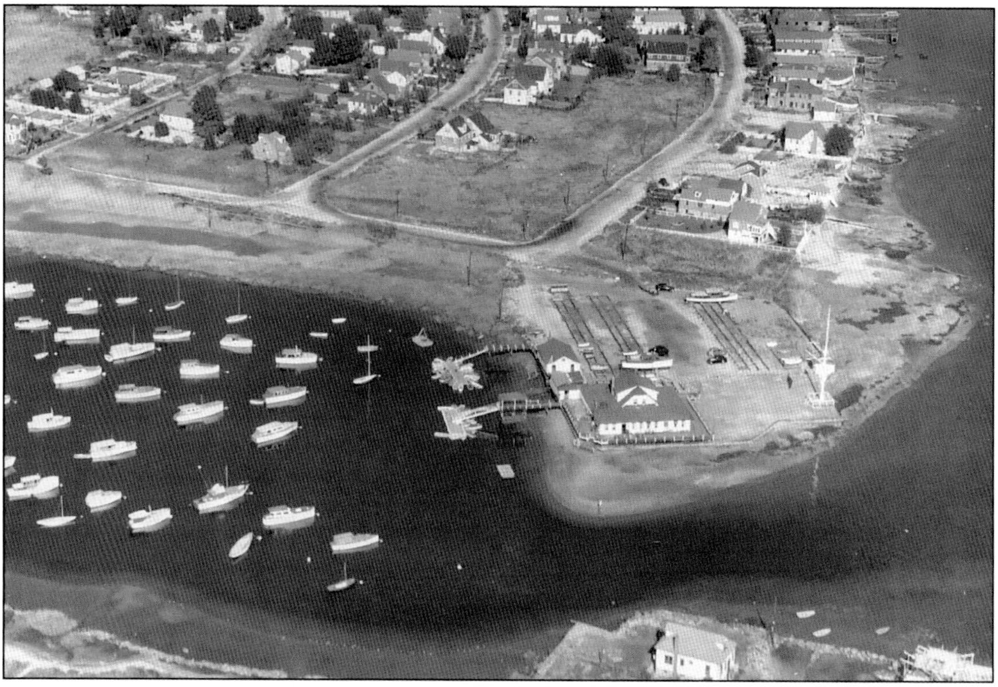

Arthur Seifert took this interesting aerial photograph of Locust Point in 1946. With its two docks, the Locust Point Marina is at the right center, and Hammond Cove, often referred to as "the lagoon," is at the left. The community of Schuyler Hill is in the foreground, and the Long Island Sound would be at the right.

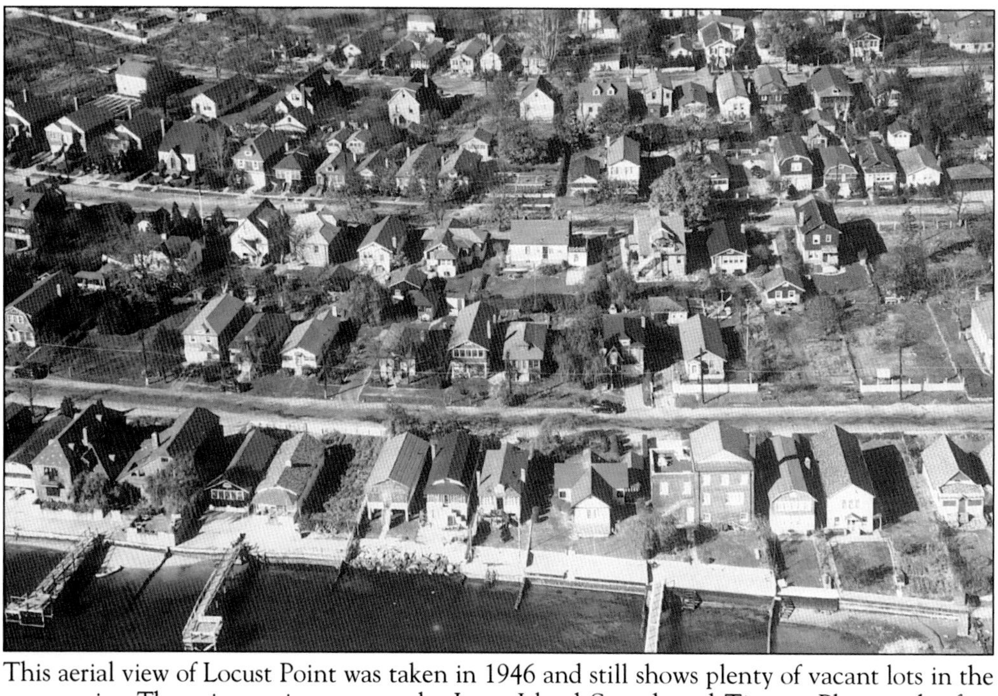

This aerial view of Locust Point was taken in 1946 and still shows plenty of vacant lots in the community. The private piers are on the Long Island Sound, and Tierney Place is the first roadway beyond the front row of houses. Arthur Seifert snapped this westward view.

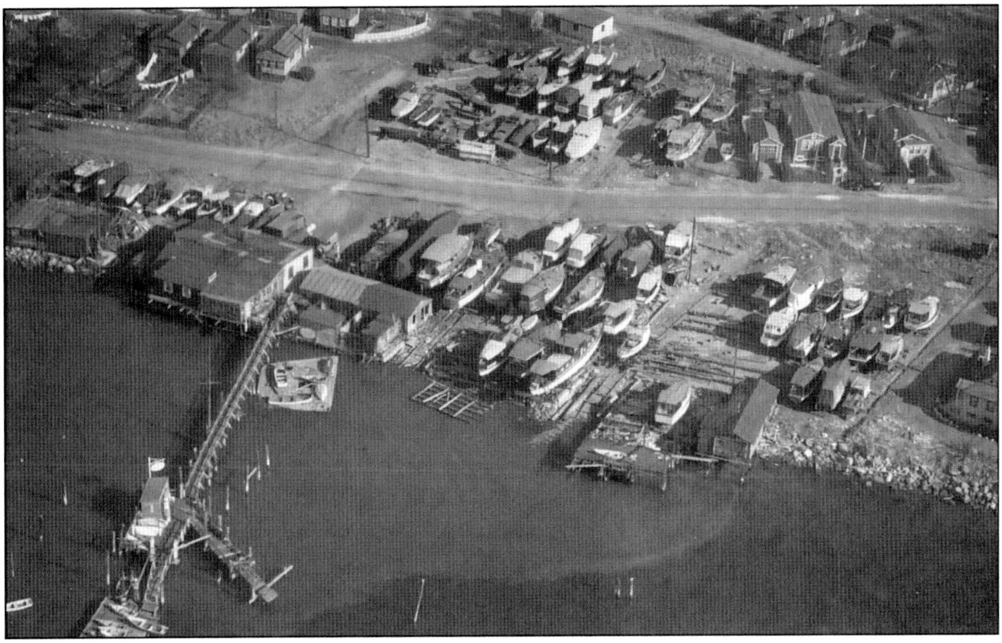

Vernon Seifert was piloting a Piper Cub out of the Flushing Airport in 1946 when he came over the East River to see this aerial view of Harding Park. His brother Arthur photographed this view, which focuses on Smith's Boat Yard.

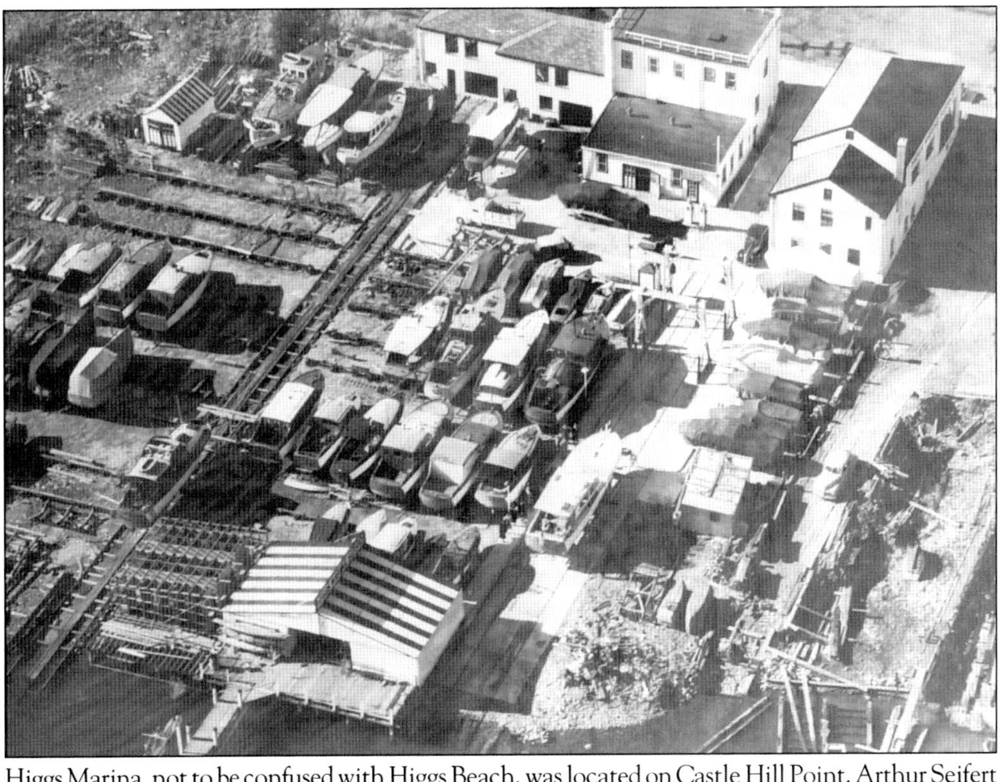

Higgs Marina, not to be confused with Higgs Beach, was located on Castle Hill Point. Arthur Seifert took this photograph from a Piper Cub in 1946, while his brother Vernon piloted.

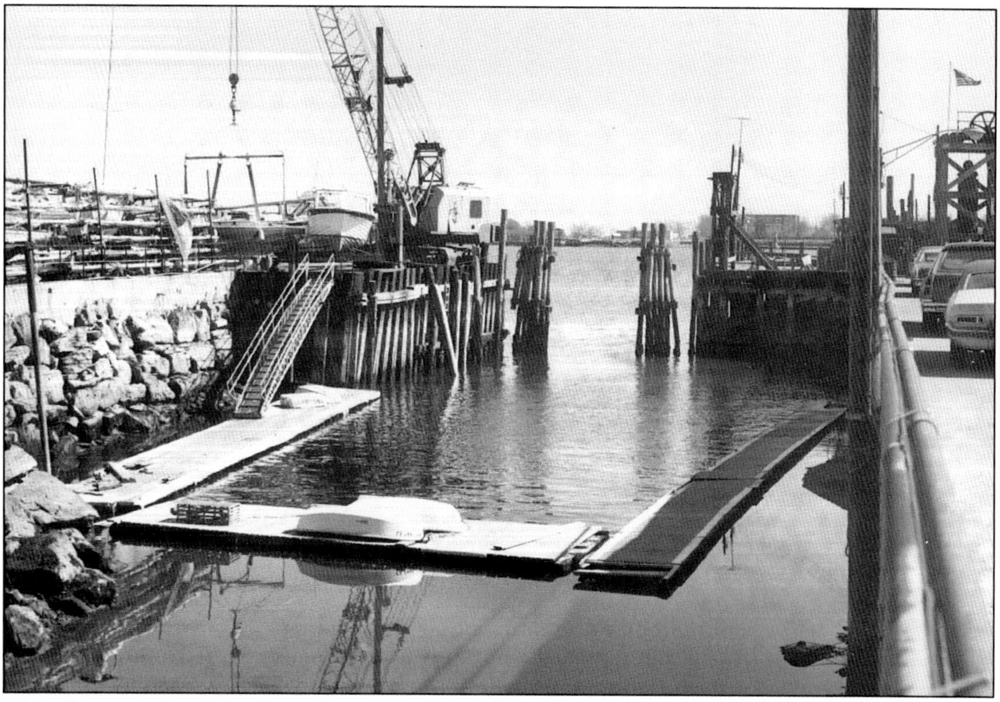

This photograph of the ferry slip at the foot of Fordham Street was taken in 1979. (Courtesy of John McNamara.)

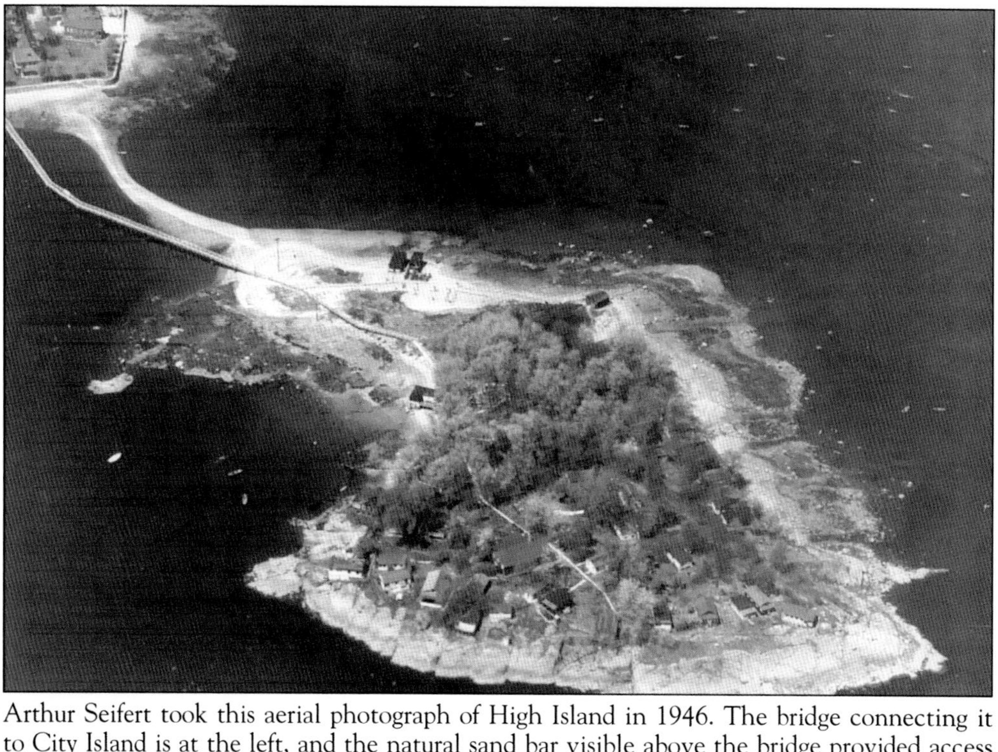

Arthur Seifert took this aerial photograph of High Island in 1946. The bridge connecting it to City Island is at the left, and the natural sand bar visible above the bridge provided access at low tide.

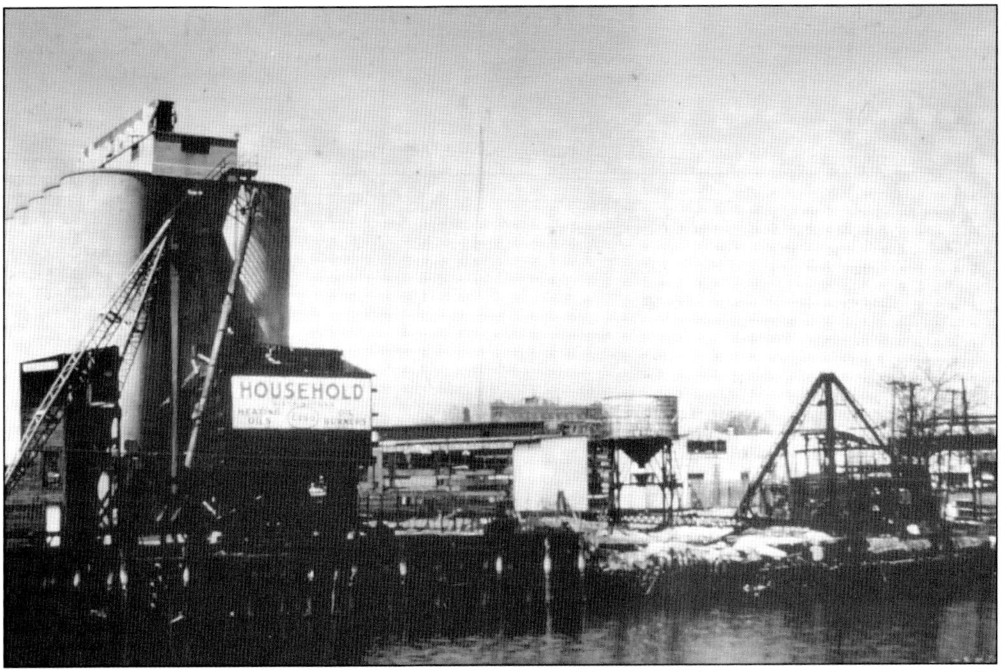

This 1968 Westchester Creek photograph was provided by Ron Schliessman. Note the coal silo at the left and the Westchester Avenue EL in the background.

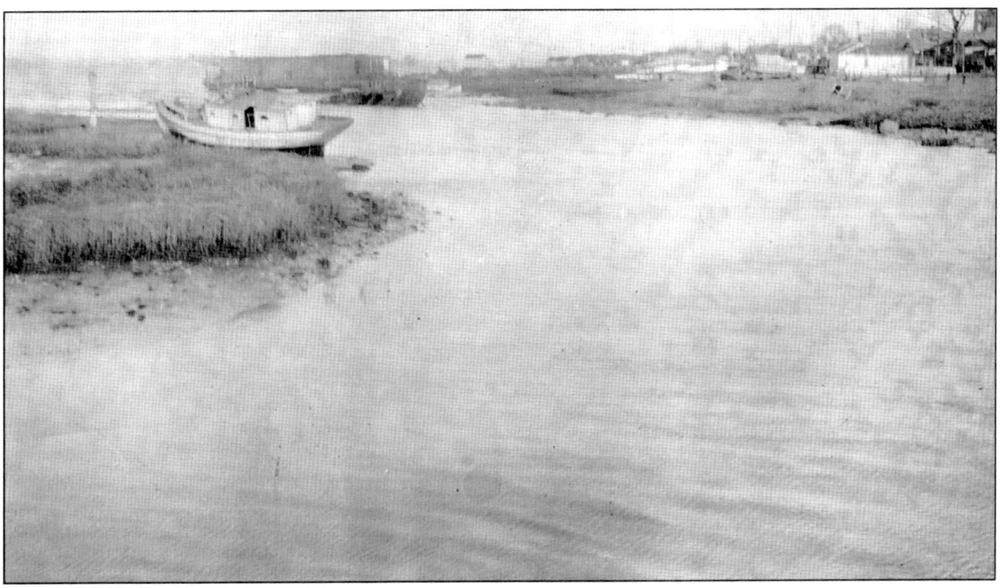

Weir Creek, now overlaid by the Throgs Neck Expressway, emptied into Eastchester Bay when this photograph was taken in 1931. The Bronxonia Yacht Club would be to the left, while Edgewater Park is to the right.

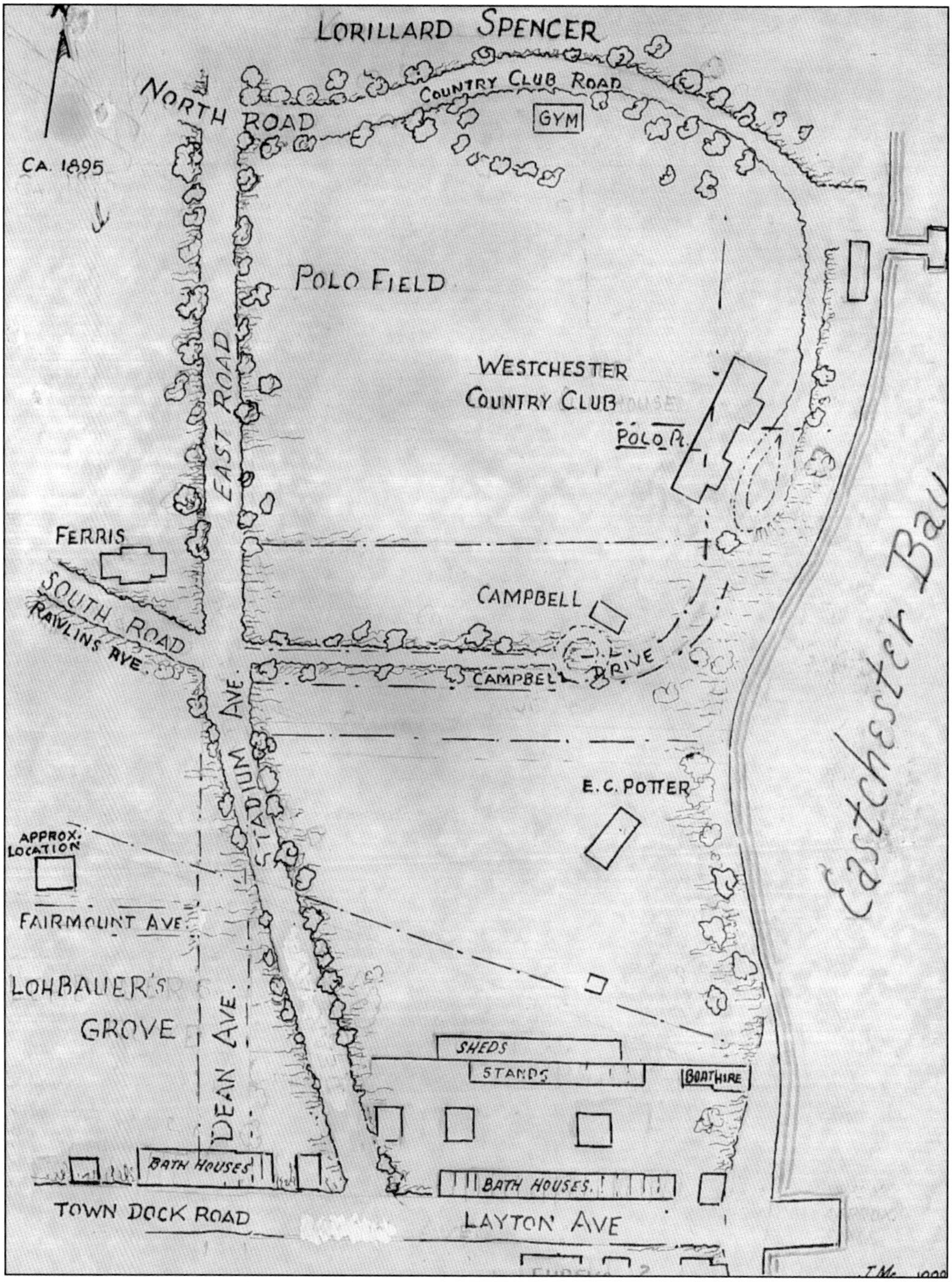

John McNamara drew this map of the Country Club waterfront, which includes Lohbauer's, just north of Town Dock Road (now Layton Avenue). Laubauer's Park was broken up into lots and auctioned off by Joseph P. Day on May 19, 1908. Henry's Bay View Inn became one of the new occupants. Note the polo field of the Westchester Country Club toward the north, from which we get the name Polo Place. During the American Revolution, the Ferris House at the left was occupied by Lord Howe when he sought to cross Westchester Creek at Crow Hill to cut off George Washington. The building later became a convent and was torn down in 1962.

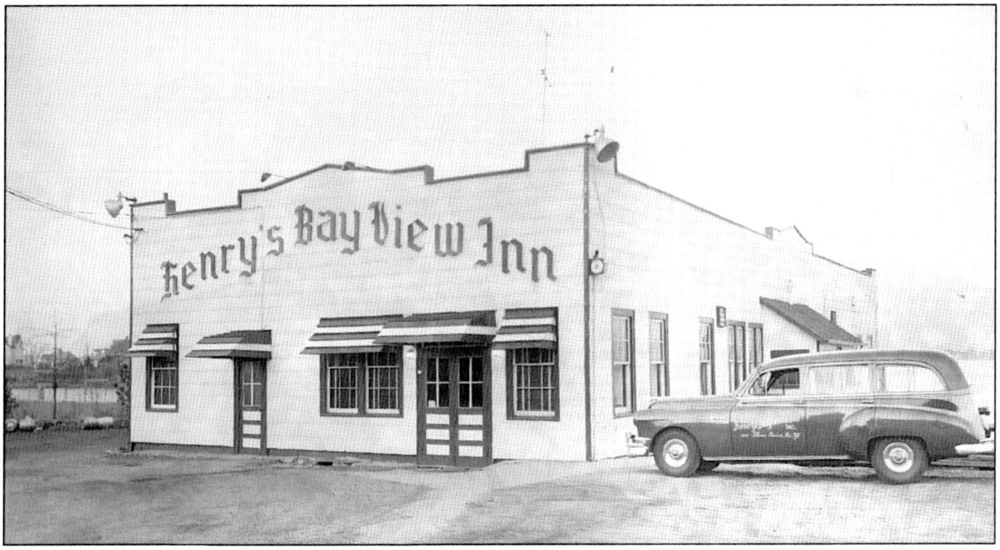

Fred Lohbauer's Bay View Villa opened in 1896 at the foot of Layton Avenue. It was a full resort with a hotel, restaurant, dancing pavilion, bowling alleys, ball fields, bathing facilities, etc. Fred died in 1904, and his wife ran the business for another four years. The property was broken up into 700 lots and auctioned off on May 19, 1908. Henry Heaffner, who owned a nearby bar, obtained the choice lots toward the water for his inn.

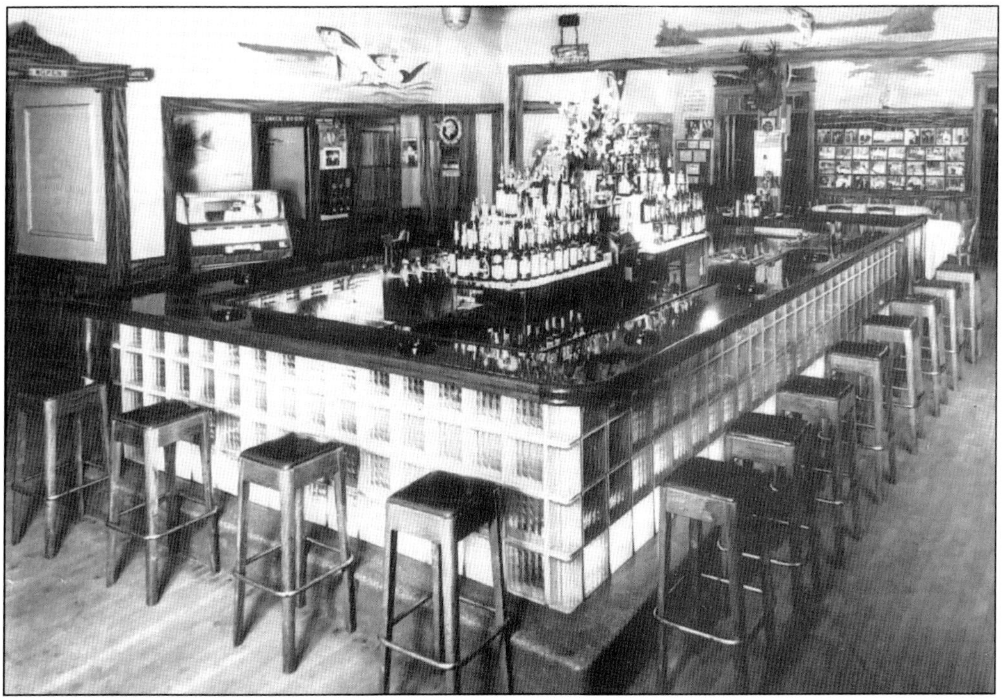

Henry's Bay View Inn owed some of its popularity to frequent visits from members of the New York Yankees baseball team. The players felt very much at home at Henry's and occasionally went behind the bar to help out when things got very busy. They, along with the local clientele, missed the place when it burned down in April of 1958. Ron Schliessman supplied both of the photographs on this page.

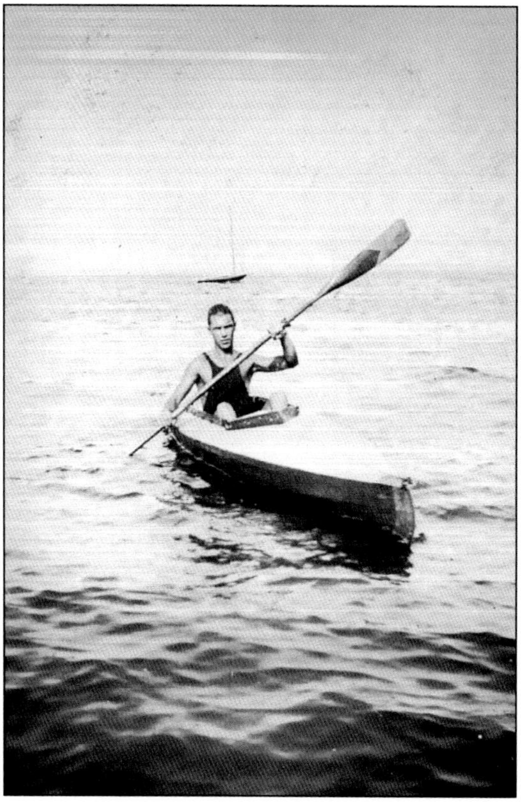

John McNamara plies the waters of the Long Island Sound in his kayak in 1932. His Kleppler model had a canvas top and a rubber hull that was stretched over a bamboo frame.

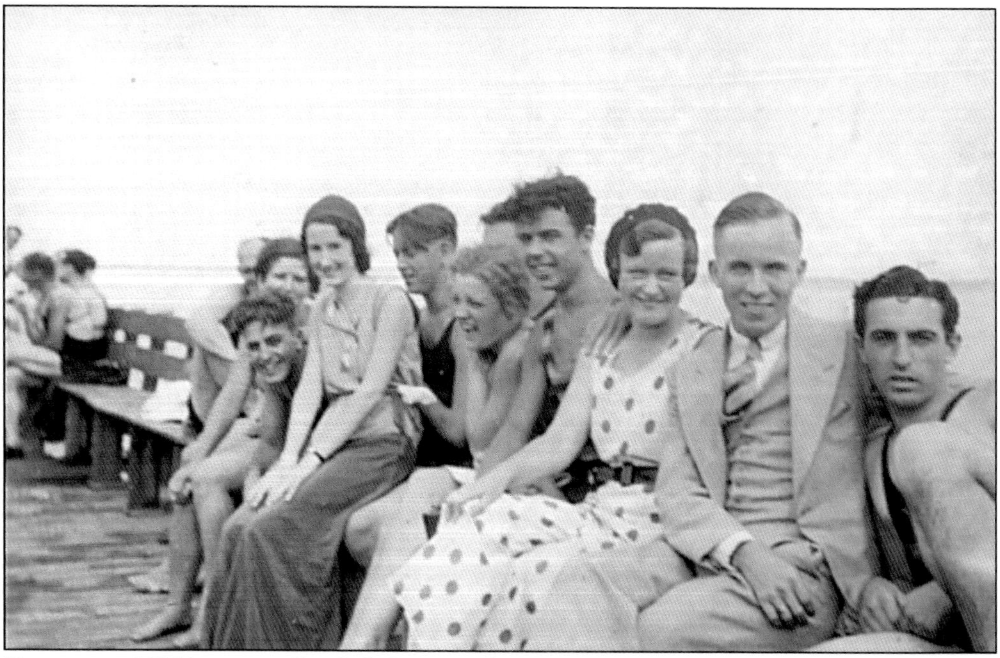

Teenagers of 1931, seen at Big Oak Pier in Edgewater Park, are, from left to right, as follows: Lillian Ferreira, Larry Bornholz, Pat Sheey, Alf Johansen, Millie Vogel, Ed McNamara, Muriel MacKenzie, Jim McGevna, and Phil Zullo.

This 1918 snapshot, taken in Edgewater Park, shows, from left to right, Henrietta McCoy, Clare Stenek, Betty McNamara, and Marion McCaffrey in the latest bathing attire. The photograph was supplied through the courtesy of John McNamara.

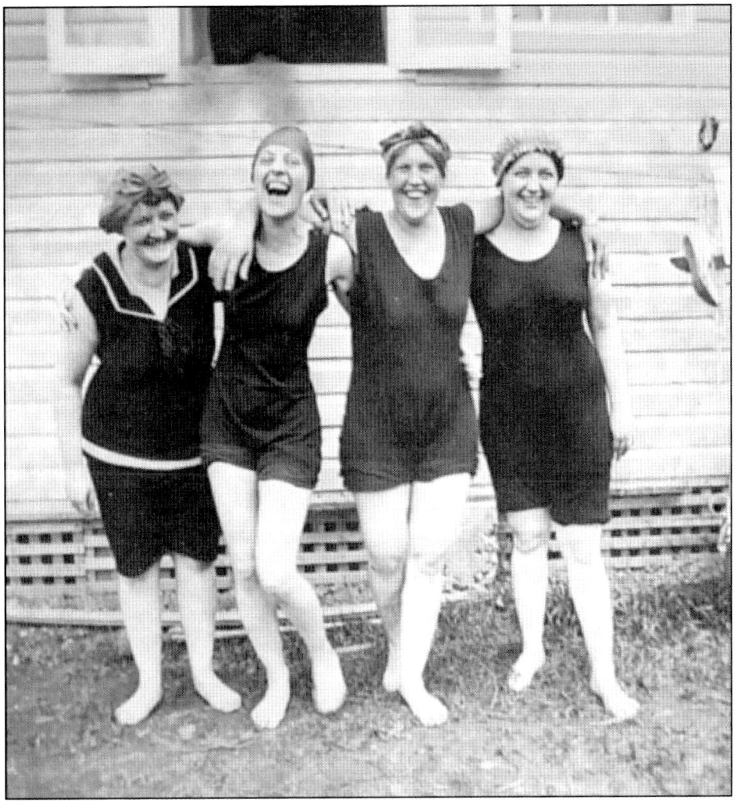

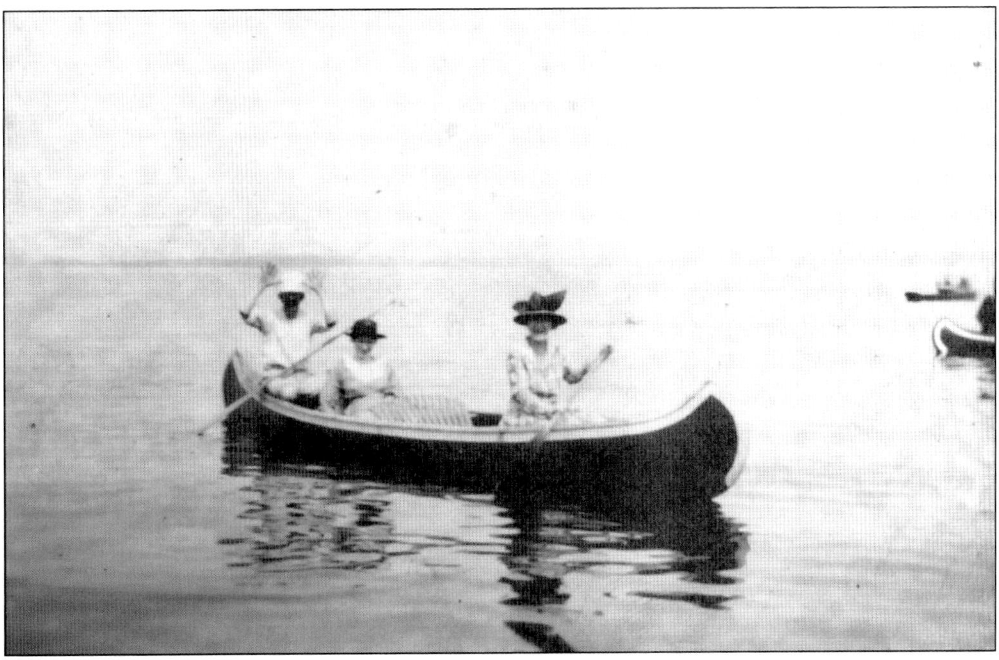

Street attire in canoes was not unusual in 1920, when Mr. Carr, his sister, and his wife relaxed after church services. Carr was an elder in the first Protestant congregation formed in Edgewater Park.

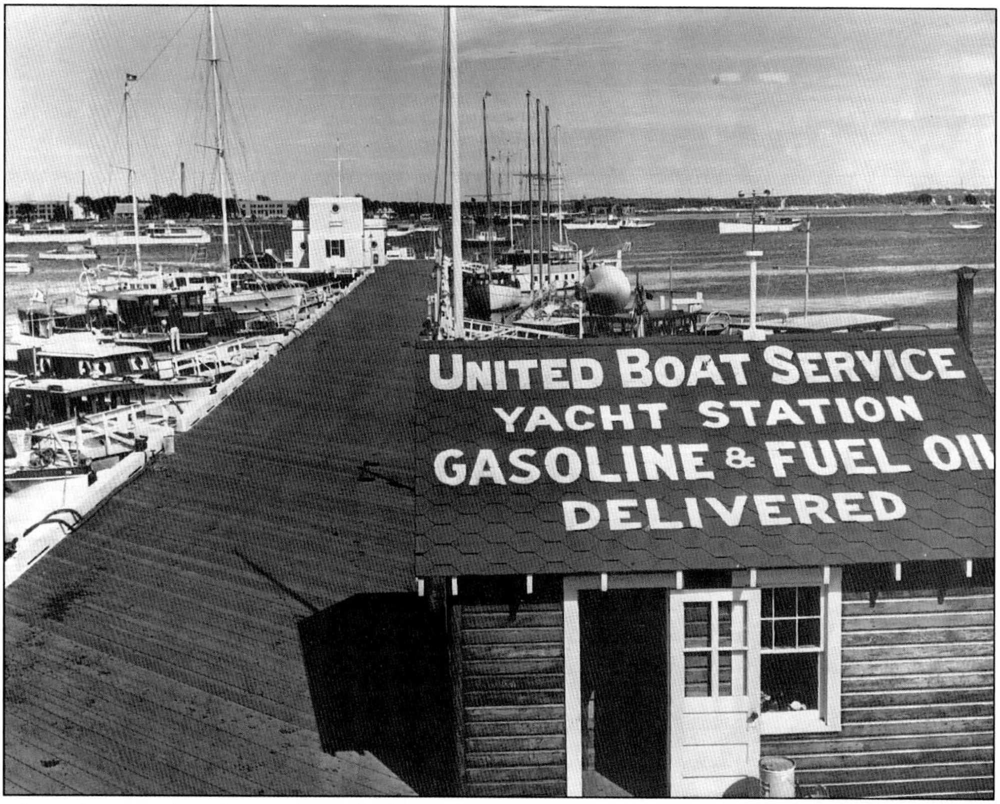

This photograph of the United Boat Service at east Carroll Street was supplied by John McNamara. The dock, shown here, was a masterpiece of design but was built east to west, which was an error as it was subject to wind damage and difficult to dock at in heavy winds. The first of its kind on the east coast, the dock was built in 1930 by Connie Esmark and owned by Victor Anderson. Robert Jenkins later acquired it.

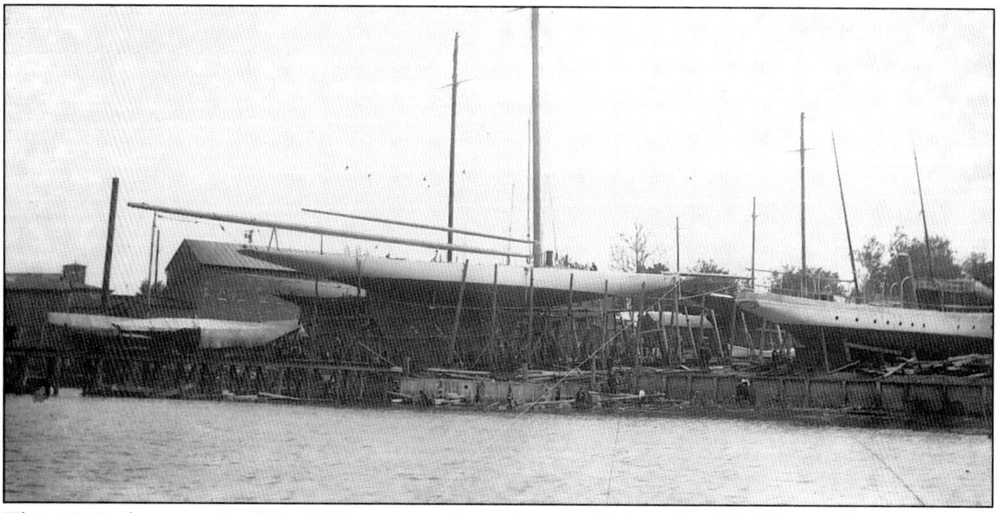

This 1903 photograph of the *Reliance*, on the railway at Robert Jacob's Shipyard, was supplied by John McNamara. Numerous 65-foot tugs and 50-foot landing barges were built at this yard, which is now the Consolidated Shipyard.

Four

Entertainment

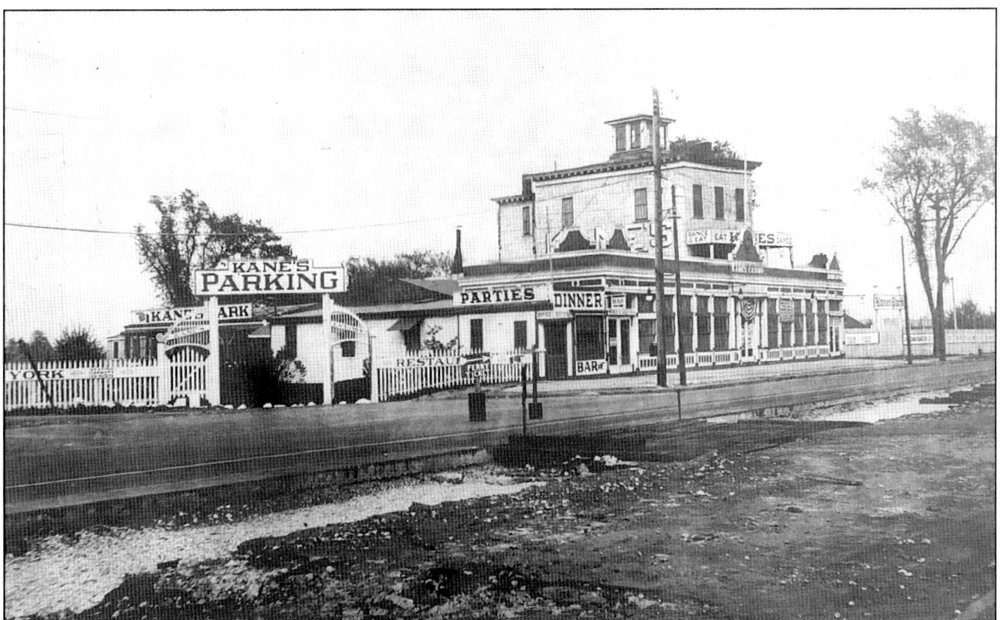

Kane's Park and Casino graced Soundview Avenue on Clason Point from 1906 through 1940. It was a popular site for clambakes, dance marathons, and other events, and Betty Boop was among the celebrities who entertained there. This *c.* 1935 photograph came from the Seifert Collection.

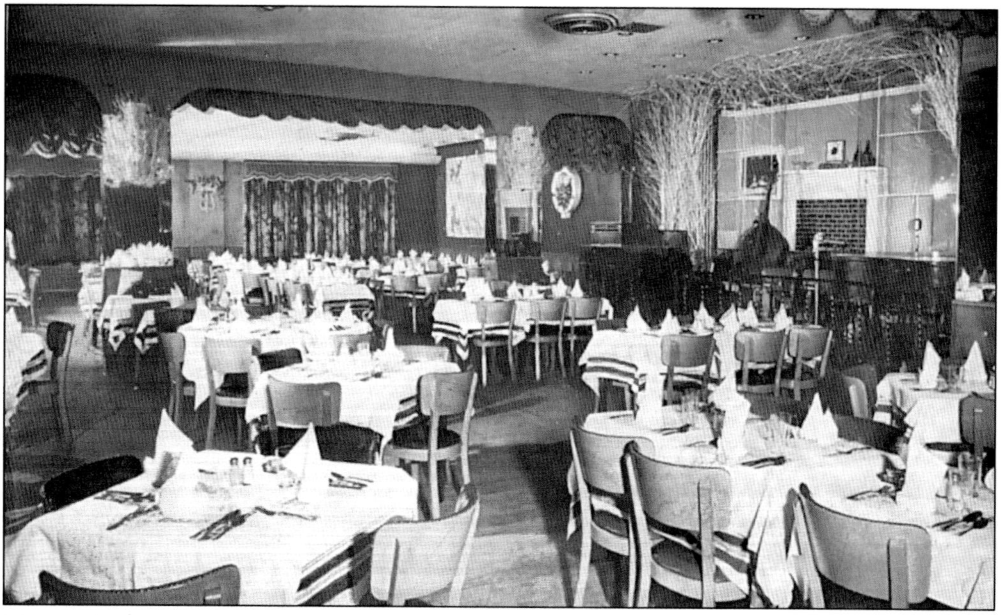

Mayer's Parkway Restaurant was established in 1902 as The Parkway and later changed its name for the owners, Mr. and Mrs. Robert Mayer. It was located at 613 East 233rd Street. This postcard rendering of the main dining room should bring back some pleasant memories.

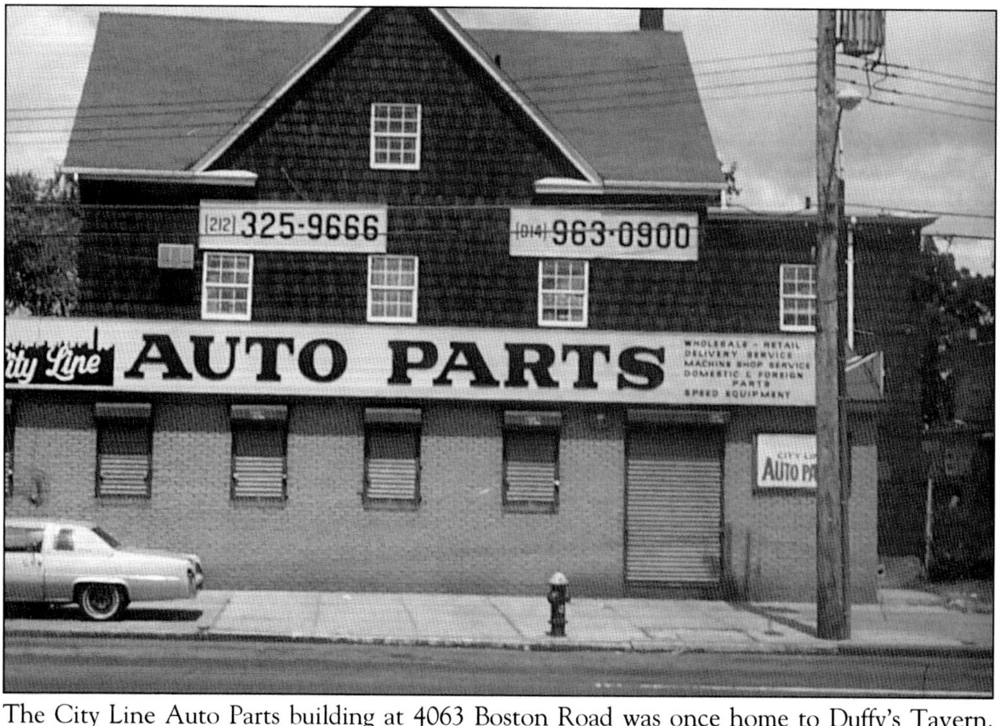

The City Line Auto Parts building at 4063 Boston Road was once home to Duffy's Tavern. John Duffy opened it and named it as much for the radio show as for his surname. Due to the popularity of the radio show and the array of cabaret singers featured, it soon became the "in place." Nick DiBrino, who knew Mr. Duffy, believes that the building was once a stage coach stop.

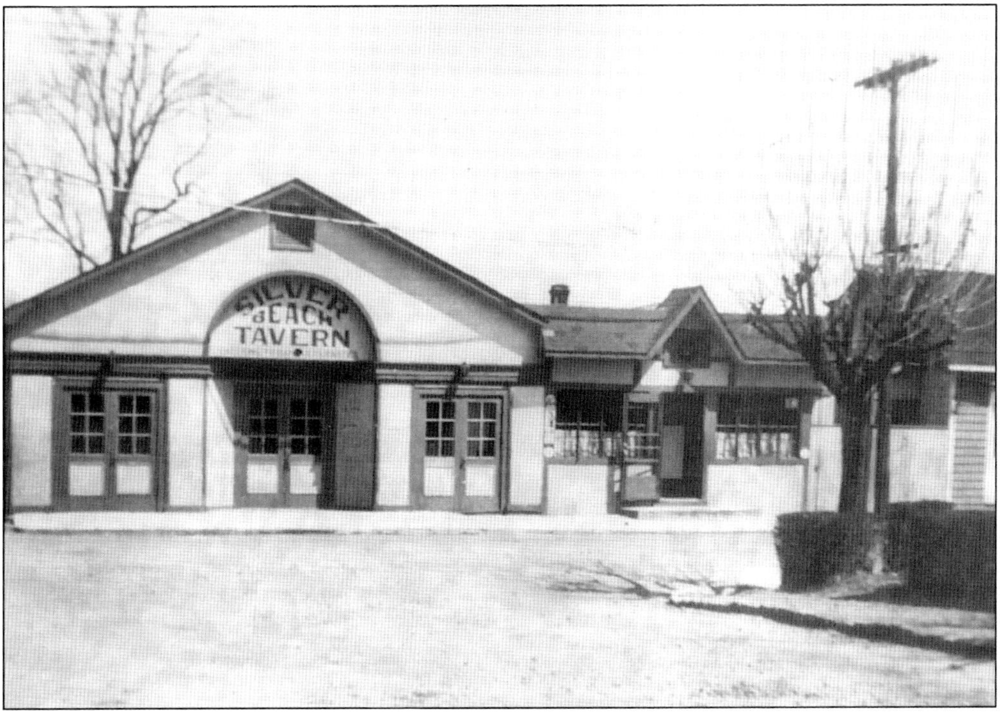

This photograph of the Silver Beach Tavern was taken shortly after it was opened by Carl Uvaro in 1934. It was destroyed by fire on Sunday, July 15, 1984. The landmark tavern and catering hall is still missed not only by the Silver Beach residents, but also by the entire community.

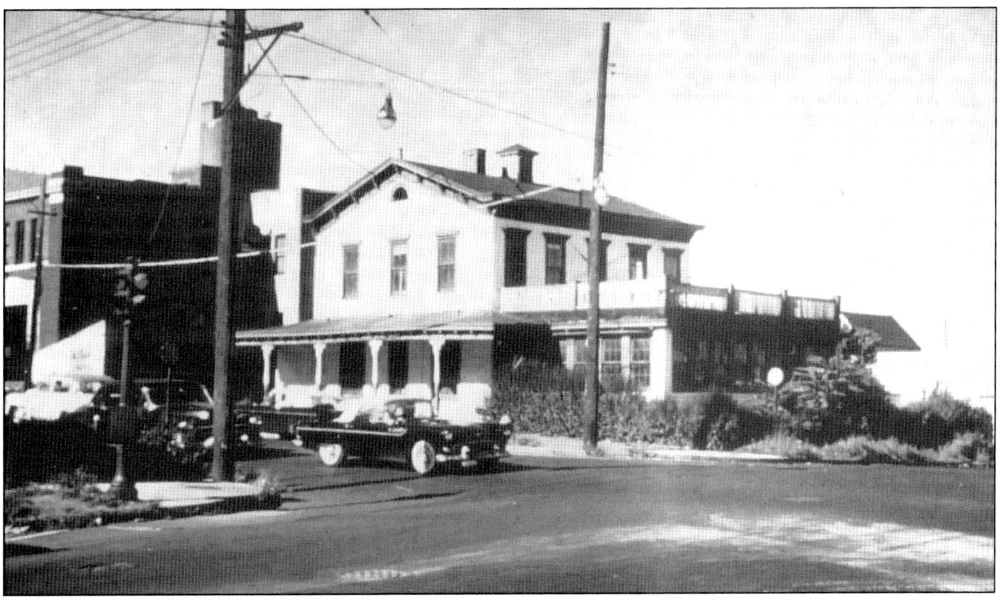

The Track Restaurant and Tavern was located on the north side of Williamsbridge Road at Eastchester Road. Charles Coleman built the structure as his home in the 1850s; it became a tavern in the 1890s. It was named after the nearby Morris Park Race Track and closed down in 1957. Ron Schliessman took this picture in 1959, shortly before the tavern was razed.

Tel. 1237 Woodlawn

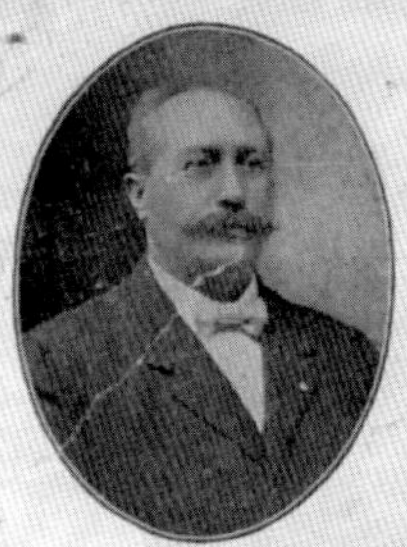

Dickert's Old Point Comfort Park

4018 BOSTON ROAD

BRONX, N. Y. CITY

No. 192

RULES and REGULATIONS

BY WHICH PARTIES MUST BE STRICTLY GOVERNED

1. A deposit is required of $ ....

2. No return checks to be issued.

3. The dancing of two gents together is strictly prohibited; also not allowed to dance with coats off.

4. Any unseemly or boisterous conduct to be instantly suppressed.

5. The right is reserved by the proprietor to expel any person objectionable to him.

6. It is distinctly understood between the parties hereto that this contract is given and the terms made by the proprietor solely upon the representations of the committee as to the standing of the Club, Lodge or Society, &c., its members, the number of members and friends expected to participate, and the benefits to be derived by the proprietor in the sale of drinkables and eatables, which representations shall not be merged in this contract, but may be proved by parole evidence—that in case of any misrepresentations or deception the Park proprietor shall have the right not only to rescind the contract or any part thereof, but also take possession of said Park and hold the said committee individually or said party or society etc., as he may choose, liable for damages.

7. The Society engages for the occasion the special officers appointed by the manager at $3.00 each.

8. The Committee or members of the Society are forbidden to bring wine, liquors or refreshments or baskets containing such on any part of the premises.

9. The Committee agree to properly advertise said Festival and make due allowance to the proprietor for loss in case the aims and purposes of the Festival shall be defeated by rain.

It is distinctly understood that in case of violation of any of the foregoing rules, or the non-performance of any of the conditions or any part thereof, the proprietor shall have the right to rescind the contract, or any part thereof, or take immediate possession of said Park.

NO INTERMISSION ALLOWED AT SUMMERNIGHT FESTIVALS

We, the undersigned, do hereby individually and as a Committee of the

____

____

an organization consisting of __________ *members, engage the above named place for* ______________________________

______________________________192____

for the purpose of ______________________________

and we do hereby agree to accept and make this contract, subject to all the conditions and rules set forth on the side, and which forms part of this contract, and for the faithful observance of said rules and the performance of the conditions, we hold ourselves individually and the said ______________

______________________________ *responsible*

For ______________________________

______________ } *Committee.*

For Proprietor ______________________________

Manager.

Dickert's Old Point Comfort Park was established at 4018 Boston Road near Dyre Avenue in the early 1900s by Henry Dickert. The 4-acre resort was a popular site for Oktoberfests, banquets, and festivals and was run by Dickert for about two decades. The rules and regulations are printed at the left in this contract from the early 1920s. Rule number three indicates "The dancing of two gents together is strictly prohibited; also not allowed to dance with coats off."

BREINLINGER'S

OLD POINT COMFORT PARK

4018 BOSTON ROAD, EASTCHESTER, N. Y.

7 Cent City Zone to Dyre Ave., Via Westchester and Boston R. R. Local Trains

TELEPHONE, WOODLAWN 1208

Up-to-Date Grounds for Picnics and Summernight Festivals

Gentlemen:

I hereby announce and recommend for the coming season's festivities my charmingly located and easily to reach Park, which affords accomoda-tions second to none in Greater New York.

The Park having ample capacity, comfortably holding 2000 to 3000 visitors and offers the following attractions for amusements : **Swings, Carousel, Long Distance Rifle Range, large Dancing Pavilion in central location of Park, 4 Bowling Alleys, Music Pavilion** ; Play-grounds for young and old, with seating capacity for 2000 shaded by hundreds of trees.

Including Dining Room and also Ball Room with elegant Restaurant annexed.

The kitchen is modern and spacious. Real German cooking prevails.

The books are now open for engagements. I respectfully invite the committees of Societies, Clubs, Lodges and Church Congregations to honor me with a visit.

Arrangements also can be made for Clam Bakes, Beefsteak Parties, Dinners and Private Celebrations.

Respectfully,

KILIAN BREINLINGER, Prop.

DIRECTIONS:

Take Second or Third Avenue Elevated to 133d Street and Change for Westchester and Boston Railroad, Get Off at Dyre Avenue Station. Or Take Subway to 180th Street, then Take Westchester and Boston Railroad to Dyre Avenue Station

117 THE J. W. BAUER CO., PRINTERS, 362 EAST 148TH STREET, THE BRONX

Kilian Breinlinger purchased Dickert's Old Point Comfort Park from Henry Dickert in 1926 and issued this flyer to announce the availability of his resort to societies, clubs, lodges, and church groups. The park held 2,000 to 3,000 visitors and offered real German cooking. Among the amenities advertised here were swings, a carousel, a long distance rifle range, a large dancing pavilion, and four bowling alleys. Breinlinger maintained the park through 1957. It was razed in 1960.

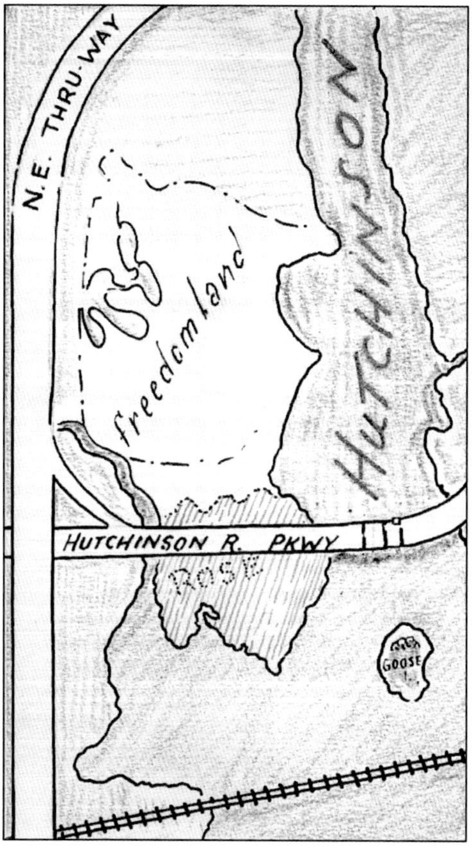

Bronx historian John McNamara was among the dignitaries at the groundbreaking ceremonies for Freedomland. Created in the shape of the U.S., it was located west of the Hutchinson River between the New England Thruway and the Hutchinson River Parkway. Construction began on August 26, 1959. John McNamara drew this map.

Freedomland opened on June 19, 1960, and was immediately hailed as the largest amusement park in the world. It boasted of 305 acres shaped in the form of a map of the U.S. New York's cold winters and the opening of the New York World's Fair contributed to its demise. The park filed for bankruptcy on September 15, 1964. Co-op City was later built on the site. The Paul Lavalle Freedomland Band was performing in Old New York in this photograph from September of 1962.

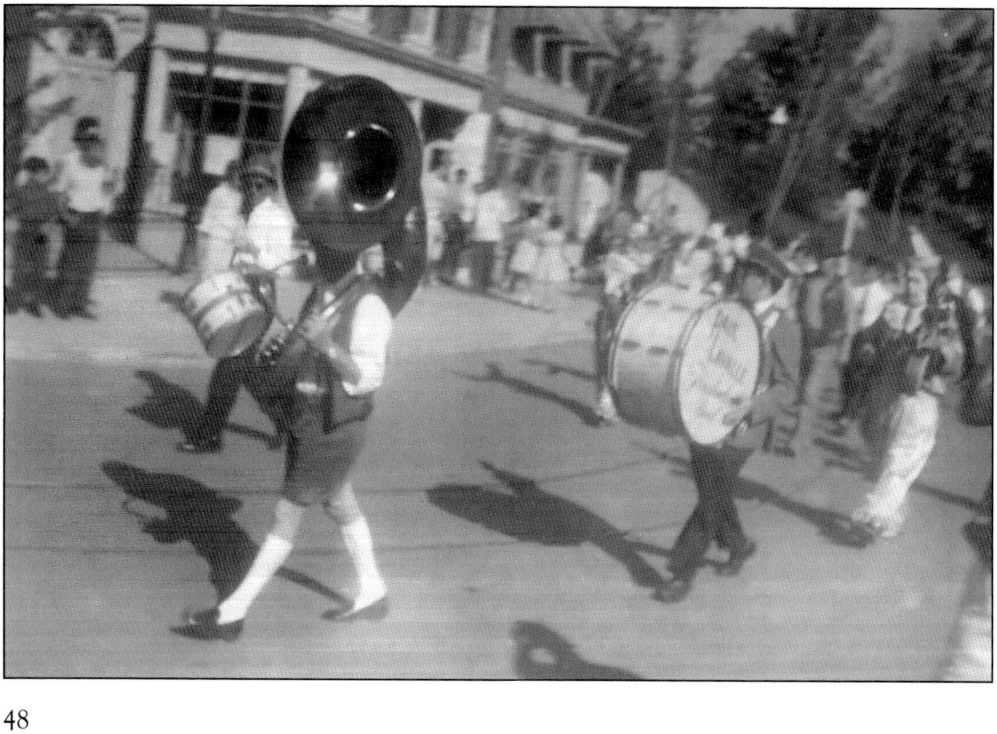

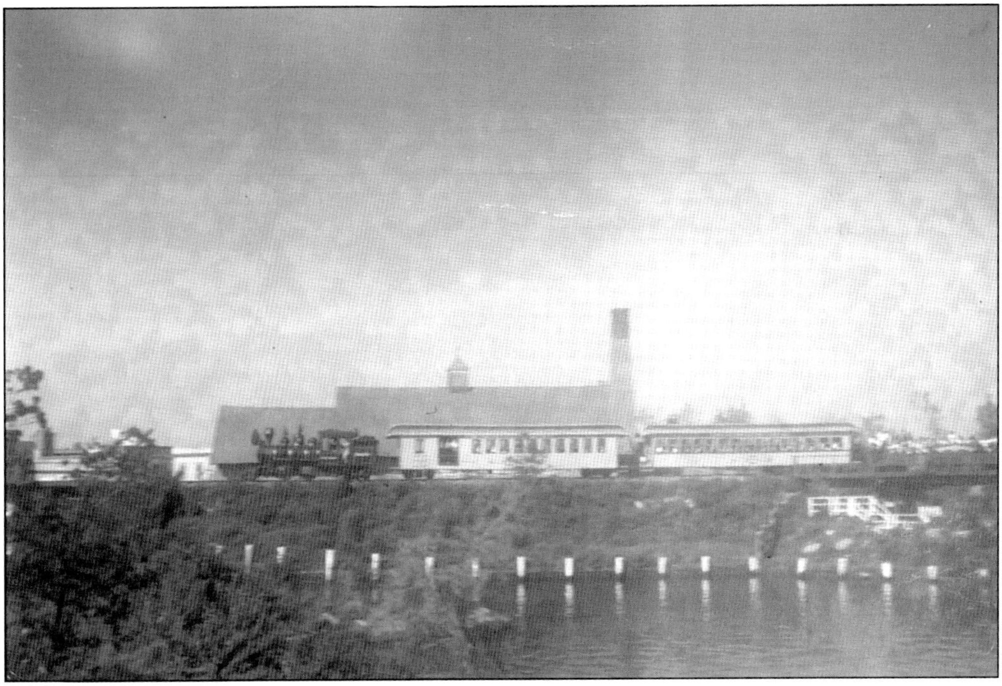

Few will forget the jingle "Mommy, Daddy, take my hand. Take me out to Freedomland." One of the popular attractions was the Sante Fe Railroad, which took you from Chicago to San Francisco, where one could experience the 1906 earthquake, visit Fisherman's Wharf, or visit Chinatown.

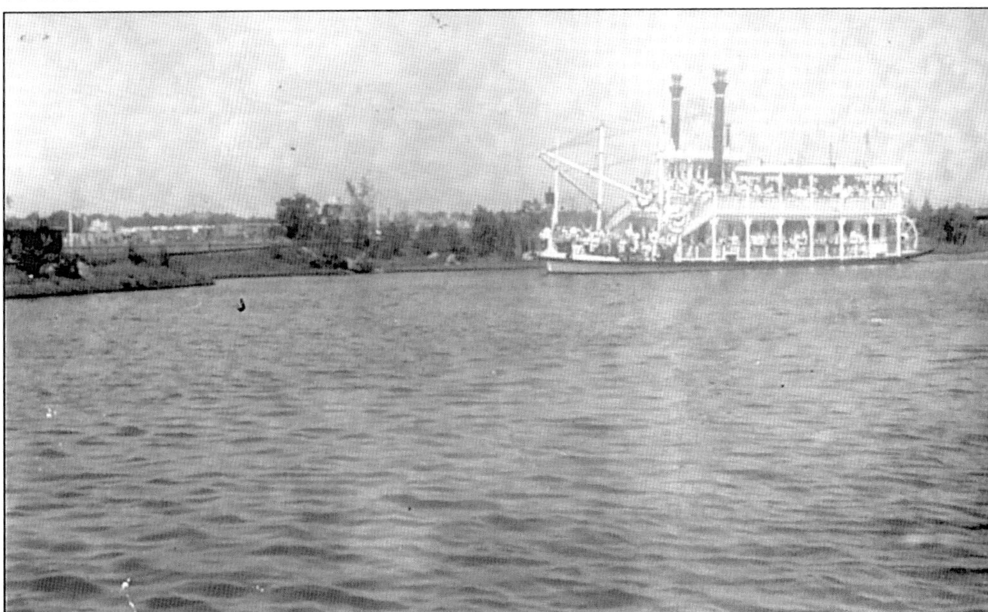

Jack McCarrick took these photographs of Freedomland; this one shows the Great Lakes Excursion Boat, a sternwheeler, traversing the waters past Native-American villages and the Canadian shore. The seven areas of Freedomland were Little Old New York, Old Chicago, San Francisco, the Great Plains, the Old Southwest, New Orleans, and Satellite City.

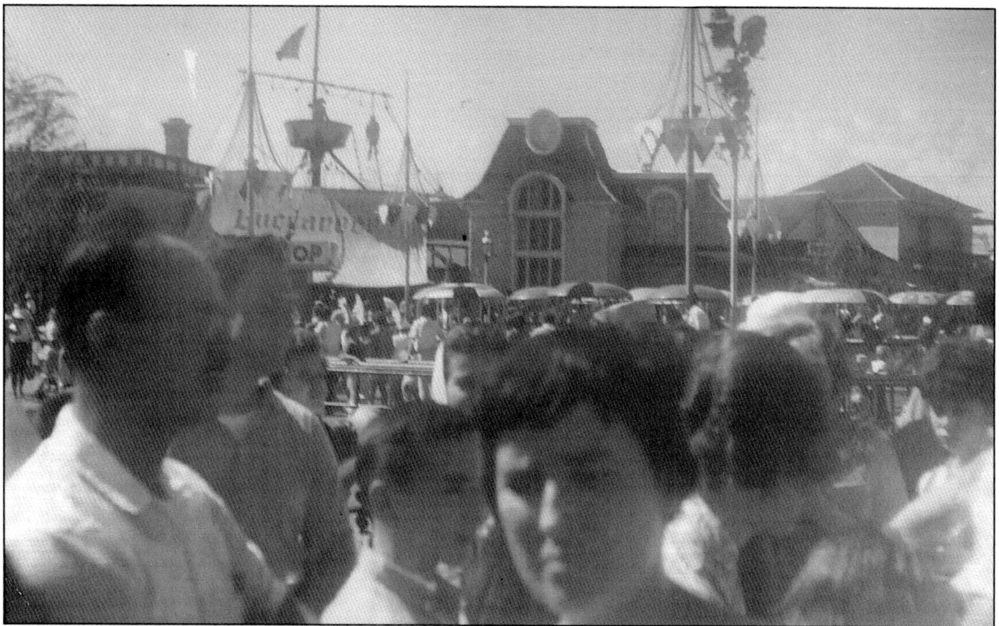

This Jack McCarrick photograph of New Orleans, one of seven Freedomland sites, was taken in September of 1962. Among the attractions in this area were the Crystal Maze, which was constructed of elaborate sets of mirrors and the Tornado. The latter allowed one to experience being in the eye of a tornado.

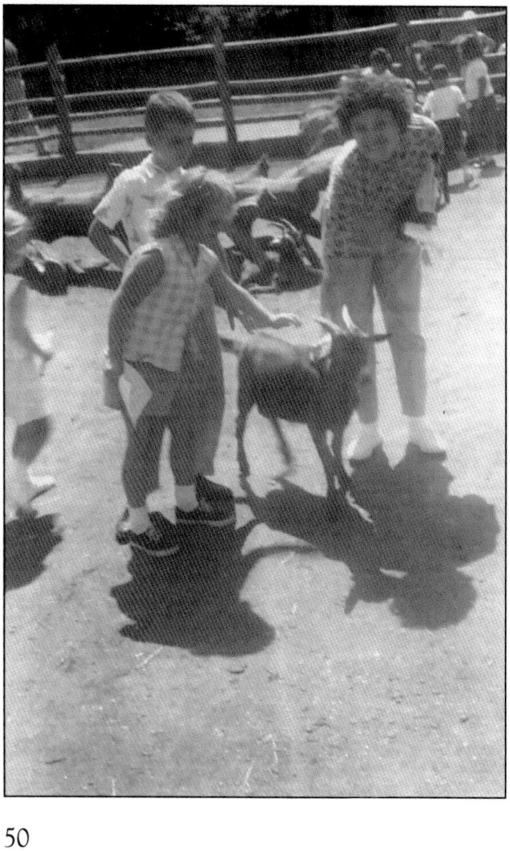

The McCarrick family were among the millions who visited Freedomland in the northeast Bronx. This photograph was taken in the area designated as the Midwest, and Jack, Ann Marie, and their mother, Ann McCarrick, are shown here with a young goat in 1962.

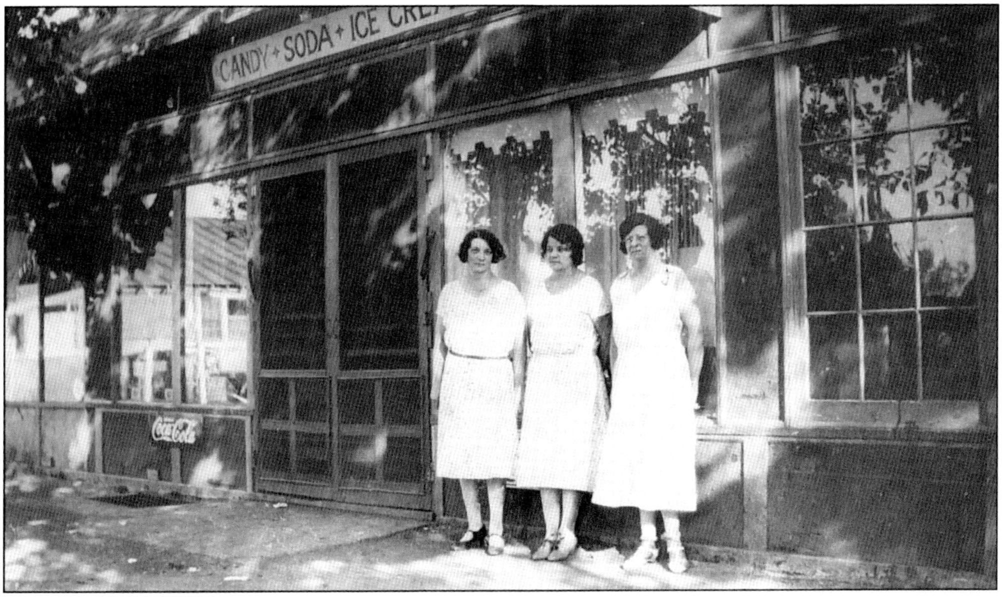

Juliet, Emily, and Dottie Willing ran the Edgewater Park Candy Store for James Shaw up to the early 1940s, when Herman O'Neill took over. Herman later sold out to Anna Wehr, who ran it with her young son Larry.

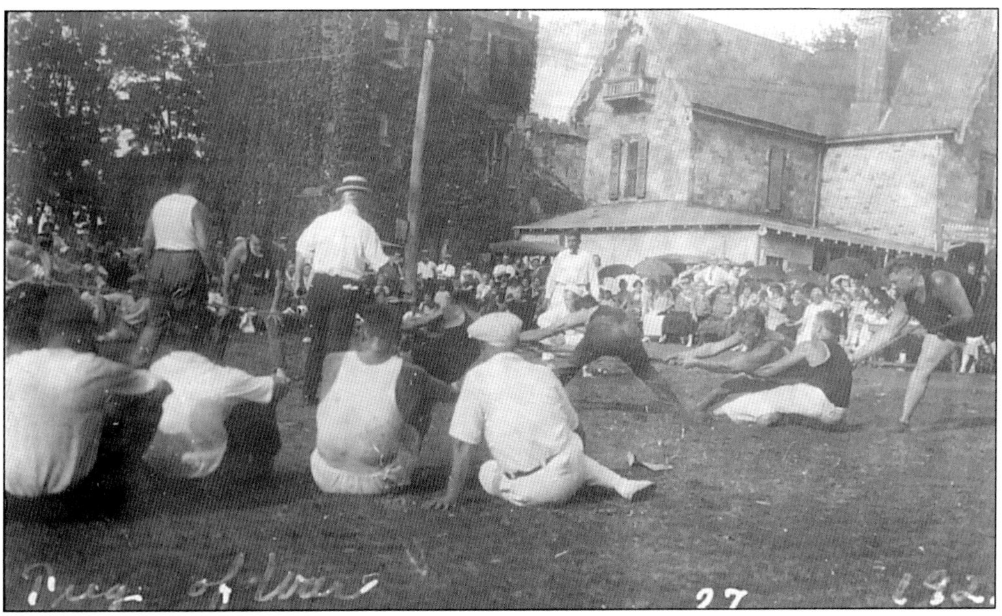
This tug-or-war contest between lifeguards and the volunteer hose company in Edgewater Park took place in 1923. The former Adee Mansion is in the background. The wooden addition in the front right was the ice cream parlor, while the general store was in the mansion.

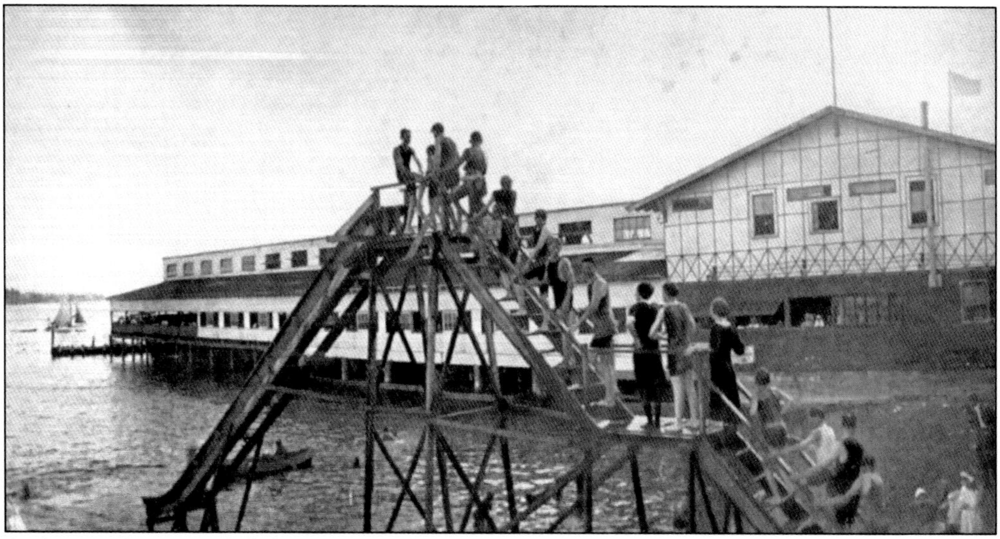

Arthur Seifert provided this picture of the giant slide at the Clason Point Amusement Park. It was taken in the 1920s, and you will readily note that all the young men have tops to their bathing trunks. The slide goes into the waters of the East River, and Gilligan's Pavilion is at the right. The park was accessible by both land and sea.

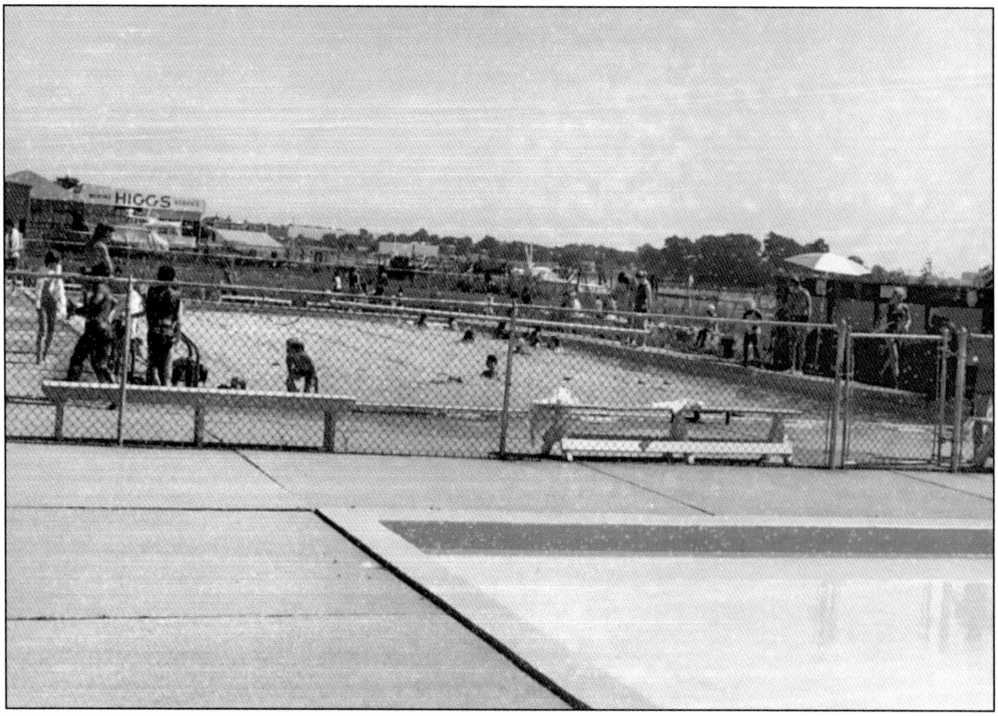

Arthur Seifert provided this photograph, taken less than two decades ago, of the Castle Hill Pool with Higgs Marina in the background.

This flier for Higgs Camp Grounds on Clason Point advertises the 1922 rates for their facilities. Shore sites rented at $80 for the summer season, while those to the rear were $75. Winter rates were $8 per family per month. Tents were replaced by bungalows that were later insulated for year-round living. The site is now called Harding Park. Arthur Seifert provided this flier.

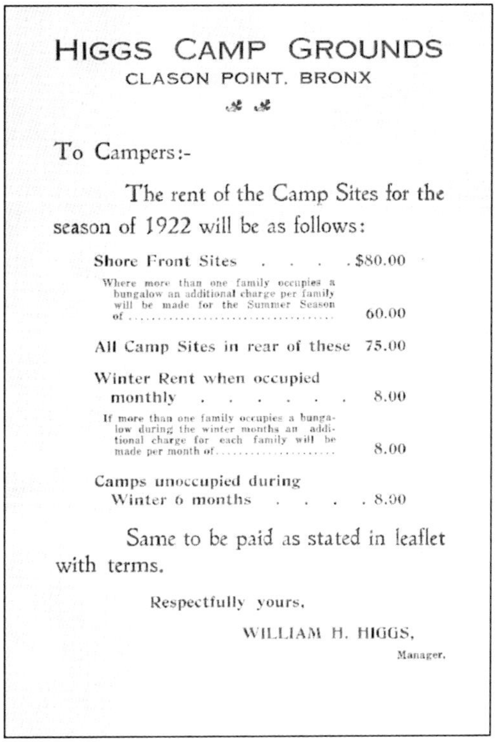

HIGGS CAMP GROUNDS
CLASON POINT, BRONX

To Campers:-

The rent of the Camp Sites for the season of 1922 will be as follows:

Shore Front Sites	$80.00
Where more than one family occupies a bungalow an additional charge per family will be made for the Summer Season of	60.00
All Camp Sites in rear of these	75.00
Winter Rent when occupied monthly	8.00
If more than one family occupies a bungalow during the winter months an additional charge for each family will be made per month of	8.00
Camps unoccupied during Winter 6 months	8.00

Same to be paid as stated in leaflet with terms.

Respectfully yours,

WILLIAM H. HIGGS,
Manager.

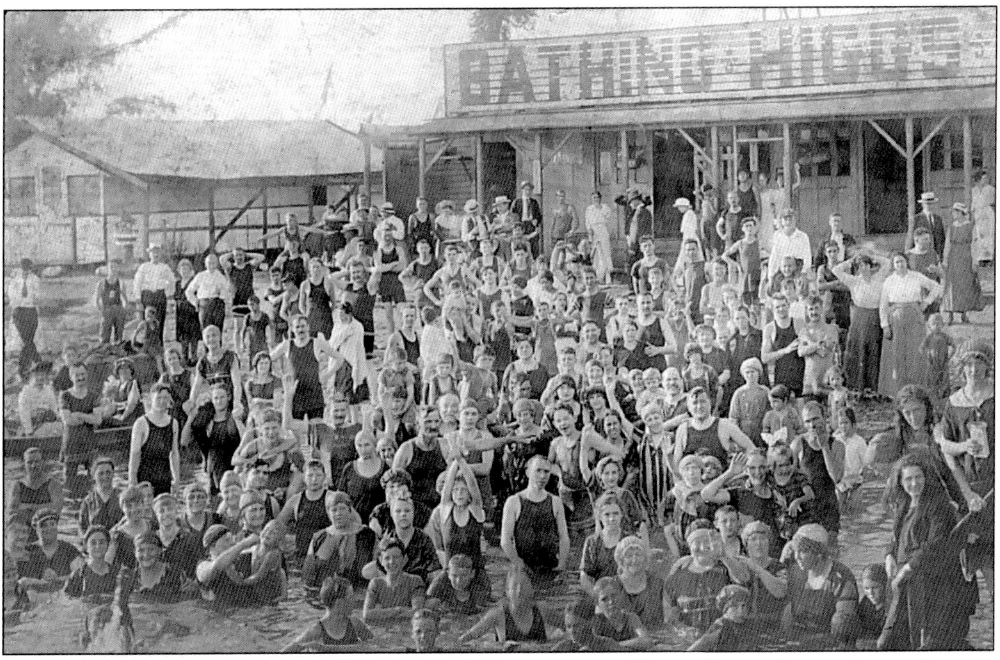

Higgs Beach and Camp Ground was a grand attraction on Clason Point during the mid-teens, as this picture of bathers shows. The recreational facility was established by Thomas Higgs and his son, William, who took over the management c. 1914. It developed into a bungalow colony, and the year after President Warren Harding died, it was renamed in his honor. Harding Park is located west of White Plains Road at the East River. Arthur Seifert provided the photograph.

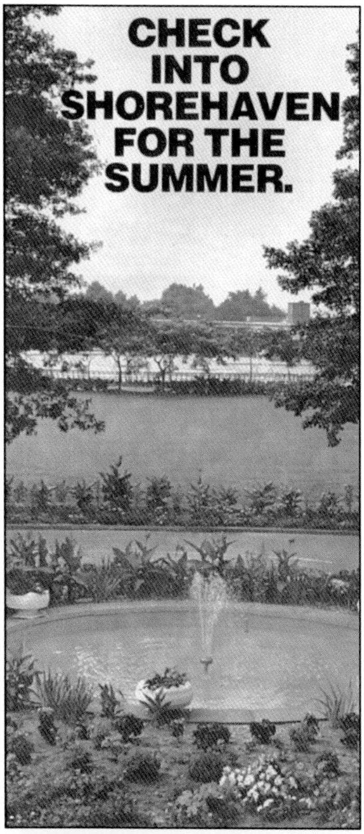

This Shorehaven brochure touts the many amenities at their beach resort at Clason Point. Located at the end of White Plains Road, it boasted of the largest saltwater pool in New York and top notch entertainment by such stars as Red Buttons, Norm Crosby, Nipsey Russell and many others. Also, they offered private transportation by the Shorehaven bus.

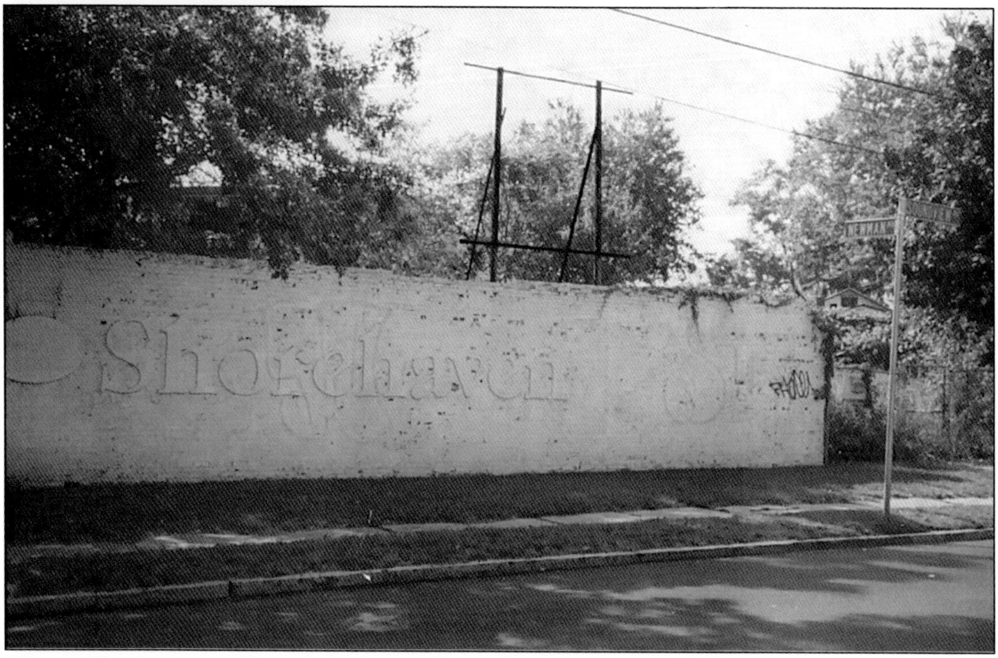

This wall, advertising Shorehaven, is still standing and brings back memories of the amiable owners, the Goldstein family; the huge pool; fantastic shows; dancing; barbecues; and various contests. Others may recall the Shorehaven Follies or Wednesday night square dancing.

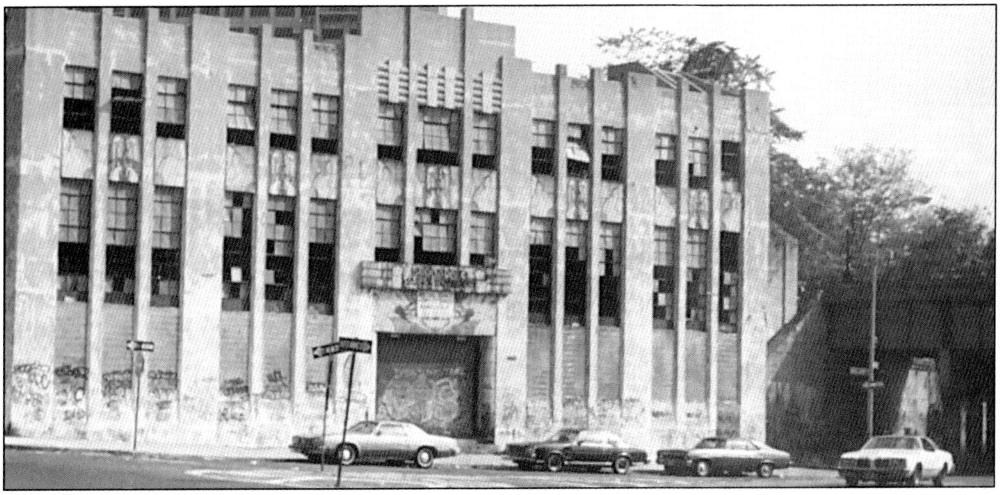

I took this photograph of the Bronxdale Pool October 16, 1988. It looked neglected enough that I thought it might soon be razed. Located on Bronxdale Avenue at Antin Place, it once played host to New York's leading talent including Milton Berle, Henny Yougman, Morton Downey, and so many others. Built after World War I, it started to decline in popularity during World War II. A principal attraction was the huge pool.

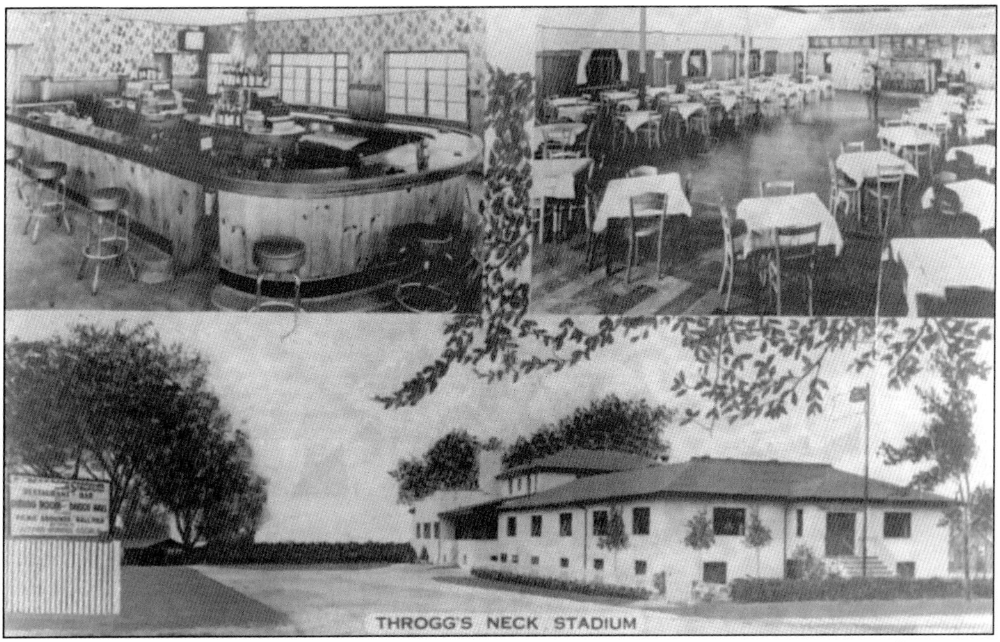

The Throggs Neck Country Club, located at Schurz and Hosmer Avenues, was once known as German Stadium. It was the site of international soccer matches, after which numerous languages were spoken around the oval bar in the upper left photograph. Many wedding receptions and reunions were hosted in the main dining hall to the right. The rear portion of the building at the bottom, where the chimney is located, was part of the old Morris mansion. It was built c. 1851 and was home to Francis Morris of horse racing fame. His grandson, Alfred Hennen Morris, later resided here and is credited with establishing the Morris Park Race Course. The Zeumer family operated the Stadium from the mid-1930s to 1970, when Marty Gilligan, Frank Hogan, and Tom Garvey purchased the complex. It was razed in 1988.

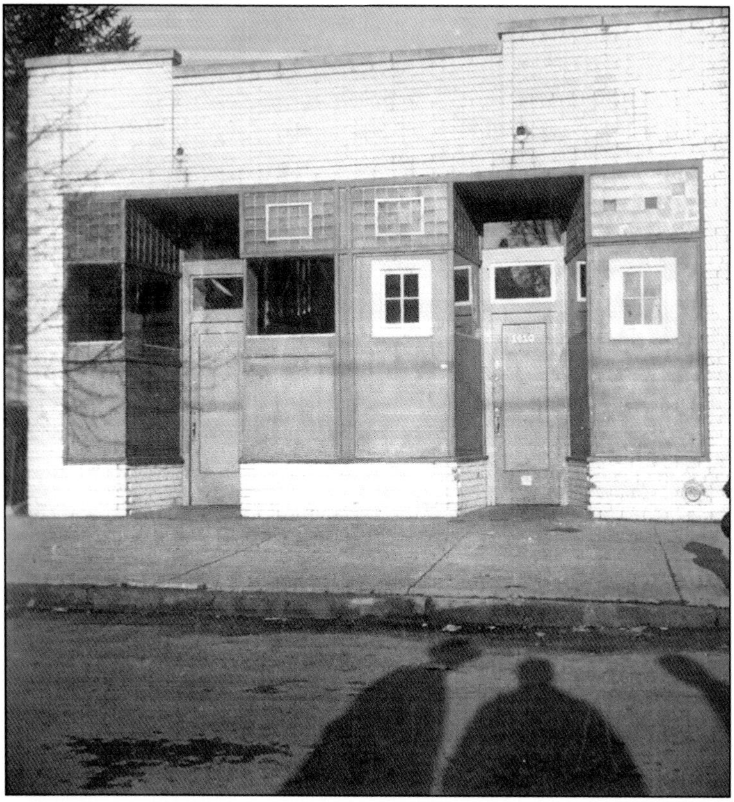

The Glover Boys Club was established at Glover Street and Westchester Avenue in 1936. It later became a canoe club and rented storage space at Lohbauer's on the Long Island Sound. This photograph was taken in 1940.

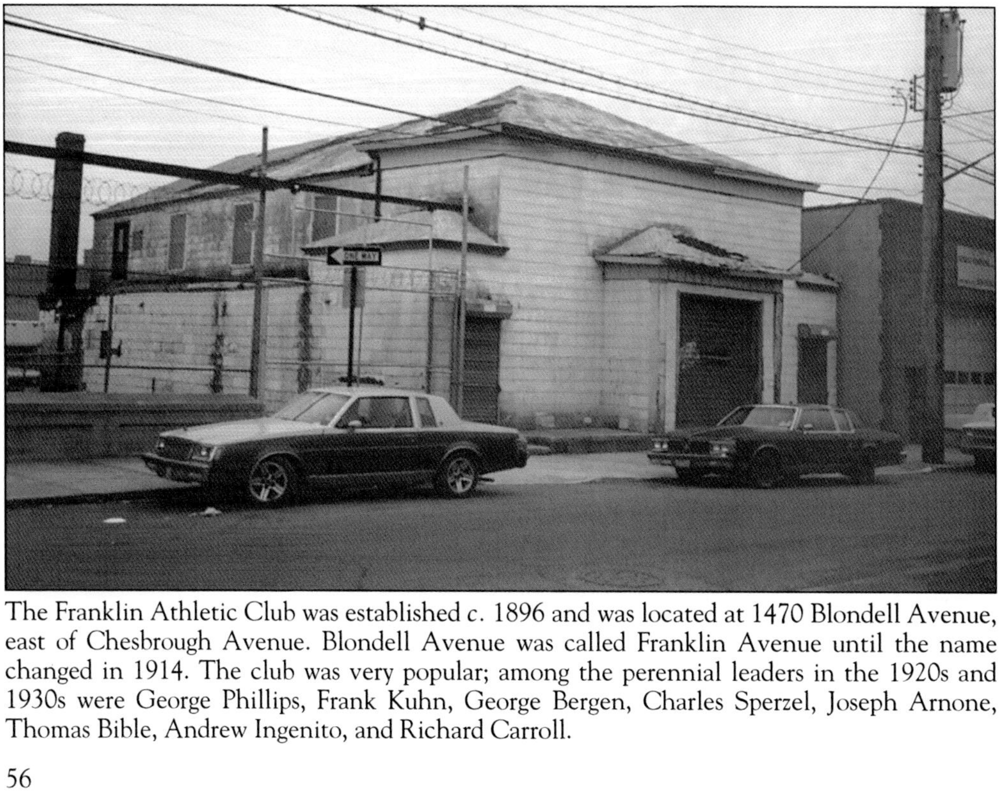

The Franklin Athletic Club was established *c.* 1896 and was located at 1470 Blondell Avenue, east of Chesbrough Avenue. Blondell Avenue was called Franklin Avenue until the name changed in 1914. The club was very popular; among the perennial leaders in the 1920s and 1930s were George Phillips, Frank Kuhn, George Bergen, Charles Sperzel, Joseph Arnone, Thomas Bible, Andrew Ingenito, and Richard Carroll.

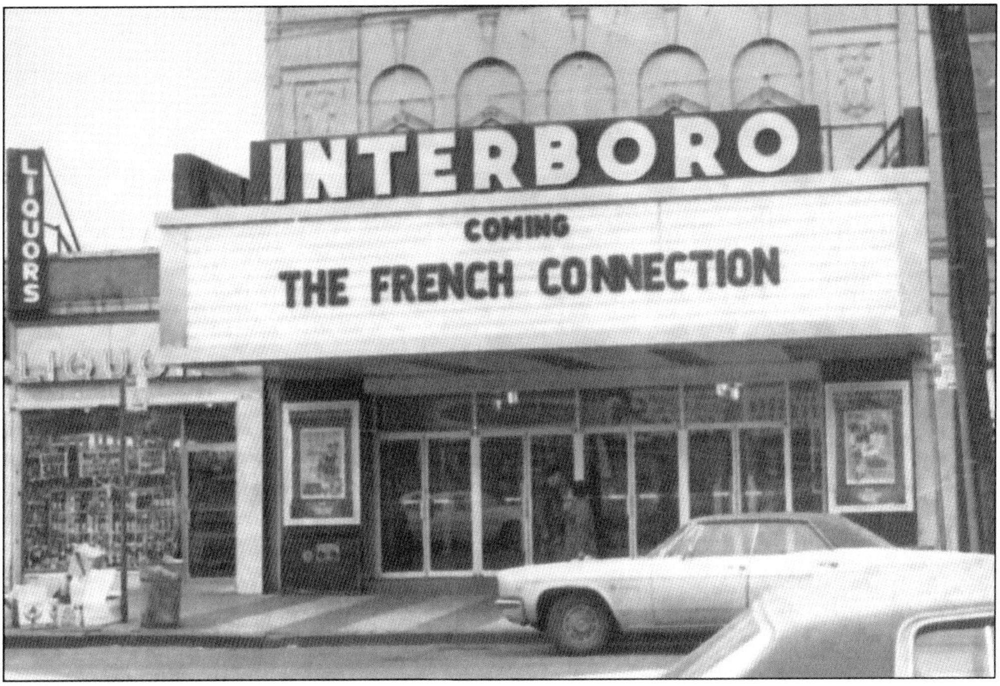

Bob Barrett provided this photograph of the Interboro Theater, taken in 1971 with the marquee advertising the coming of *The French Connection*. The theater, located at 3462 E. Tremont Avenue, opened in 1925 and was named for the Interborough Rapid Transit, which had planned a crosstown line that would have terminated on East Tremont Avenue at East 177th Street.

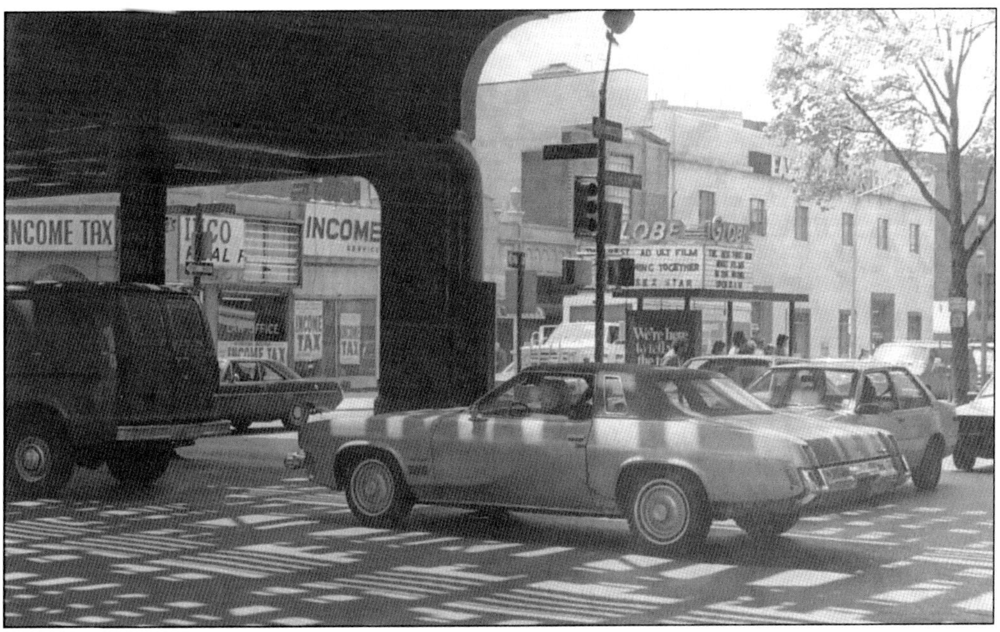

The Globe Theater, at 640 Pelham Parkway South west of White Plains Road, opened in 1938 as a family theater. When this picture was taken almost 50 years later, the clientele had changed.

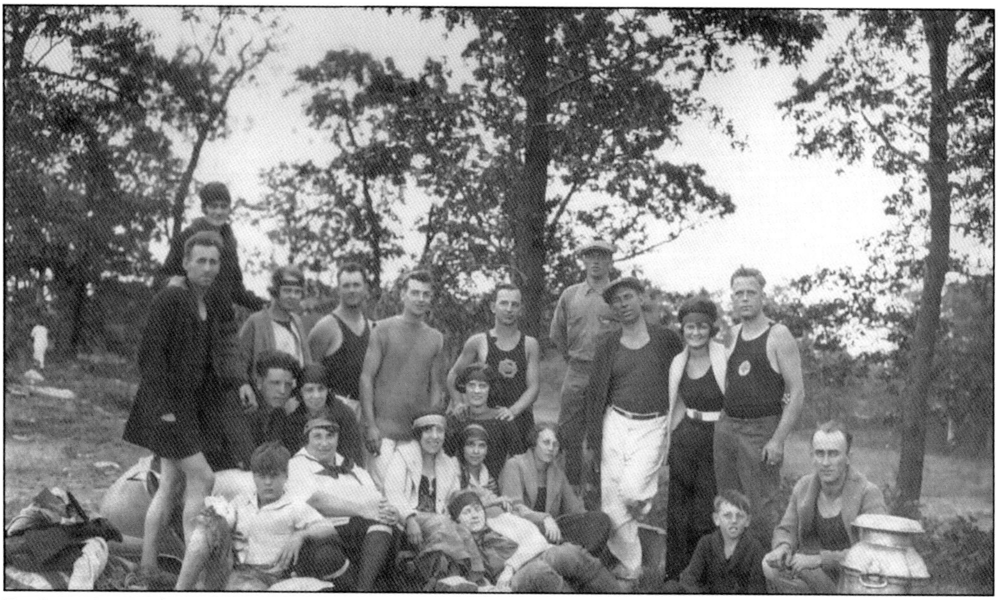

Rodman's Neck means many things to many people. This photograph was taken in 1924, when the area was often used as a picnic ground. This group paddled from Edgewater Park in canoes. The police currently use one end for a firing range, and the Parks Department use another area, but you can still find groups hosting picnics in the area. John McNamara provided this photograph.

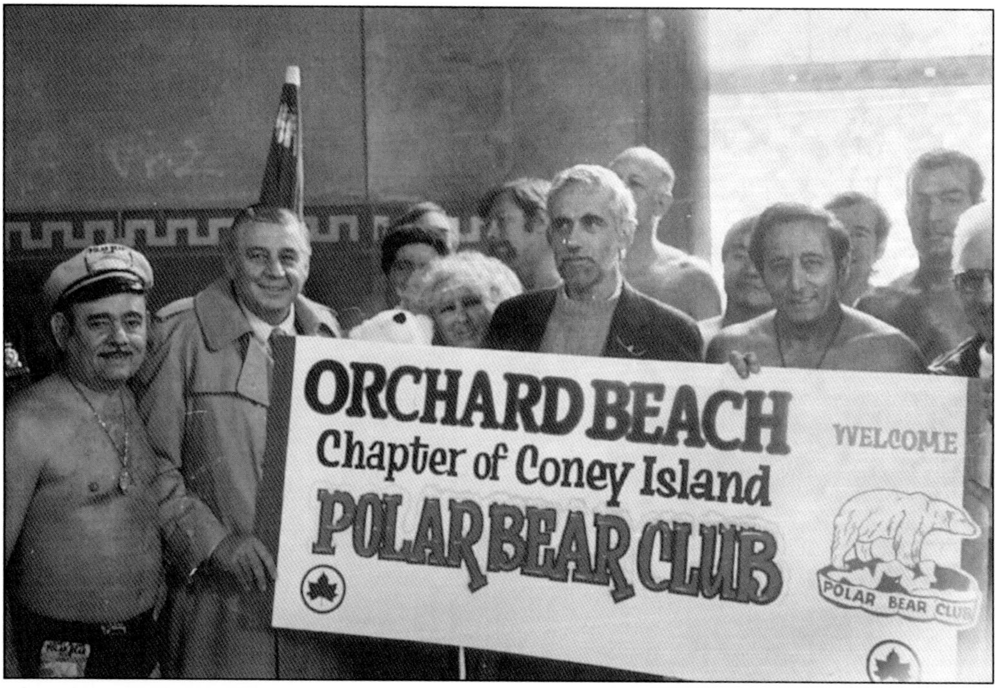

This photograph from the late-1980s shows that Orchard Beach can be fun at any time of the year. The Coney Island chapter of the Polar Bear Club braves even the coldest weather at the beach. Councilman Jerry Crispino is second from the left, and Parks Commissioner Henry Stern (with the beard) can be seen in the center.

Five

School Days

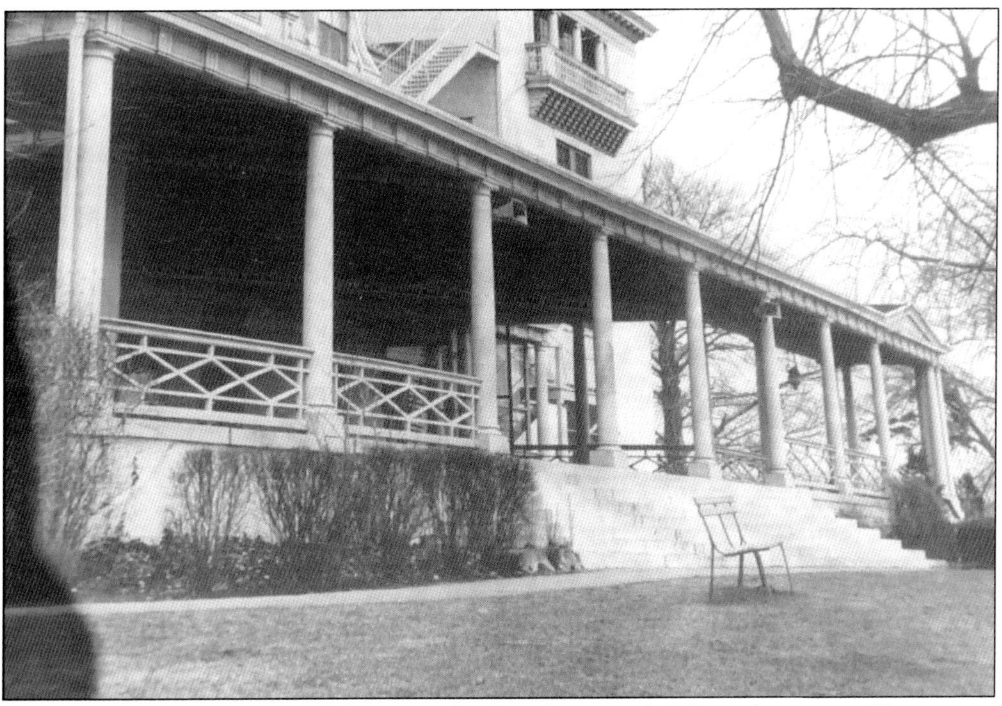

Preston High School, situated between the East River and Schurz Avenue at Huntington Avenue, affords one a spectacular view of both the Throgs Neck and Whitestone Bridges. Housed in a mansion built in 1864 for Frederick C. Havemeyer, it later became home to railroad tycoon Collis P. Huntington. The school was established in 1947 by the Sisters of Divine Compassion. Sister Lucille Coldrick currently serves as principal.

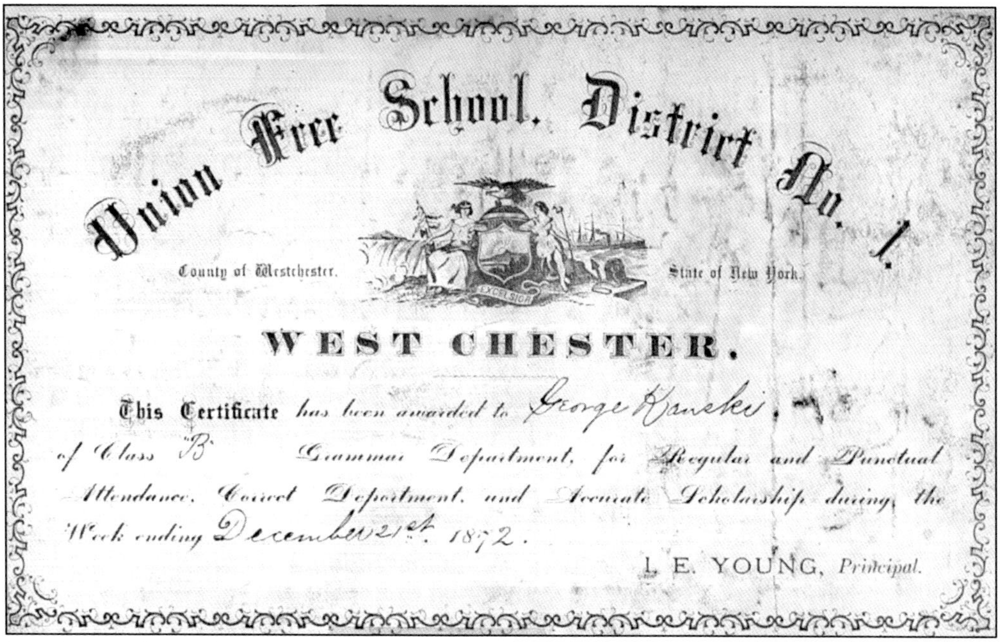

Union Free School, District No. 1.

County of Westchester. State of New York.

EXCELSIOR

WEST CHESTER.

This Certificate has been awarded to George Kanski, of Class B Grammar Department, for Regular and Punctual Attendance, Correct Deportment, and Accurate Scholarship during the Week ending December 21st 1872.

I. E. YOUNG, Principal.

The Union Free School, District No. 1 was a little brown wooden building on the Pelham Road between Zulette and Roebling Avenues. It was built in 1842 and was in use until the new schoolhouse on Frisby Avenue was built in 1886. This certificate, provided by John McNamara, is dated December 21, 1872 and is made out to George Kanski. John Burke bought the old building and used it as a barn. It was razed for the construction of the Hutchinson River Parkway.

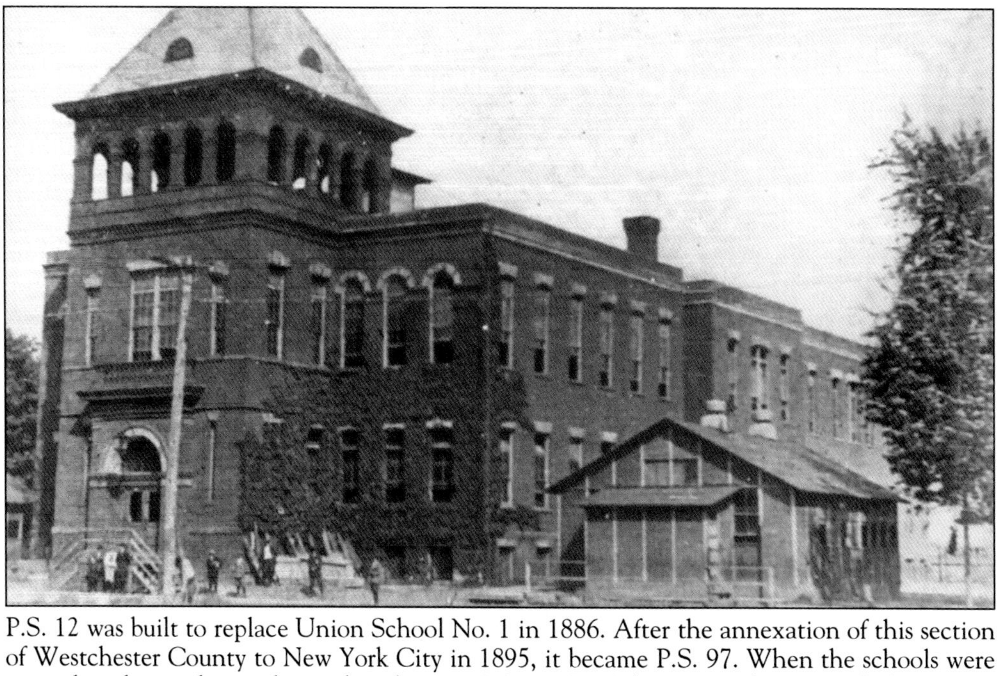

P.S. 12 was built to replace Union School No. 1 in 1886. After the annexation of this section of Westchester County to New York City in 1895, it became P.S. 97. When the schools were renumbered according to borough, it became P.S. 12. Dr. John F. Condon is recalled as one of the most popular early principals. Ron Schliessman provided the photograph.

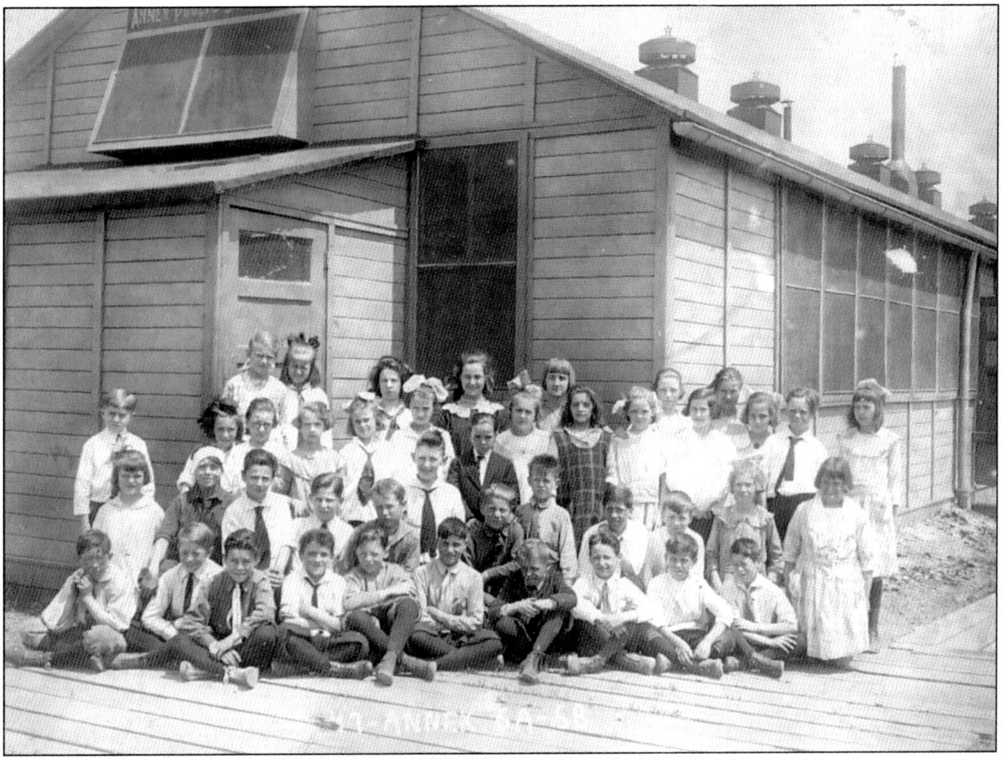

P.S. 47 is on East 172nd Street, but this photograph from the Seifert Collection was taken at their old annex on Soundview Avenue, across from Patterson Field. This image shows the 5th grade class and the building that was affectionately called the chicken coops.

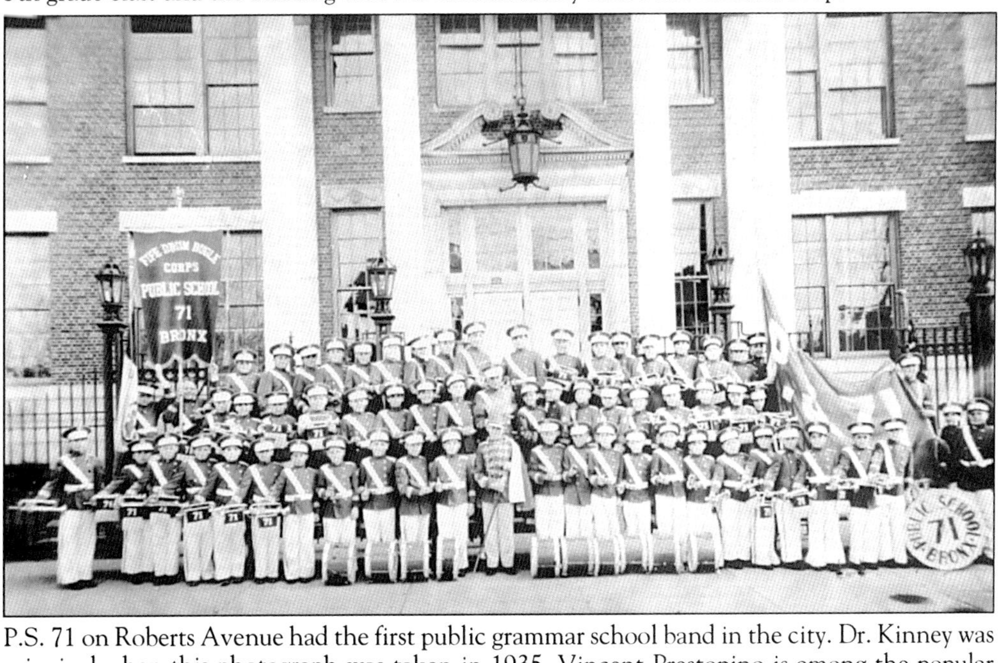

P.S. 71 on Roberts Avenue had the first public grammar school band in the city. Dr. Kinney was principal when this photograph was taken in 1935. Vincent Prestopino is among the popular locals in the picture.

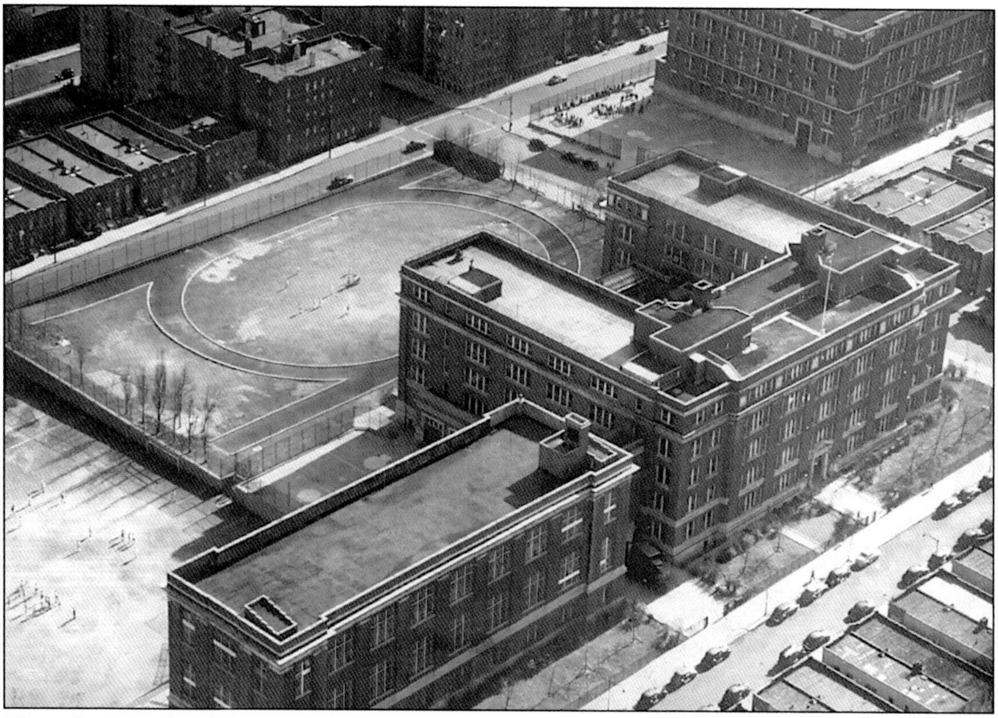

This photograph of James Monroe High School on Boynton Avenue was taken from the air by Arthur Seifert in 1946. P.S. 77 on Ward Avenue is at the right rear. This view looks to the north.

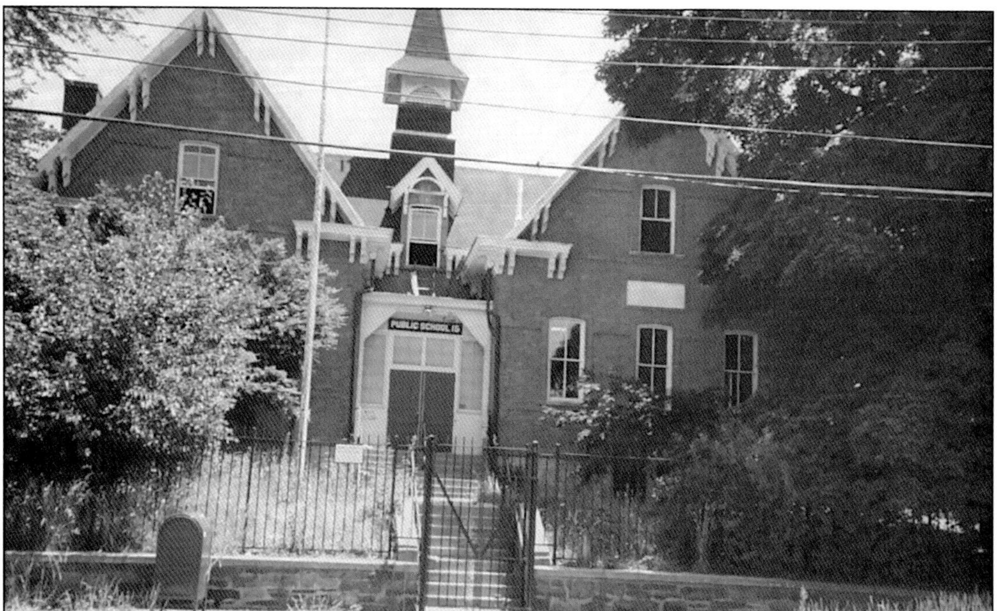

The "Little Red Schoolhouse," located at 4010 Dyre Avenue, was founded in 1877 when the area was still part of Westchester County. The official designation later became P.S. 15. When the enrollment shrank to only 84 students in 1955, its value as an educational facility was questioned; it later became a community cultural center.

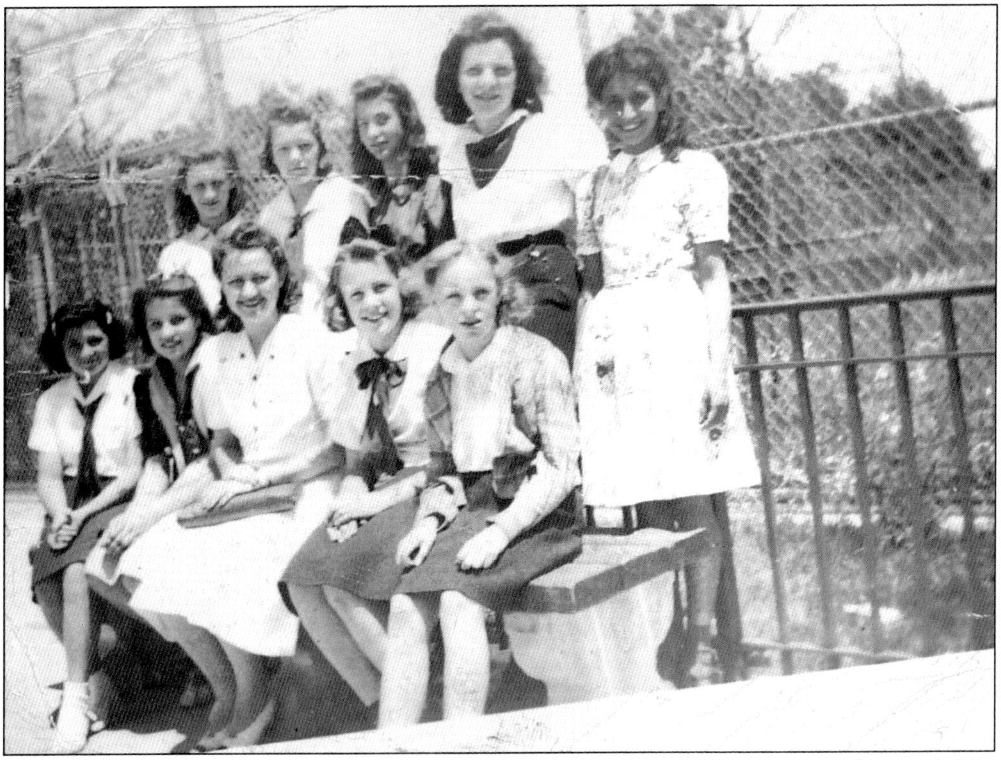

This photograph of the girls in 7A3 at P.S. 14 was taken on June 11, 1941 and provided by Kate Converso. Seen here are, from left to right, as follows: (front row) Orsolia Bonacorso, Eugenia Cuite, Miss Dunn (the teacher), Marion Kirchner, and Patricia Shanley; (back row) Rose Piscatelli, Catherine Reilly, Jean Lemonoff, Doris Timmoney, and Caroline Uhl.

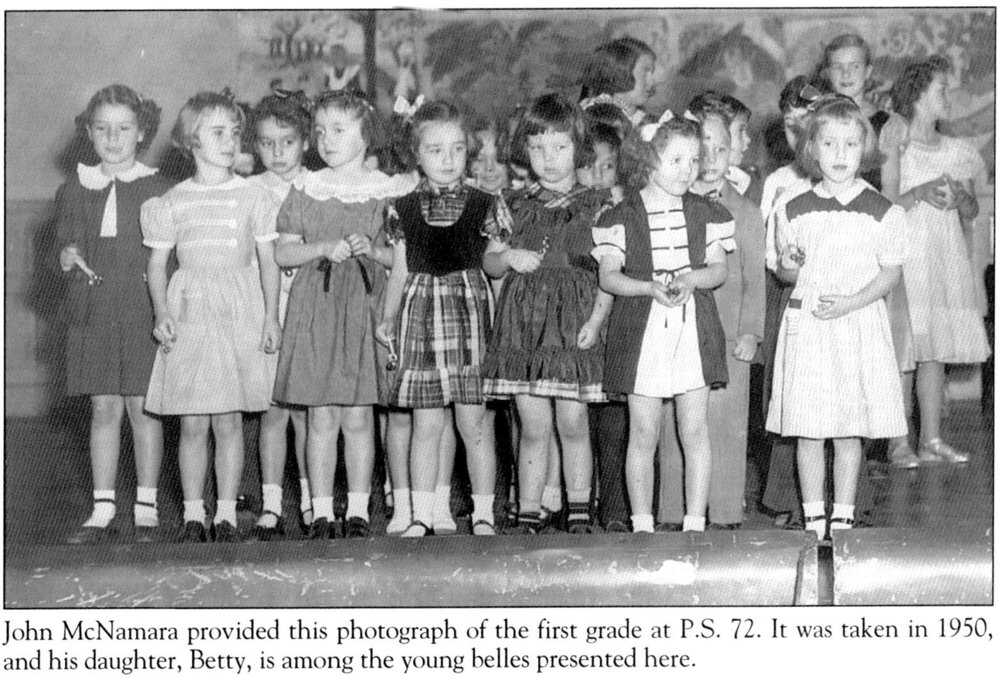

John McNamara provided this photograph of the first grade at P.S. 72. It was taken in 1950, and his daughter, Betty, is among the young belles presented here.

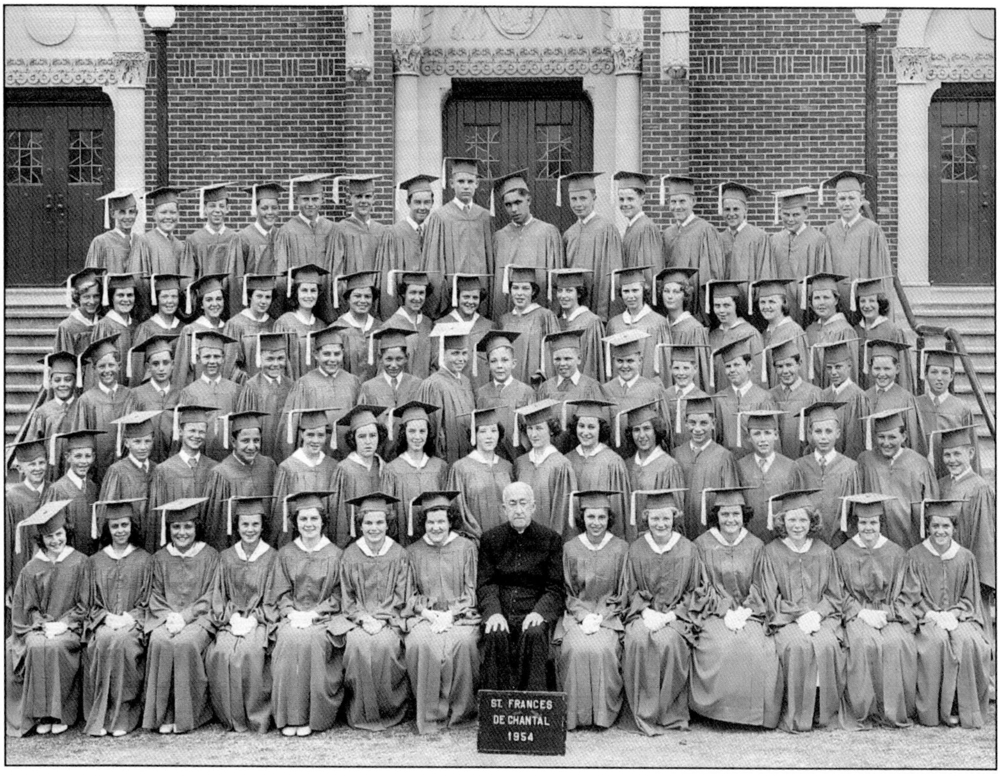

Father William Jordan poses with the 1954 graduation class of St. Frances de Chantal School in front of the church and school on Harding Avenue. This class picture was the last he posed in, as he passed away before the next graduation. Frank Twomey Jr. provided the picture.

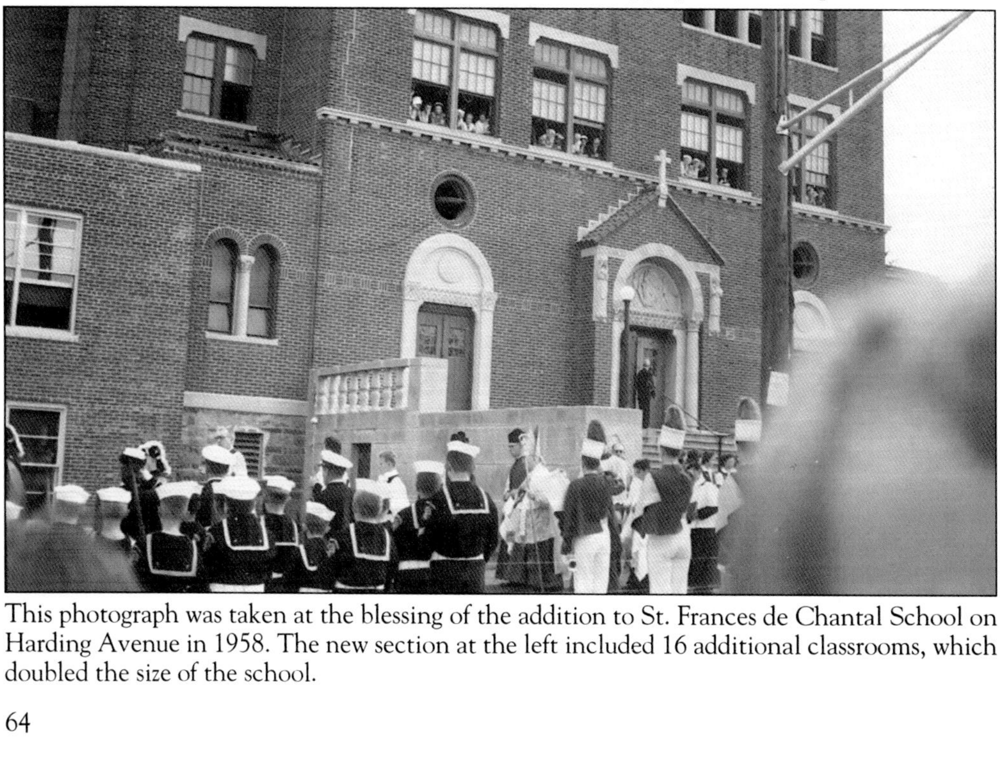
This photograph was taken at the blessing of the addition to St. Frances de Chantal School on Harding Avenue in 1958. The new section at the left included 16 additional classrooms, which doubled the size of the school.

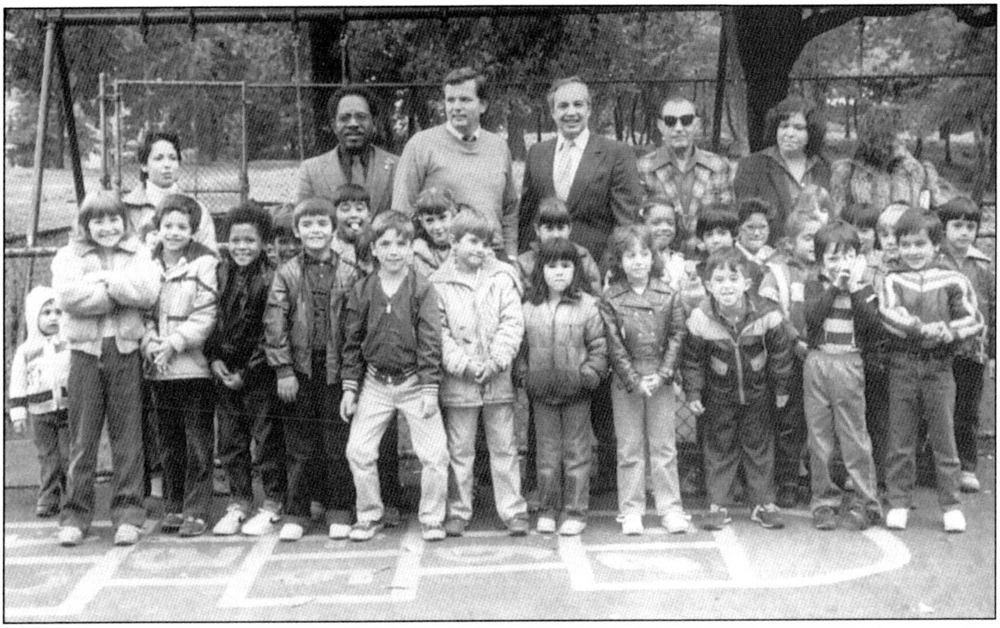

Students from P.S. 105, located at 725 Brady Avenue, strike a pose with leaders in this photograph from the late 1980s. Among those in the back row center are Sid Richards and Barrett Taylor of the Parks Department, Councilman Mike DeMarco, and Jerry Drillings.

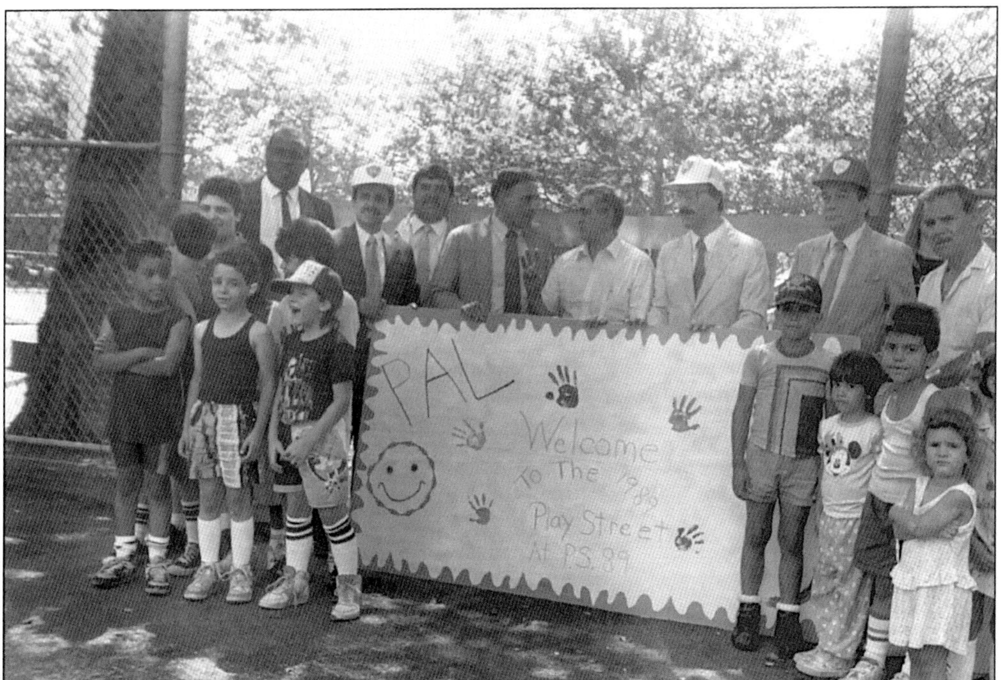

P.S. 89, located at 980 Mace Avenue, celebrated the opening of their play street in 1989 with local leaders.

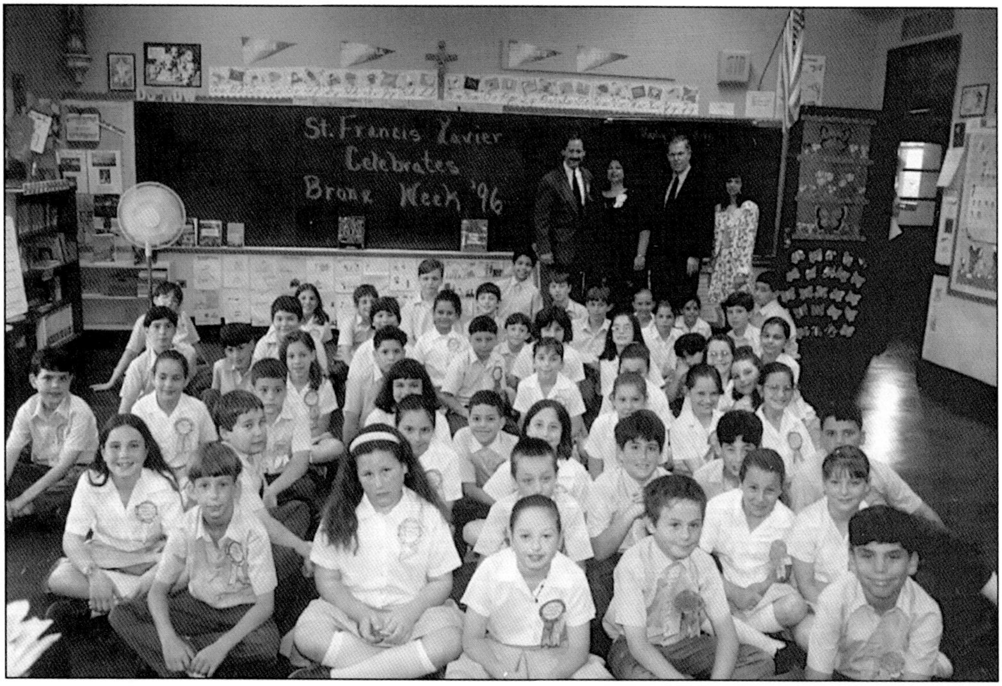

St. Francis Xavier Elementary School was celebrating Bronx Week in 1996 when this scene was photographed. Helping to celebrate the occasion is Fernando Ferrer, borough president; Mrs. Carolyn Cremonese, a teacher; Robert Heckmann, the principal; and Miss Jo Ann Rocco, a 4th grade teacher. The school is located at 1711 Haight Avenue.

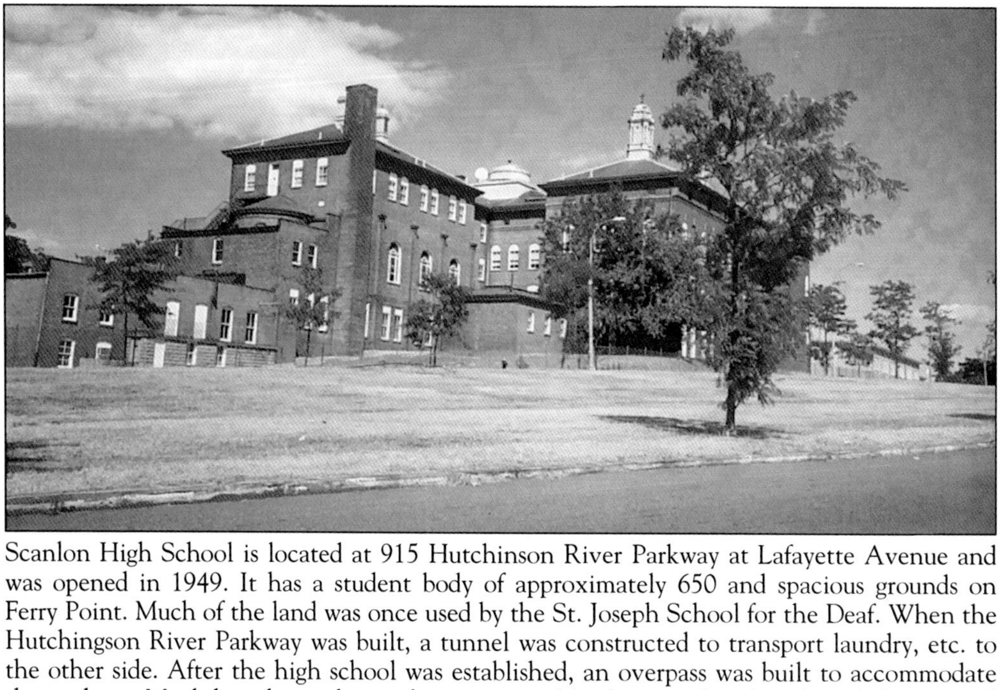

Scanlon High School is located at 915 Hutchinson River Parkway at Lafayette Avenue and was opened in 1949. It has a student body of approximately 650 and spacious grounds on Ferry Point. Much of the land was once used by the St. Joseph School for the Deaf. When the Hutchingson River Parkway was built, a tunnel was constructed to transport laundry, etc. to the other side. After the high school was established, an overpass was built to accommodate the students. Much has changed over the years, yet this photograph, taken from Lafayette and Brush Avenues in 1995, affords us a fine view of the school and grounds.

Six

Changing Scenes

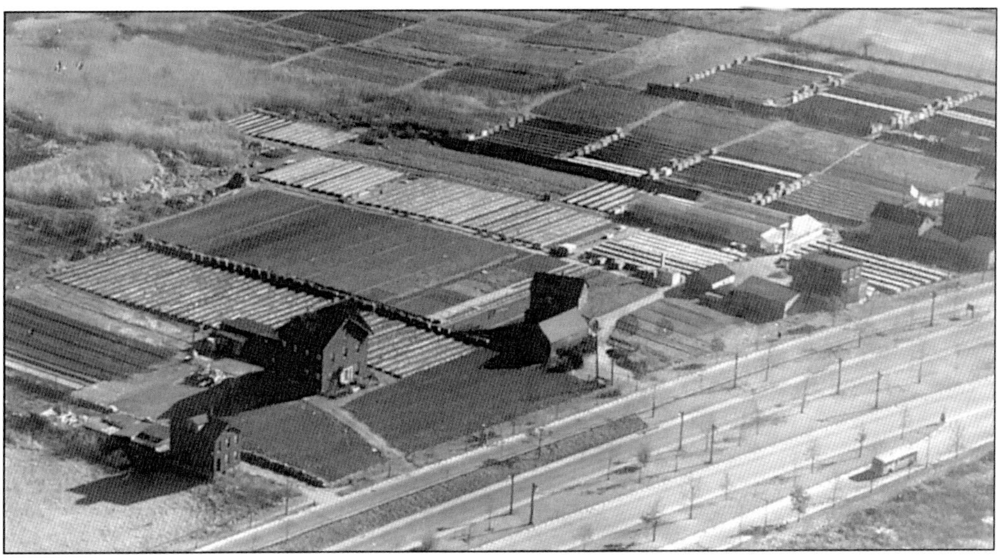

This aerial photograph, by Art and Vernon Seifert, was taken from a Piper Cub looking southeast at Ferry Point in the fall of 1946. The Hutchinson River Parkway is in the foreground. Only one bus is traveling on the lonely road. Note the farms that still occupied the area.

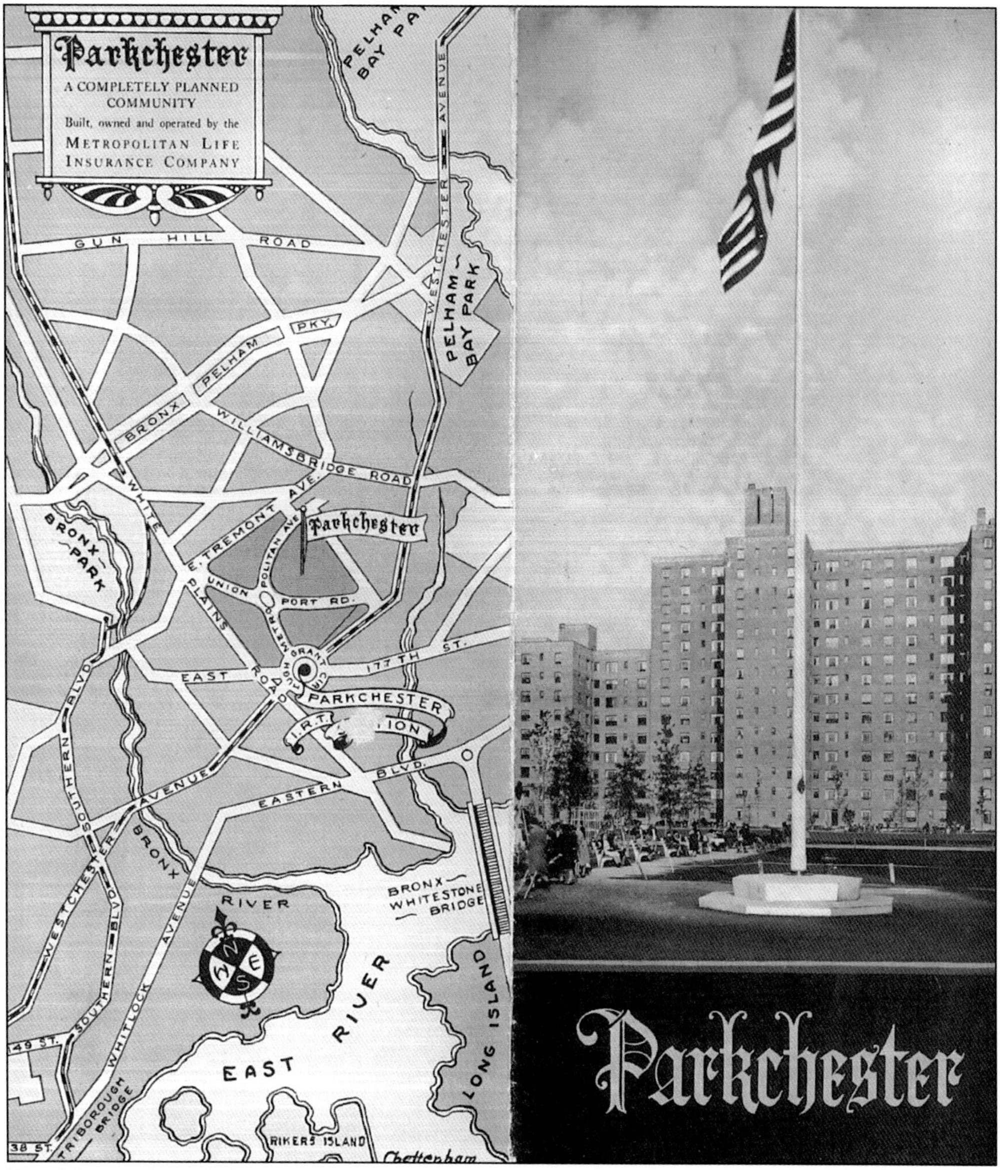

The Metropolitan Life Insurance Company acquired 129 acres, most of it from the Catholic Protectorate, to create one of the most beautiful communities in America. They called it Parkchester, and it proved so popular that there were over 50,000 applicants for the 12,272 apartments. Their efficient construction methods allowed them to keep the rent to approximately $14 a room, which included gas and electricity and was well below average for the fine amenities they offered. They produced this brochure c. 1941.

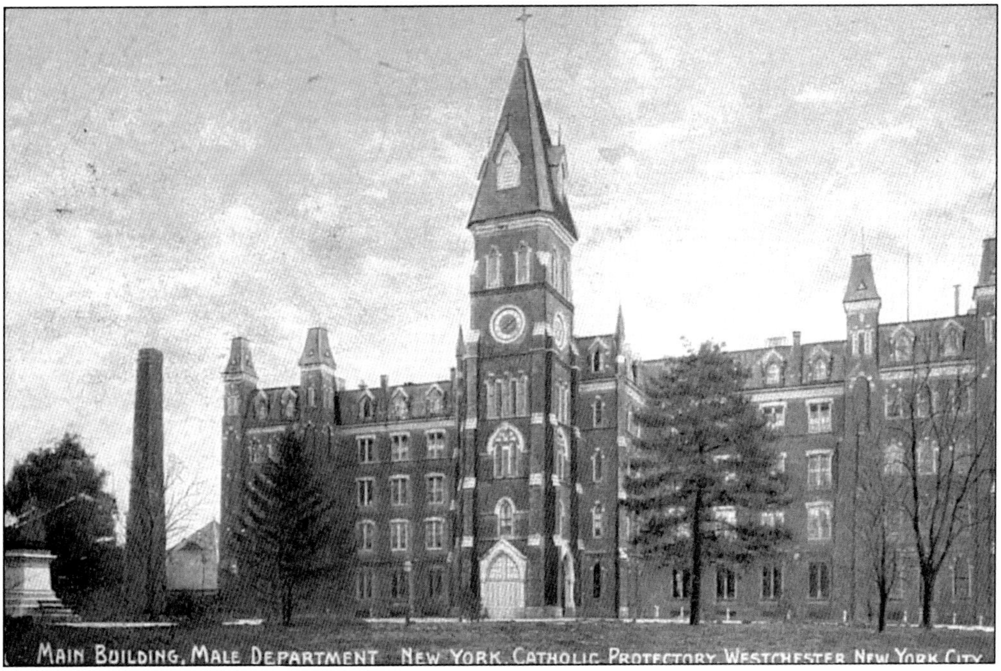

This picture of the Catholic Protectorate was taken from an old postcard of the American News Company that was postmarked September 16, 1907. It shows the main building of the Male Department. The protectorate was established here in 1865 and catered to the needs of destitute children. It was razed in 1939 for the construction of Parkchester. It may be of interest to note that their oval served as a major league ballpark from 1923 to 1936. The Lincoln Giants and the Cuban Stars West played there.

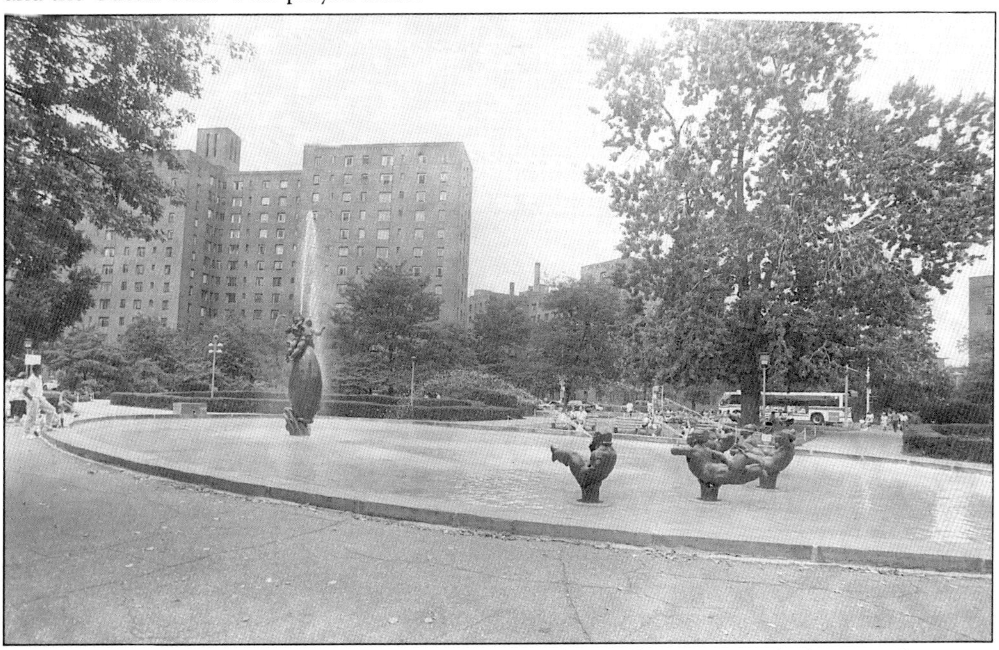

Metropolitan Oval in Parkchester was referred to earlier as the center park, due to its location. It was a central meeting place for residents, and many official ceremonies took place there.

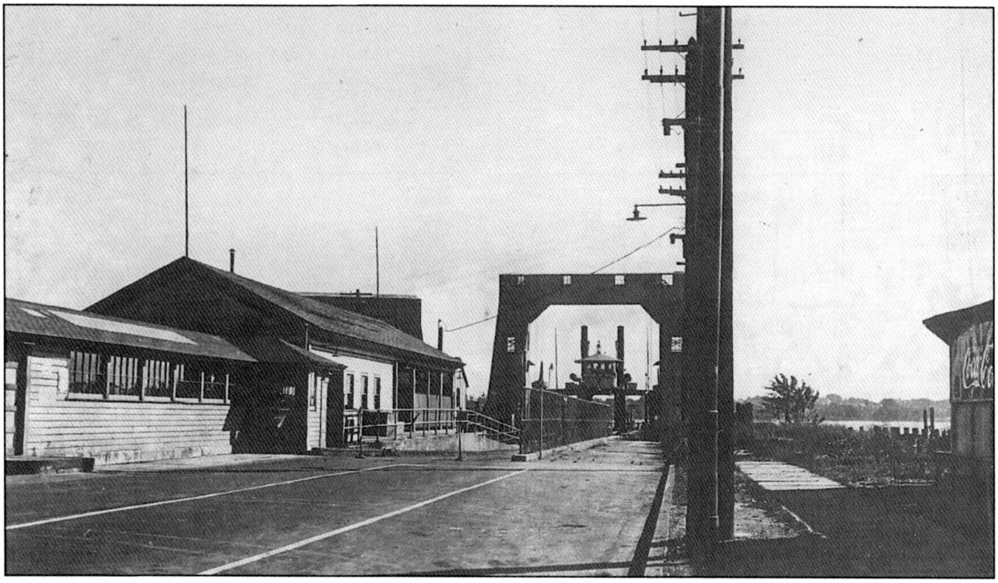

This photograph of the Clason Point Ferry House at the end of Soundview Avenue was taken in 1938. The ferry was disbanded on April 29, 1939, at 1 p.m., and the new mode of transport to the borough of Queens became the Bronx-Whitestone Bridge on Ferry Point.

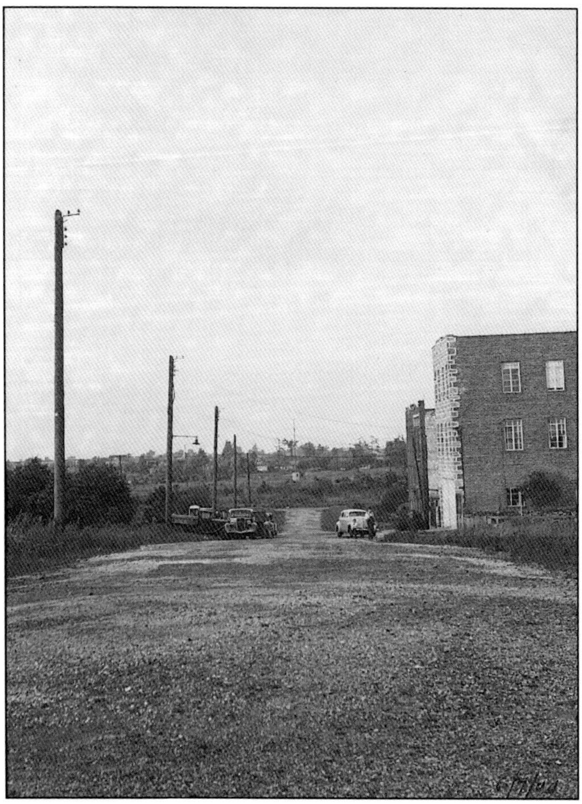

Italo Mazzella provided this photograph of Solon Place on Castle Hill Point. The view is from Castle Hill Avenue east toward Havemeyer Avenue; Ferry Point can be seen in the far background. Westchester Creek cannot be seen due to the foliage of the trees. The little white structure in the center is the air raid warden's post. The picture was taken on June 7, 1944.

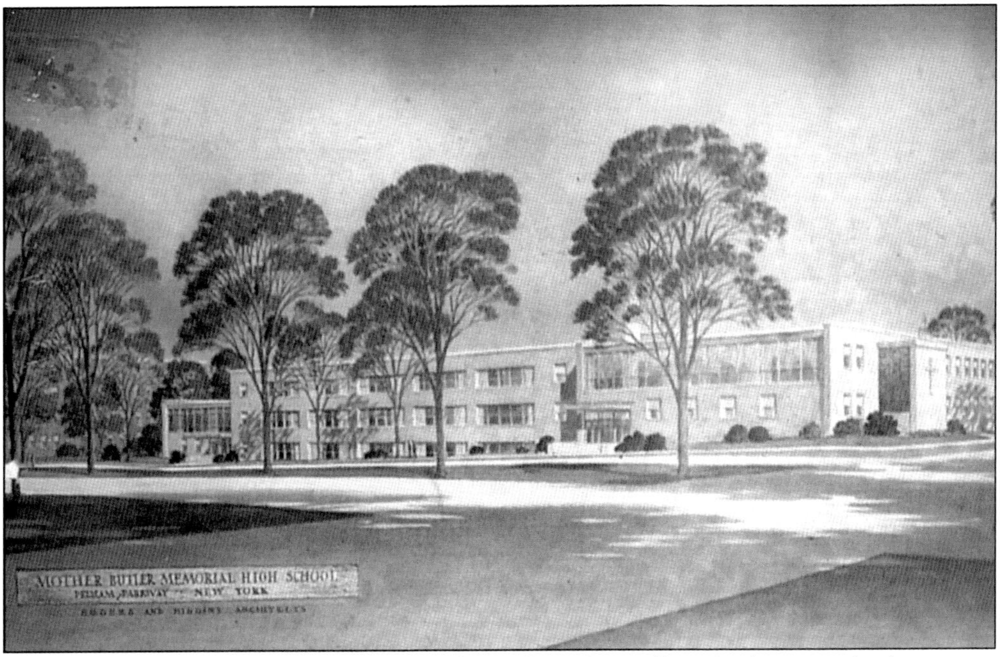

Mother Butler Memorial High School was located at 1500 Pelham Parkway on the former site of the Knickerbocker Inn and the Pelham Heath Inn.

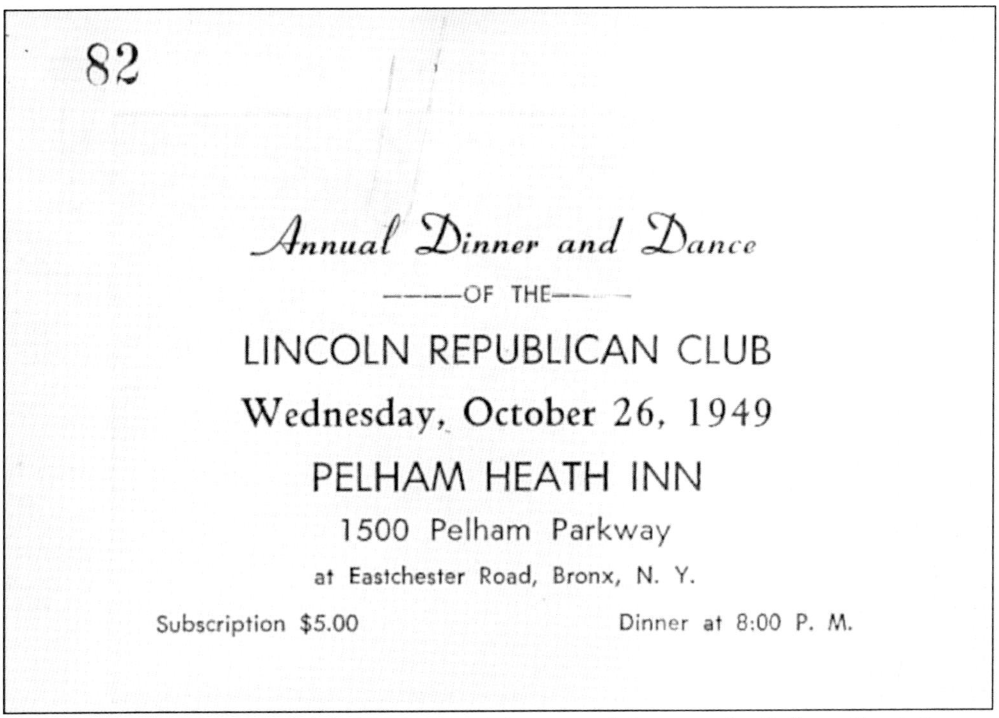

82

Annual Dinner and Dance

—OF THE—

LINCOLN REPUBLICAN CLUB

Wednesday, October 26, 1949

PELHAM HEATH INN

1500 Pelham Parkway

at Eastchester Road, Bronx, N. Y.

Subscription $5.00 Dinner at 8:00 P. M.

The Lincoln Republican Club held an annual dinner and dance at the Pelham Heath Inn on Wednesday, October 26, 1949. This ticket, which bears number 82, shows that the cost of the event was $5. The inn, located on the southeast corner of Pelham Parkway and Eastchester Road, was razed c. 1953. The site later became home to Mother Butler Memorial High School.

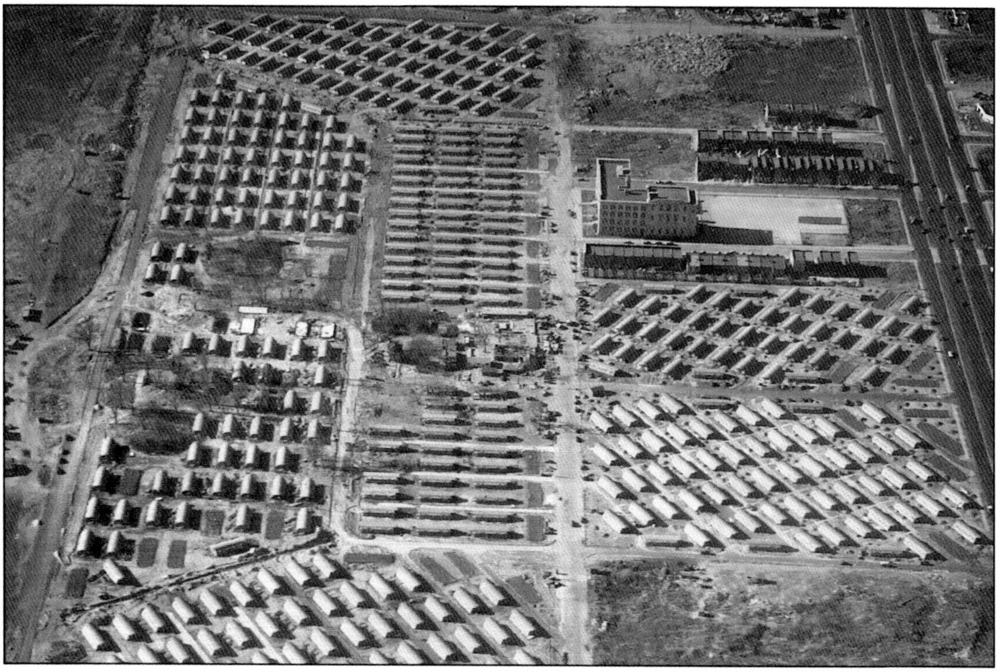

Vernon Seifert was the pilot and Arthur Seifert was the photographer of this aerial view of this N.Y.C. Housing Authority Quonset Hut Project for veterans. This westward view was taken in 1946 at Bruckner Boulevard and Metcalf Avenue. P.S. 93 on Story Avenue is the large building at the top right. The 450 huts housed 900 families.

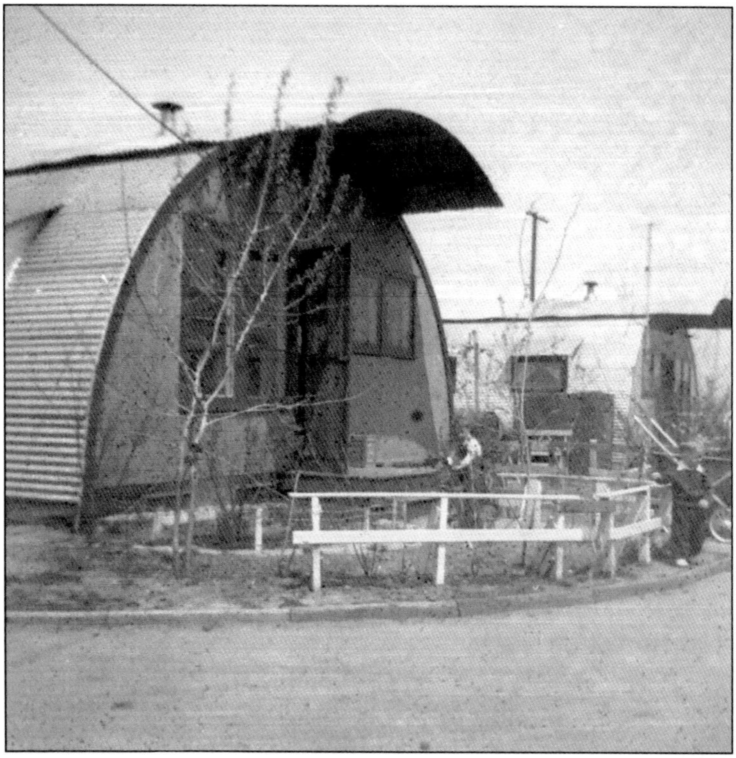

Quonset huts are steel-shelled domed structures named after the Quonset Point Naval Station in Rhode Island, where they were constructed by the Seabees during World War II. They were created as temporary housing for military personnel but were pressed into service by the N.Y C. Housing Authority to house returning servicemen and their families. Two families occupied each hut, one at either end. John McNamara supplied this picture taken in 1952 at the Castle Hill Houses.

The Bruckner Houses were comprised of about 450 Quonset huts, which were erected *c.* 1946 for veterans of World War II. This picture was taken in July of 1948 at Metcalf Avenue and Bruckner Boulevard and shows Pauline and John McNamara with their daughter, Betty. Each hut housed two families, with one at either end.

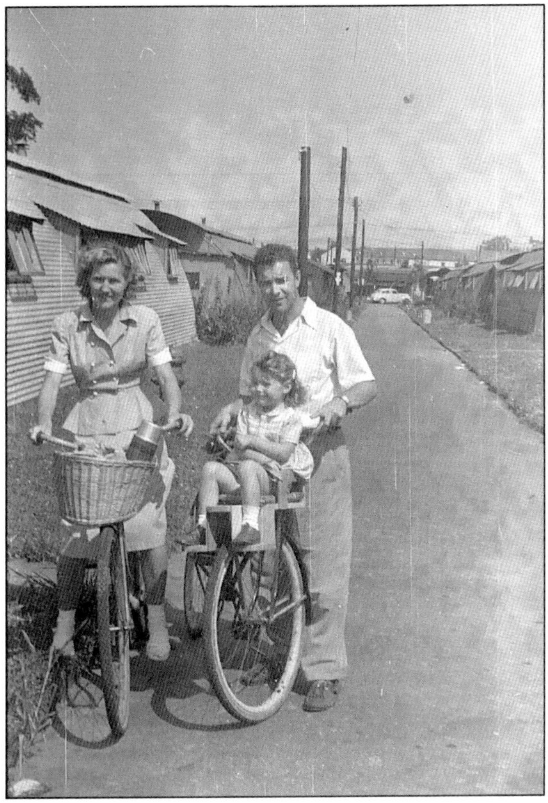

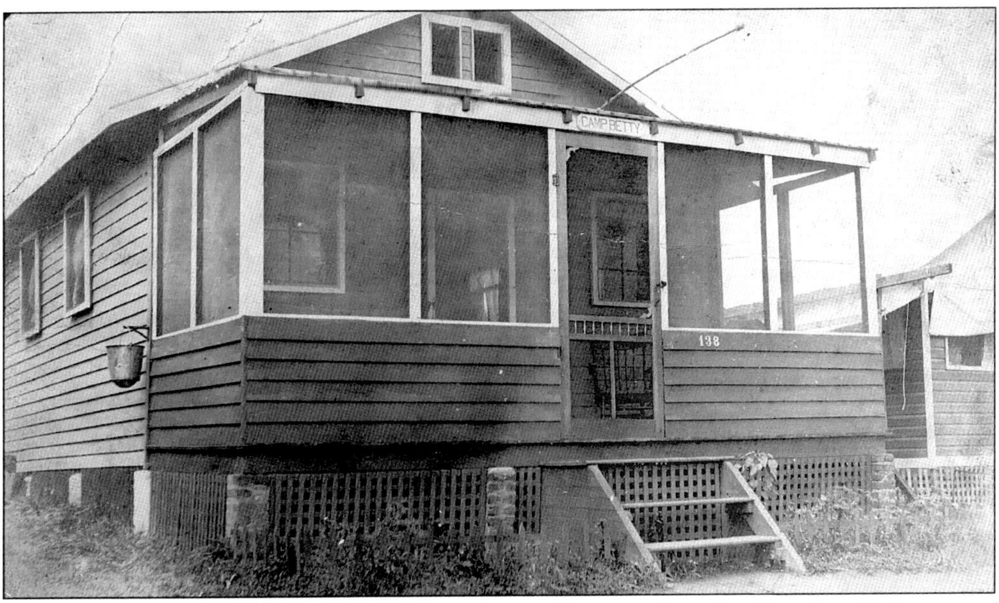

This typical bungalow of the 1920s had a red round-bottomed sand pail at the side in case of fire. This particular house was not winterized until 1955, after the death of its original owner. The sign above the door reads "Camp Betty" for Betty McNamara, and the house is numbered 138 Edgewater Camp. The number and letter system was not yet in use, and the name Park has since been substituted for Camp.

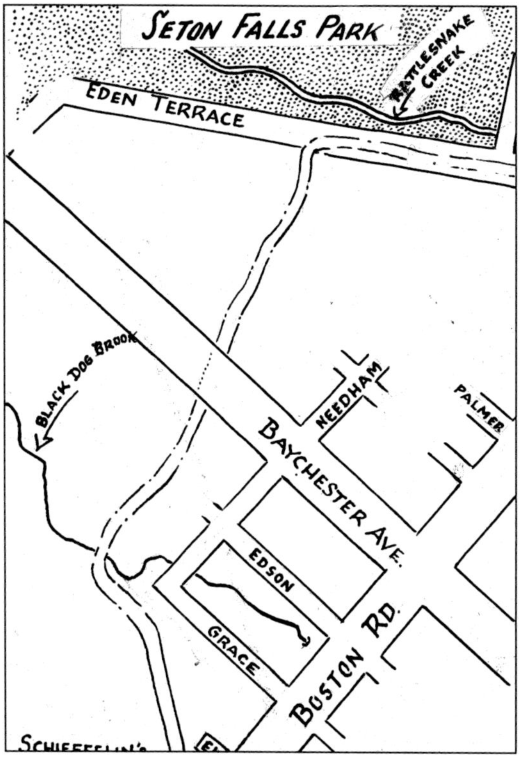

John McNamara drew this map several decades ago, and much has changed. Rattlesnake Brook has flowed through Seton Falls Park for centuries, but Seton Falls, once so majestic, has been reduced to a trickle. Eden Terrace, once known as Schieffelin's Lane, underwent another name change in 1968 to Marolla Terrace. Little has remained the same.

John McNamara supplied this 1972 photograph. The parking lot at the left was once the site of a beer garden. The lot is located on the west side of White Plains Road at East 238th Street. The sign on the upper right of the building reads "A. Herzing, Roofing and Sheet Metal Work." During the 1930s, a saloon belonging to Mr. Herzing was located here.

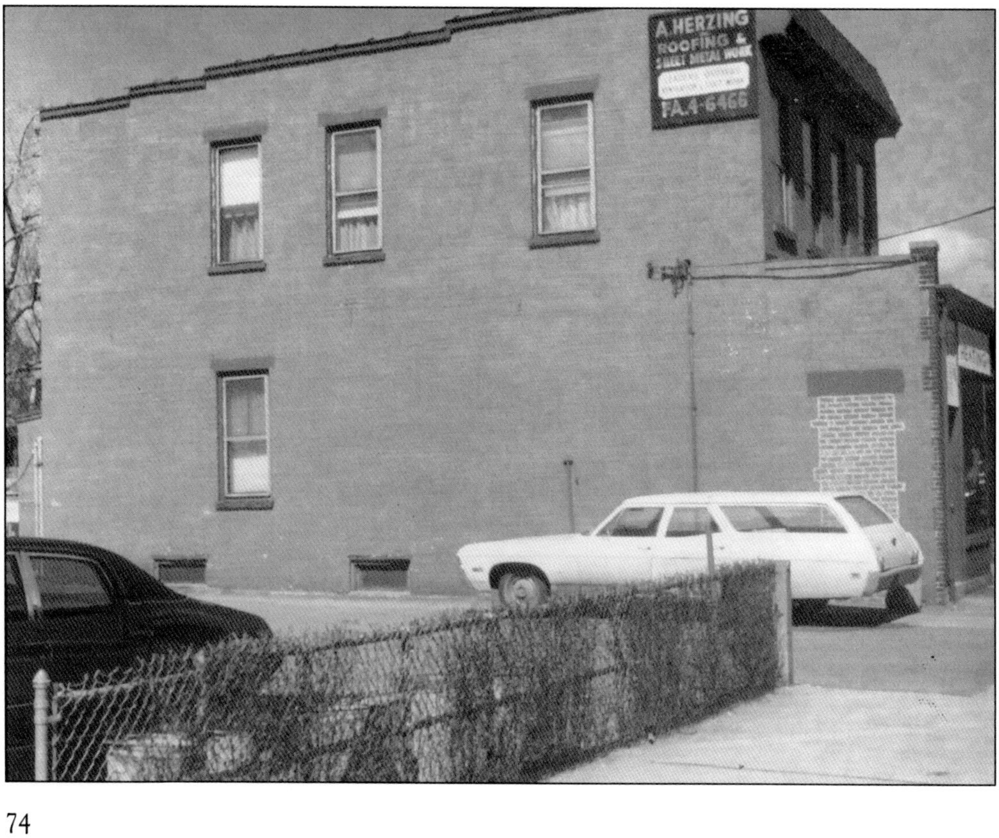

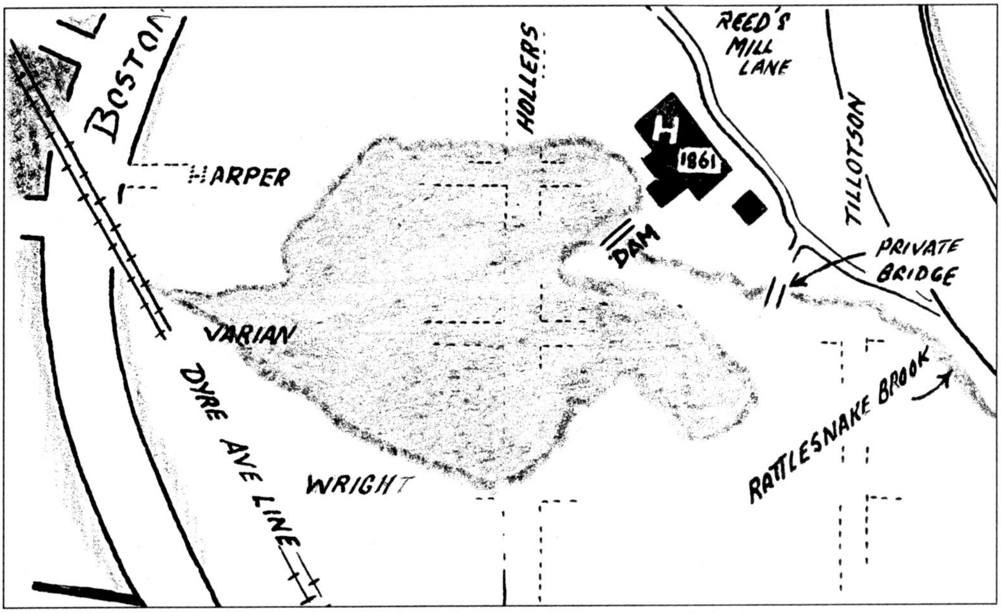

Not far from Reed's Mill Lane stood Holler's Pond, 15 acres of freshwater that was created for harvesting ice when Rattlesnake Brook was dammed. The dam was south and east of the current junction of Harper and Hollers Avenues. It was filled *c.* 1951, and local children ice-skated there no more. Bronx historian John McNamara drew the sketch.

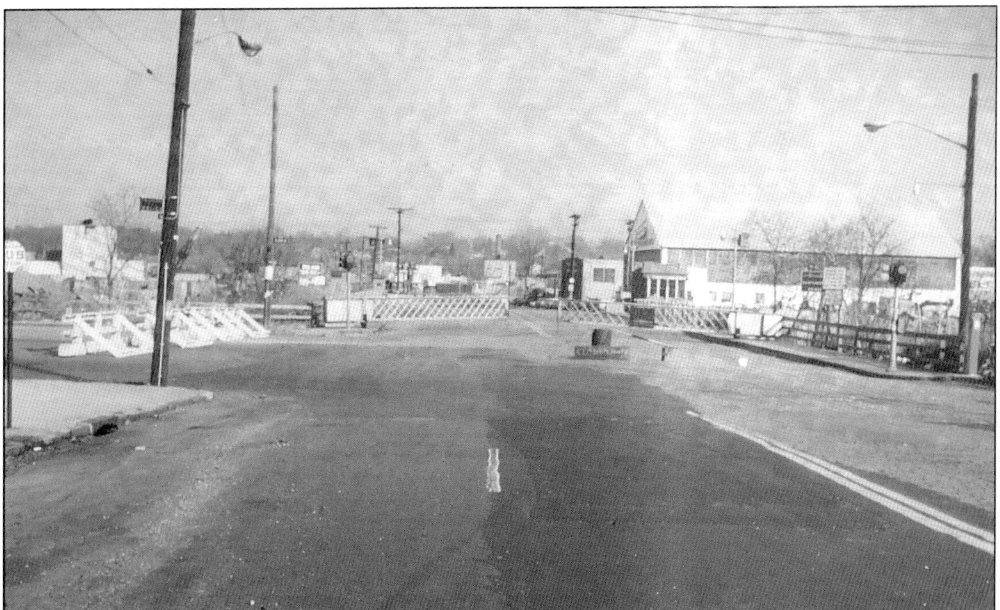

East 233rd Street is at the left in this Ted Schliessman photograph from December 1965. The view looks north along Boston Road with the drawbridge over the Hutchinson River in the background.

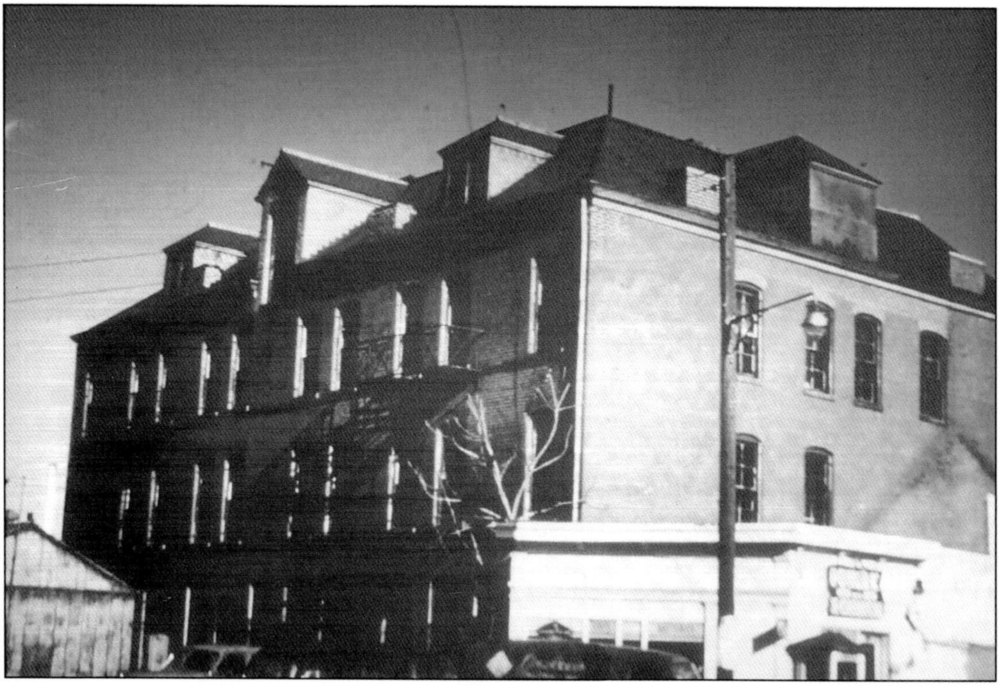

This photograph of the 43rd Precinct on Williamsbridge Road was taken in 1955 and was provided by Ron Schliessman. The view looks southward.

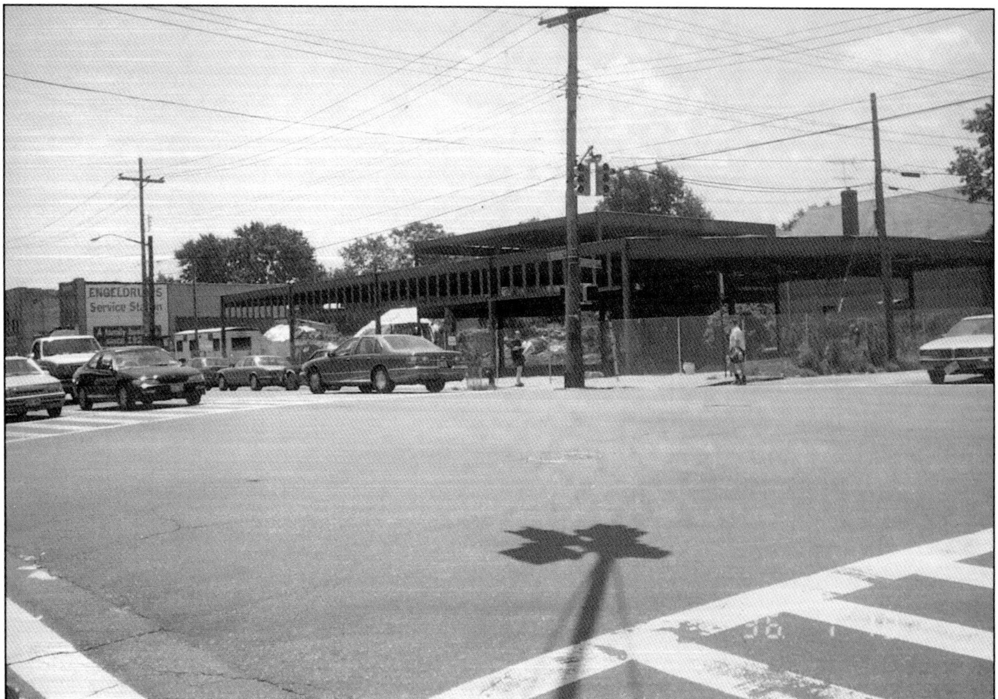

A Genovese pharmacy is under construction in this photograph taken by Sean Twomey on July 18, 1996, at the southwest corner of E. Tremont and Lafayette Avenues. Engeldrum's Service Station had previously occupied the site.

Seven

Awards, Ceremonies, and Parades

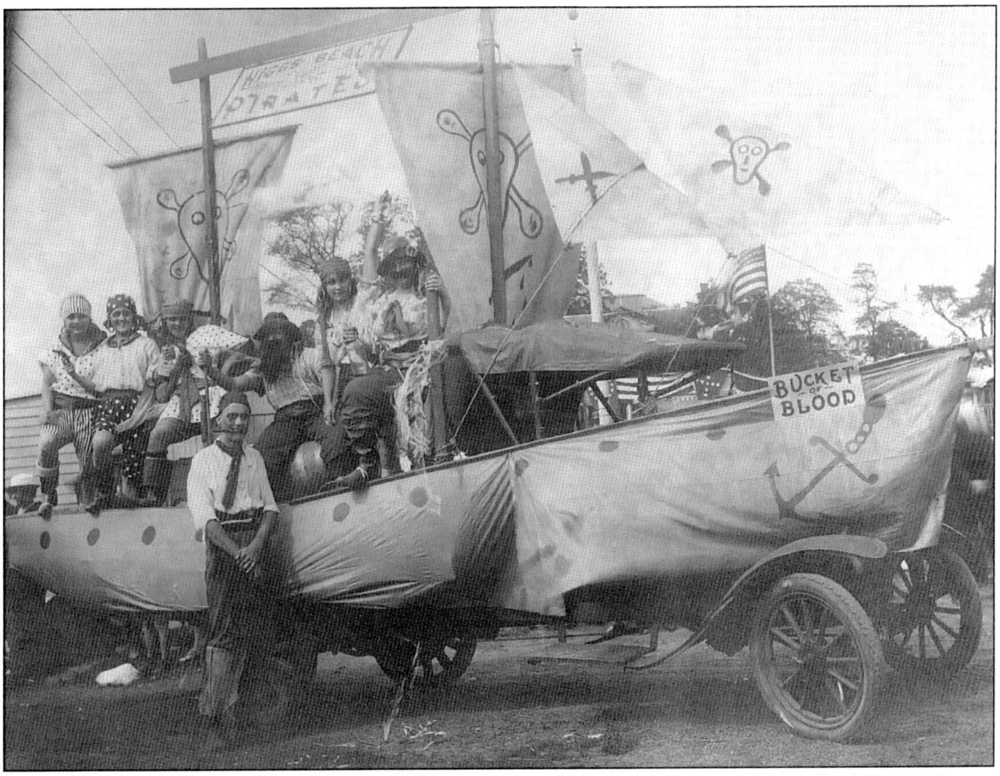

Higgs Beach was the former name of Harding Park. Thomas H. Higgs established the 100-acre beach and campground c. 1898; it lasted until about 1924. This float was part of one of their Labor Day parades during that period. Arthur Seifert provided the photograph.

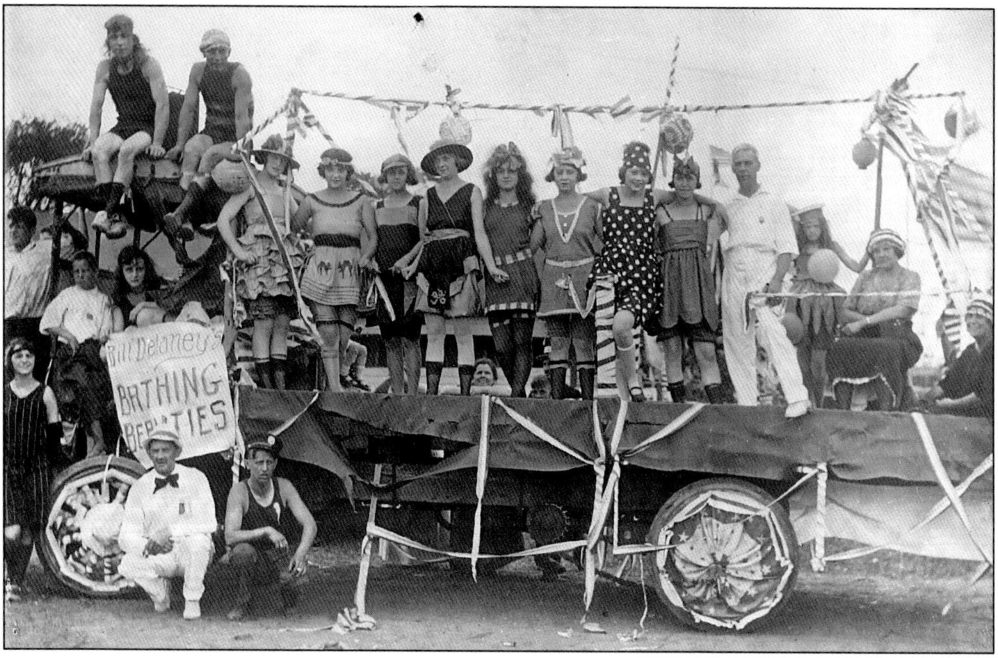

Higg's Beach and Campground held annual Labor Day parades. This parade, held in 1922, featured Bill Delaney's Bathing Beauties. The site is now known as Harding Park. Arthur Seifert provided the photograph.

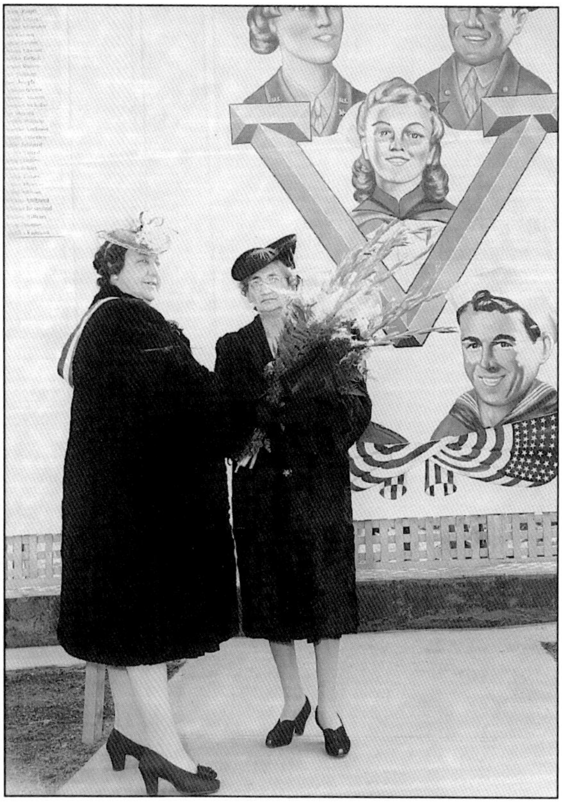

During World War II, a giant billboard honoring the men serving in the Armed Forces was erected at the southwest corner of East Tremont and Miles Avenues. Margaret Moore, a civic leader, presided at the unveiling ceremony and is shown, at left, presenting a bouquet of flowers to one of the honored women.

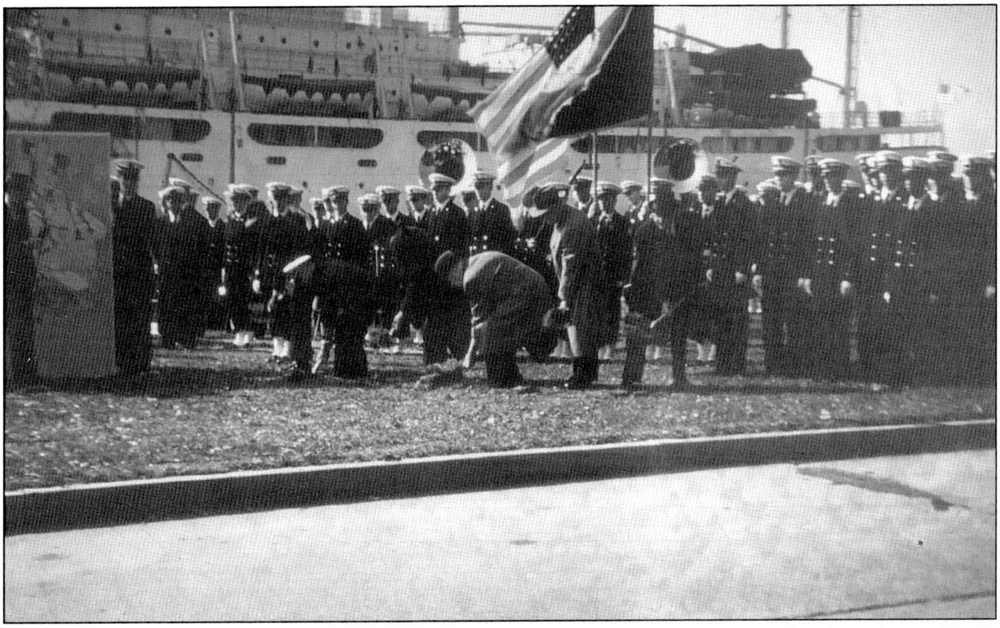

Ted Schliessman took this photograph of the groundbreaking ceremonies for the Throgs Neck Bridge at Fort Schuyler on October 22, 1957.

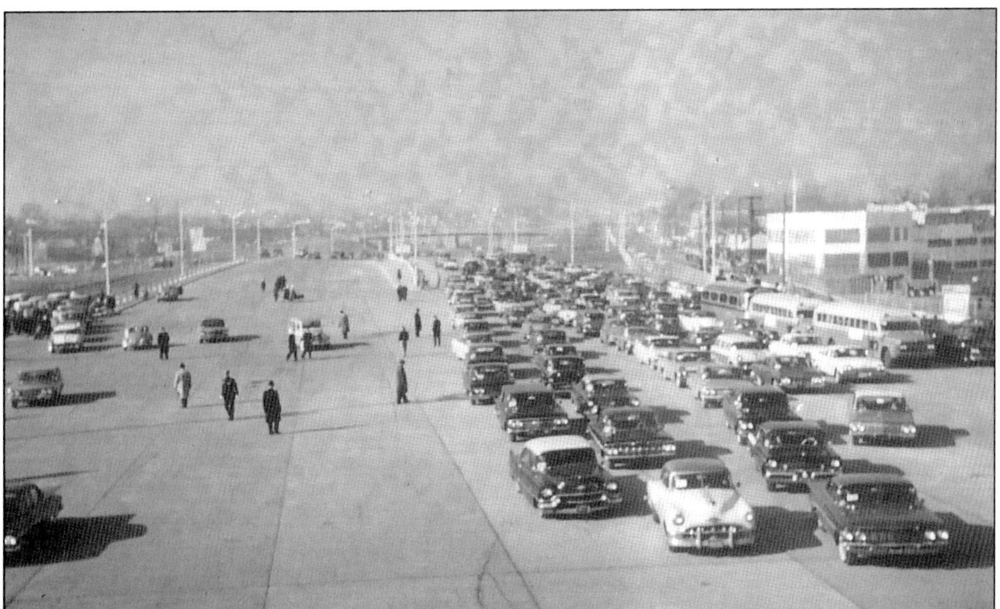

The Throgs Neck Bridge was opened to much fanfare on January 11, 1961. There was no shortage of vehicles wishing to traverse the bridge on opening day. John McNamara Sr. and Jr. crossed the span earlier that day by bicycle. Bronx Beach and Pool is in the right background. (Courtesy of the Schliessman Collection.)

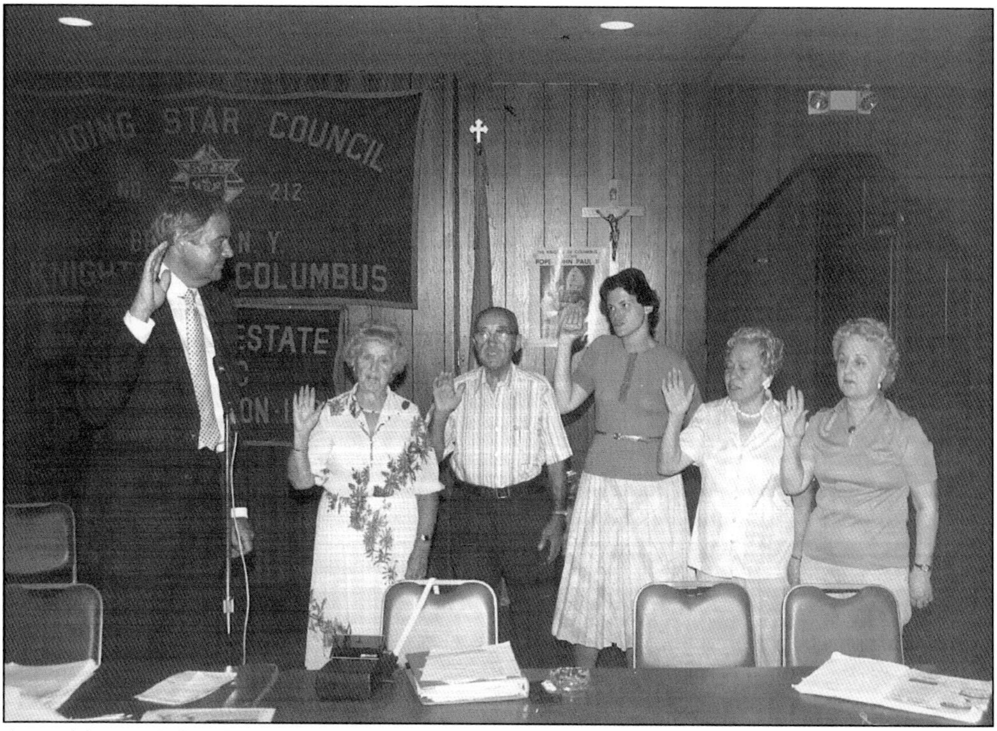

Assemblyman John Dearie is swearing in the 1984–85 officers of the Spencer Estate Civic Association in this photograph taken on July 18, 1984.

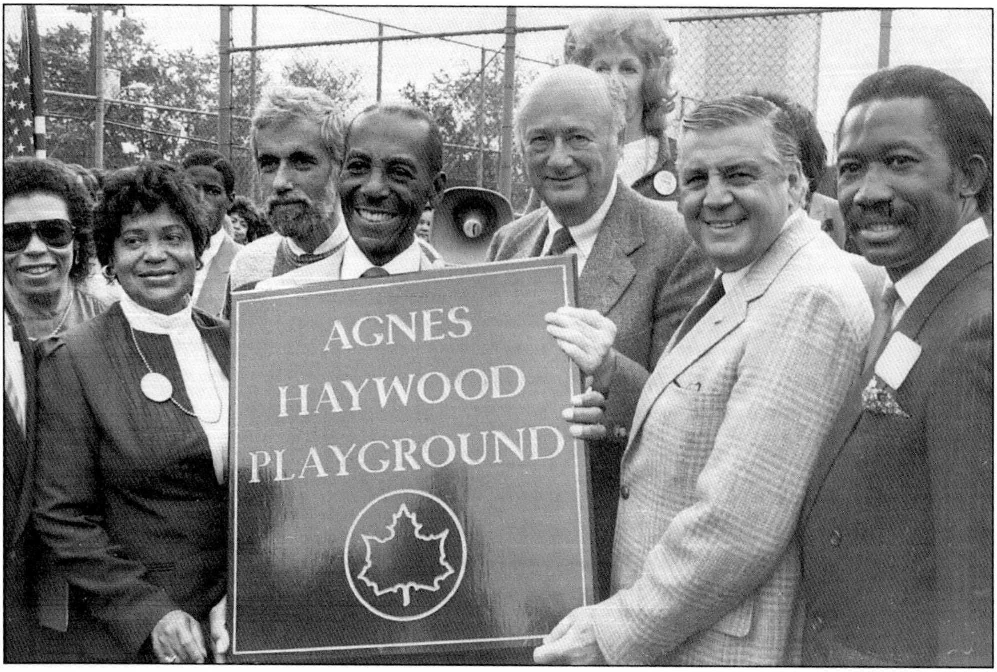

Agnes Haywood Playground in Olinville was dedicated to the loved and admired community leader in October of 1985. Parks commissioner Henry Stern and Mayor Ed Koch are joined by local officials and friends at the ceremony.

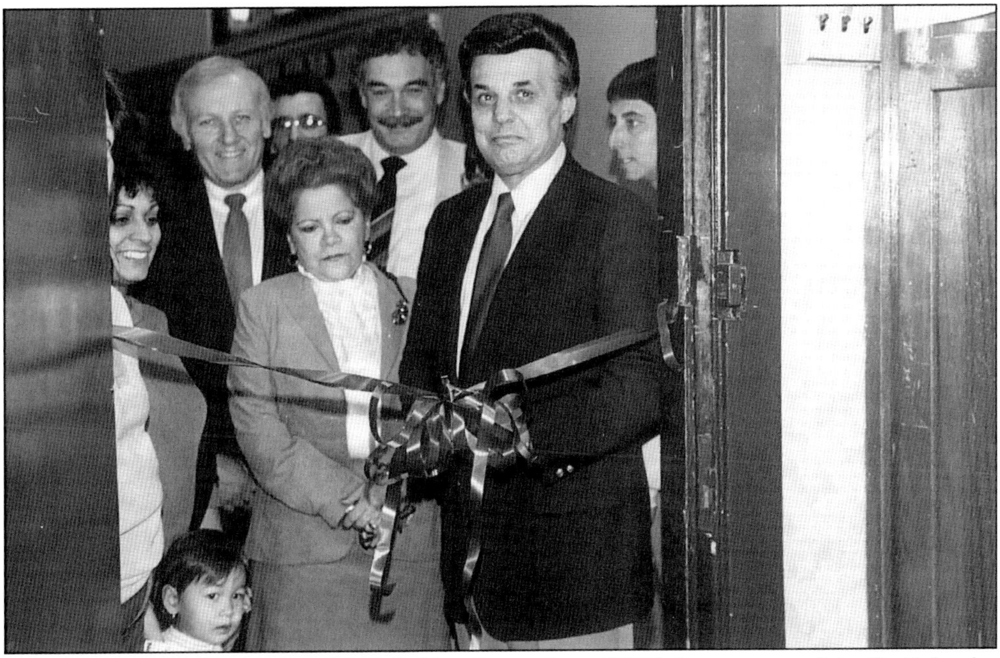

A new computer lab was opened at P.S. 71 in December of 1985. State senator John D. Calandra is about to cut the ribbon, while district supervisor Max Messer, school board 8 member Julia Rodriguez, and Principal Charles Lamontanaro look on with others.

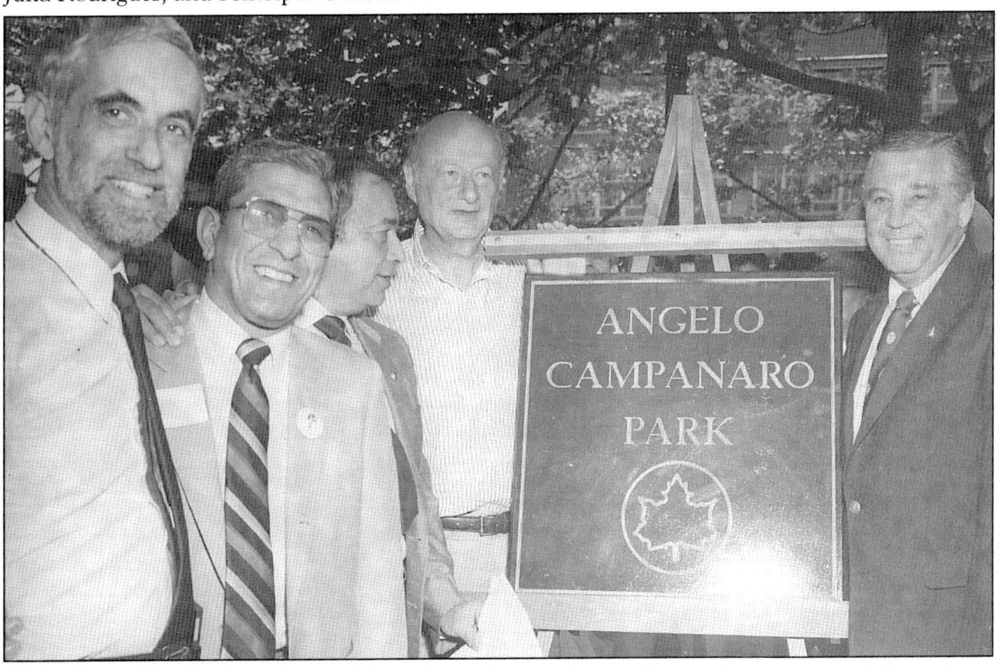

Angelo Campanaro Park, located at Gun Hill and Eastchester Roads, was dedicated on June 15, 1985. The honoree was chairman of the community planning board 12 and president of the Chester Civic Association. Seen here, from left to right, are N.Y.C. parks commissioner Henry Stern, Phil Rizzo, borough president Stanley Simon, Mayor Ed Koch, and Councilman Jerry Crispino.

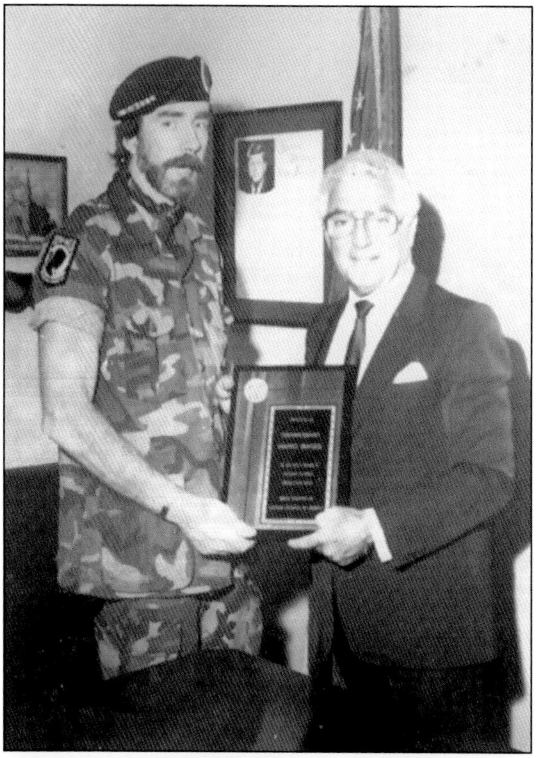

The Bronx chapter of the Vietnam Veterans Association held their swearing in ceremony on December 19, 1984. President Tom Wolf is shown here presenting a plaque to Congressman Mario Biaggi. The other officers sworn in were Ralph Ianucelli, vice-president; Guy Miata, assistant vice-president; Ron Lipshitz, secretary; Edwin Olavarria, treasurer; and Richard Calbo, membership chairman.

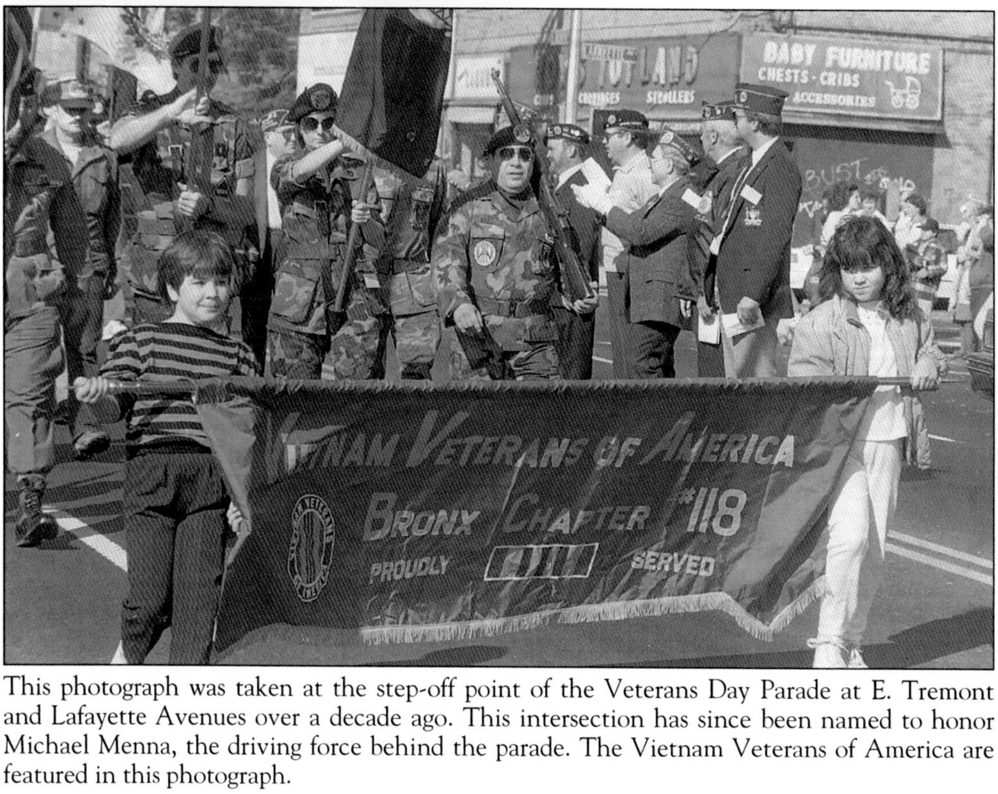

This photograph was taken at the step-off point of the Veterans Day Parade at E. Tremont and Lafayette Avenues over a decade ago. This intersection has since been named to honor Michael Menna, the driving force behind the parade. The Vietnam Veterans of America are featured in this photograph.

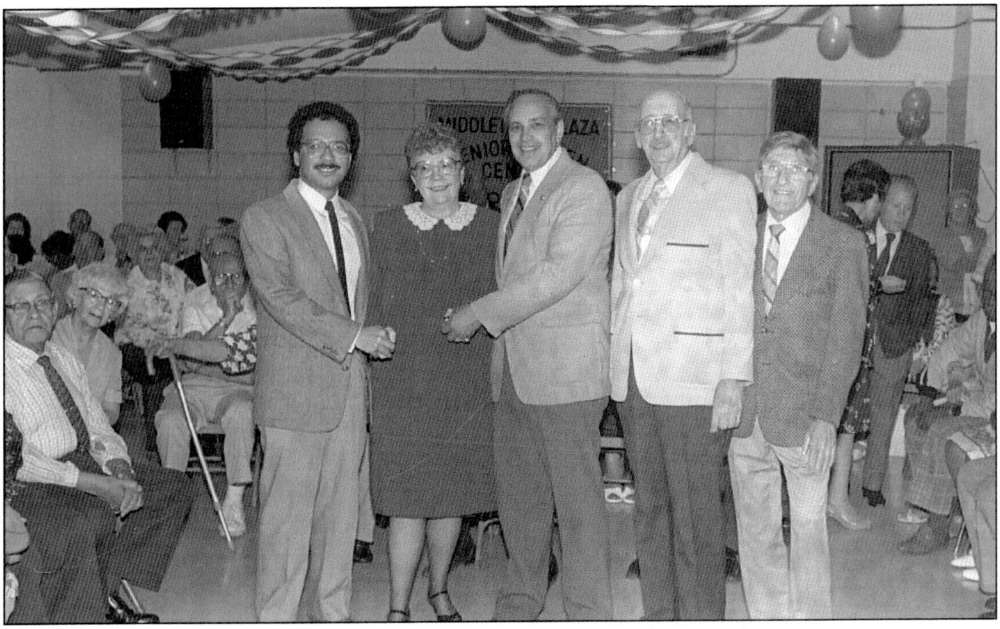

The Middletown Senior Center received their allocation for new bus service to transport the handicapped in this July 1985 photograph. Seen here, from left to right, are Jimmy Vacca of Community Planning Board 10, the center director Helen Woodstock, Councilman Mike DeMarco, STOP Chairman Al Morelli, and the center's advisory board chairman Bill Rescigno.

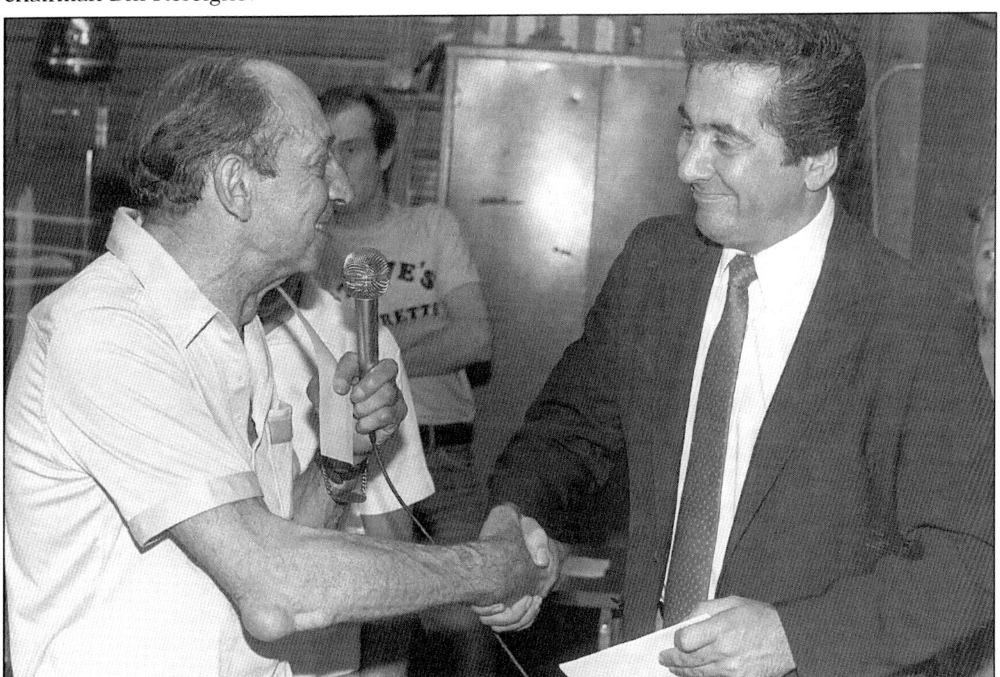

State senator Guy Velella is presenting a $300 check to Dominick Gregory, president of the Morris Park Seniors Association, to be used for a seniors bus trip. The picture was taken on July 21, 1986.

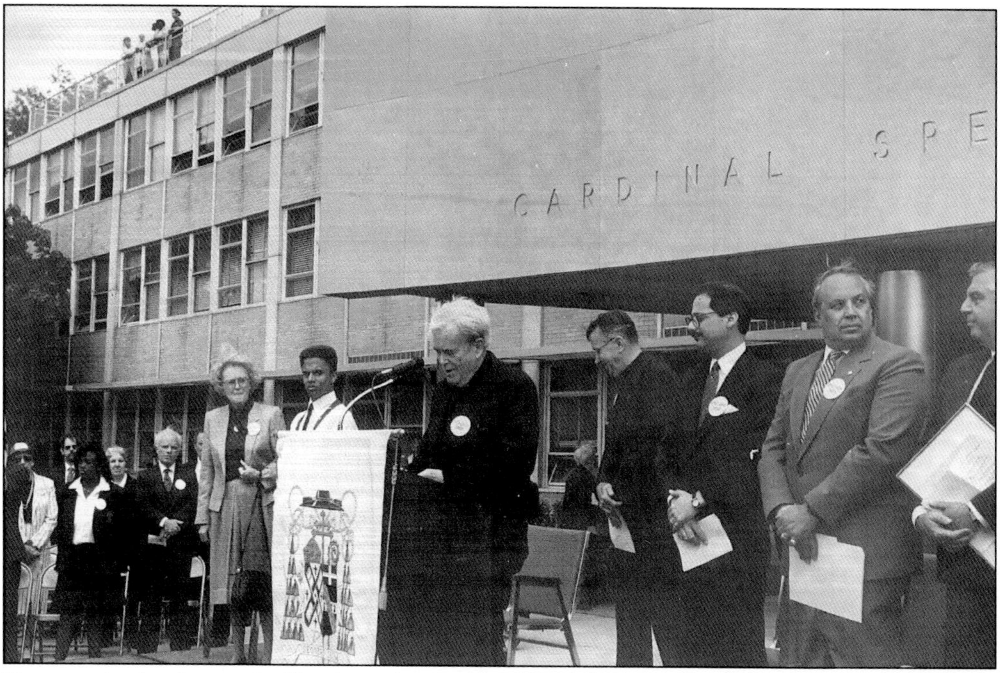

Community leaders and officials gather at Needham Avenue for the unveiling of Cardinal Spellman Place on May 18, 1990. Cardinal Spellman High School is in the background and is a further reminder of Francis Cardinal Spellman who served as Archbishop of New York from 1939 to 1967.

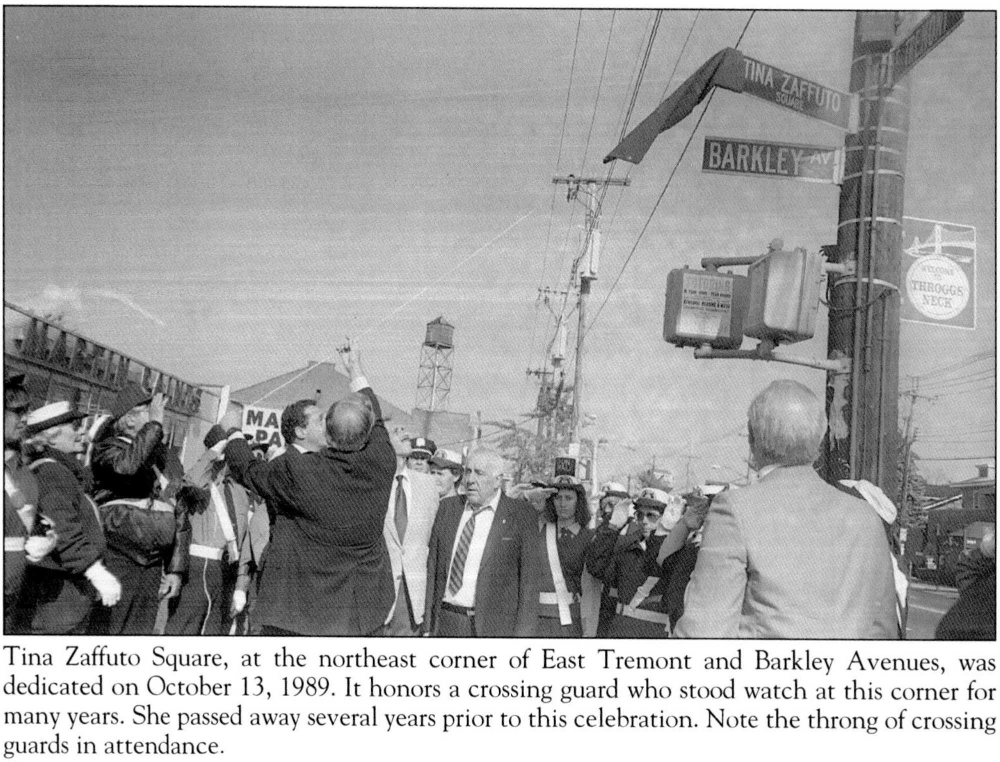

Tina Zaffuto Square, at the northeast corner of East Tremont and Barkley Avenues, was dedicated on October 13, 1989. It honors a crossing guard who stood watch at this corner for many years. She passed away several years prior to this celebration. Note the throng of crossing guards in attendance.

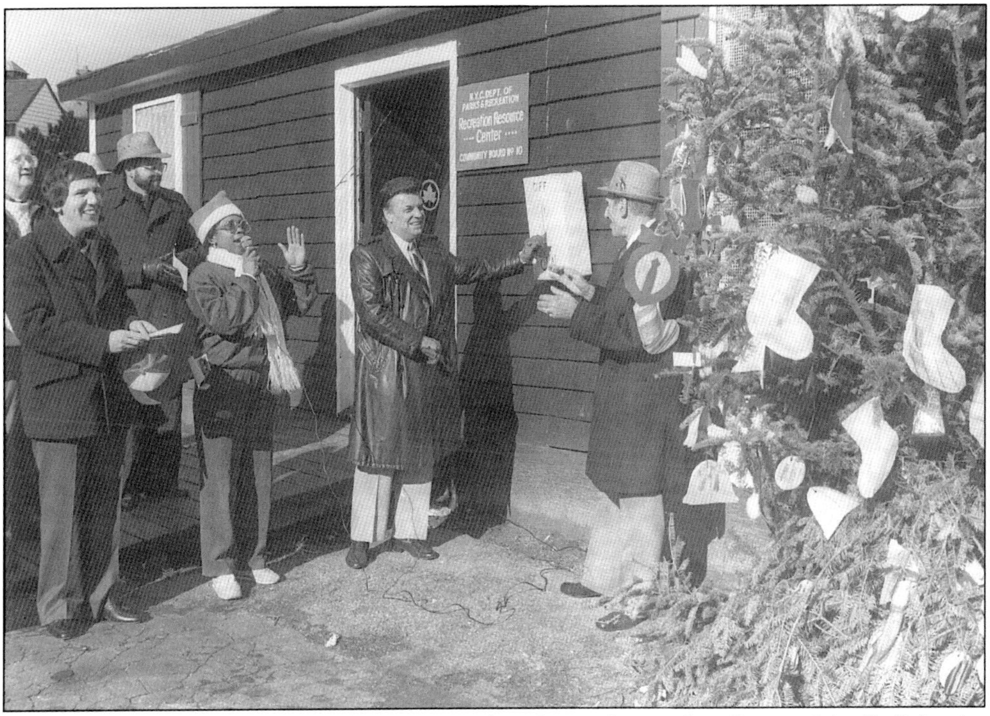

The Pelham Bay Taxpayers 1985 Christmas Parade is about to begin when Senator John D. Calandra pushes the switch to turn on the lights on the Christmas tree. Seen here are, from left to right, as follows: (front row) Vinny Tolentino, Helen Boone, Calandra, and Michael Crescenzo; (back row) Mike Barry and Father Tyrell.

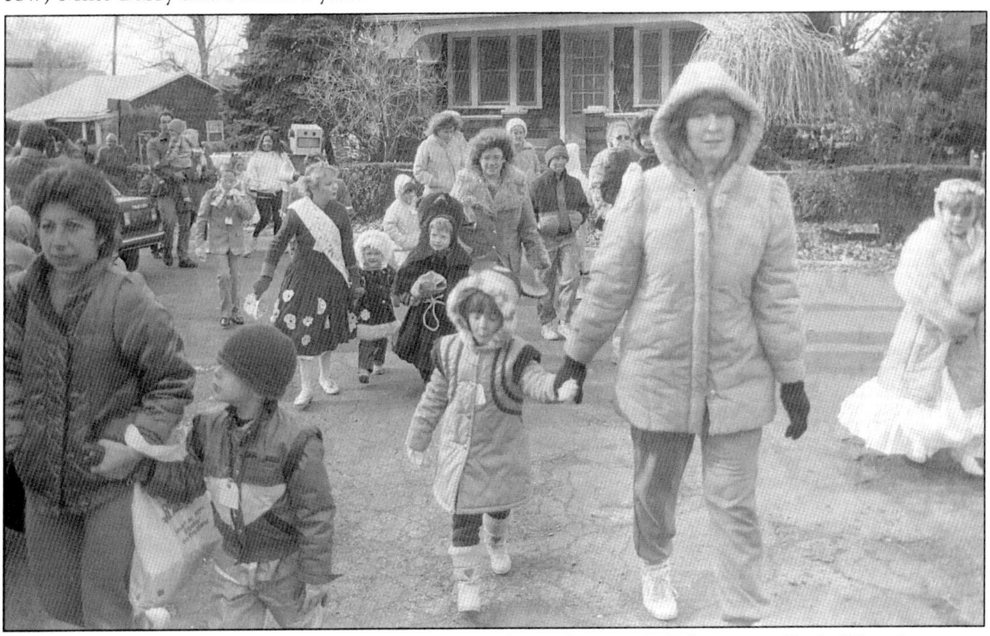

One hundred and twenty children participated in the 1987 Edgewater Park Thanksgiving Ragamuffin Parade, which was held in freezing weather. The parade ended at the Volunteer Hose Company, where hot chocolate was served and winners were chosen.

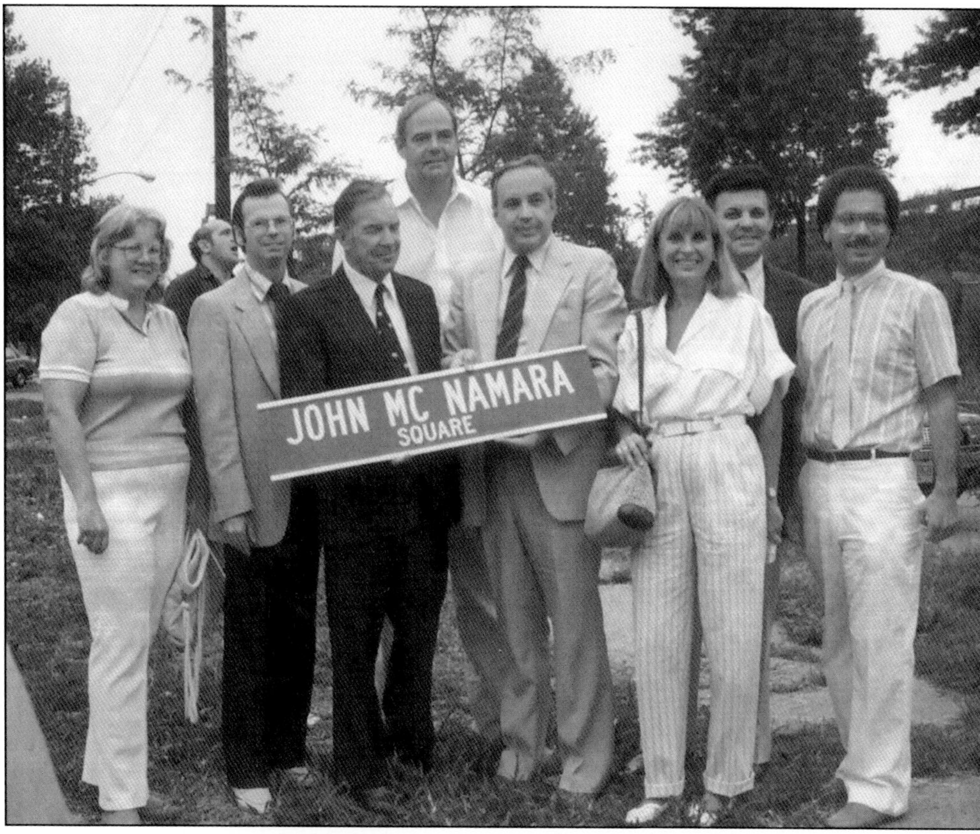

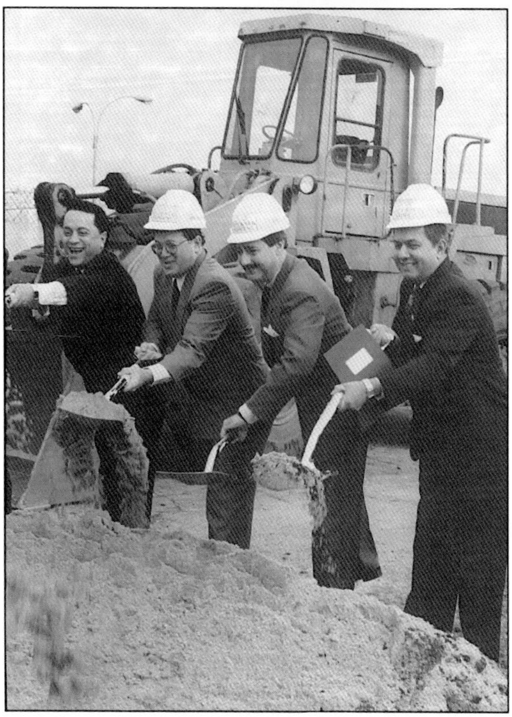

The unveiling of the John McNamara Square signs at Randall and Calhoun Avenues took place on August 22, 1985. Seen here, from left to right, are Peggy Vega, Bill Twomey, John McNamara, Assemblyman John Dearie, Councilman Mike DeMarco, Jane Gover of the BCHS, Senator John D. Calandra, and Jimmy Vacca. Carol Twomey took the photograph.

Groundbreaking for the shopping center on White Plains Road south of Story Avenue took place on November 28, 1995. Seen here, from left to right, are Bruce Ratner, Senator Pedro Espada, Assemblyman Stephen Kaufman, Borough President Fernando Ferrer, and Assemblyman Peter Rivera. Old Navy, Pergament, and Seaman's were among those slated to open at the new mall.

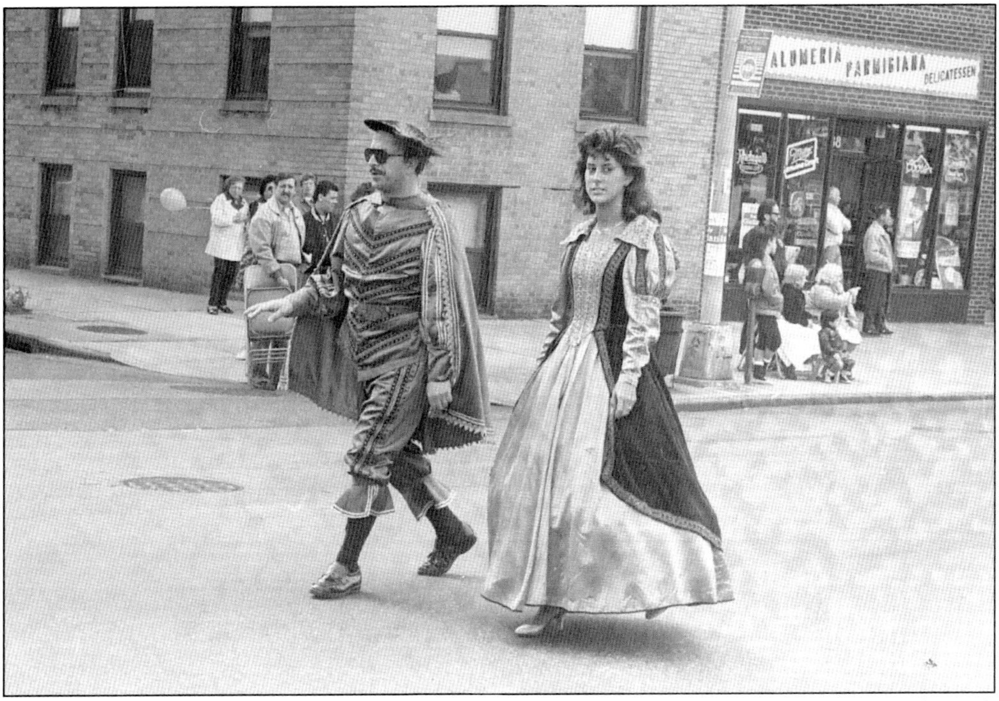

The Bronx Columbus Day Parade is one of the largest and most grandiose in the U.S. Carol Kunik was Queen Isabella, and John Soccodato was Columbus in the one portrayed here in the late-1980s. They are marching along Morris Park Avenue and just passing the intersection of Barnes Avenue. The Salumeria Parmigiana and Deli is in the background at 788 Morris Park Avenue.

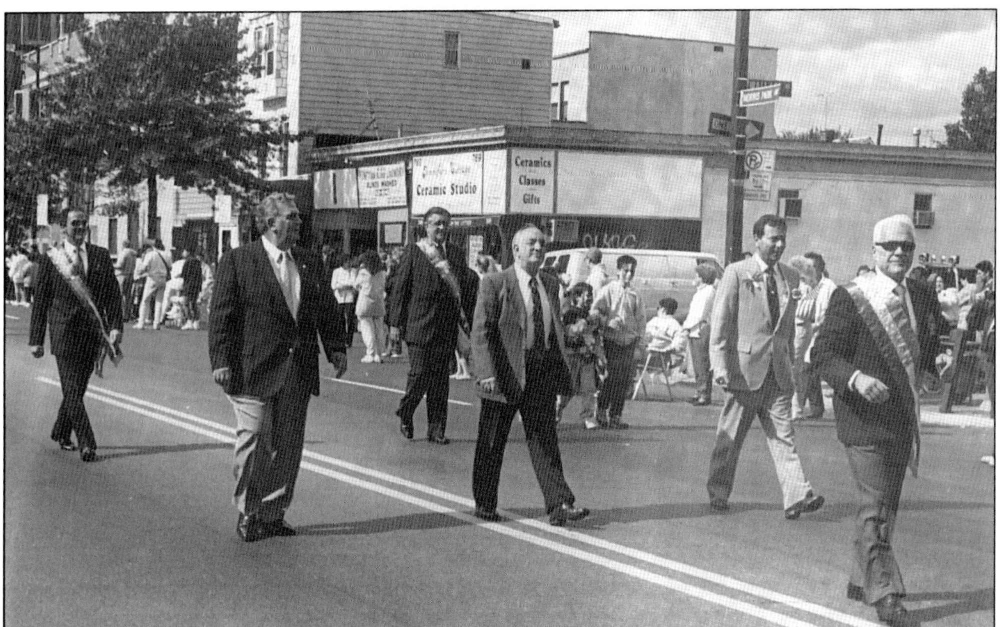

Another photograph from the same parade shows the grand marshall and dignitaries leading the way. They have just passed Jennifer's Cottage at 769 Morris Park Avenue.

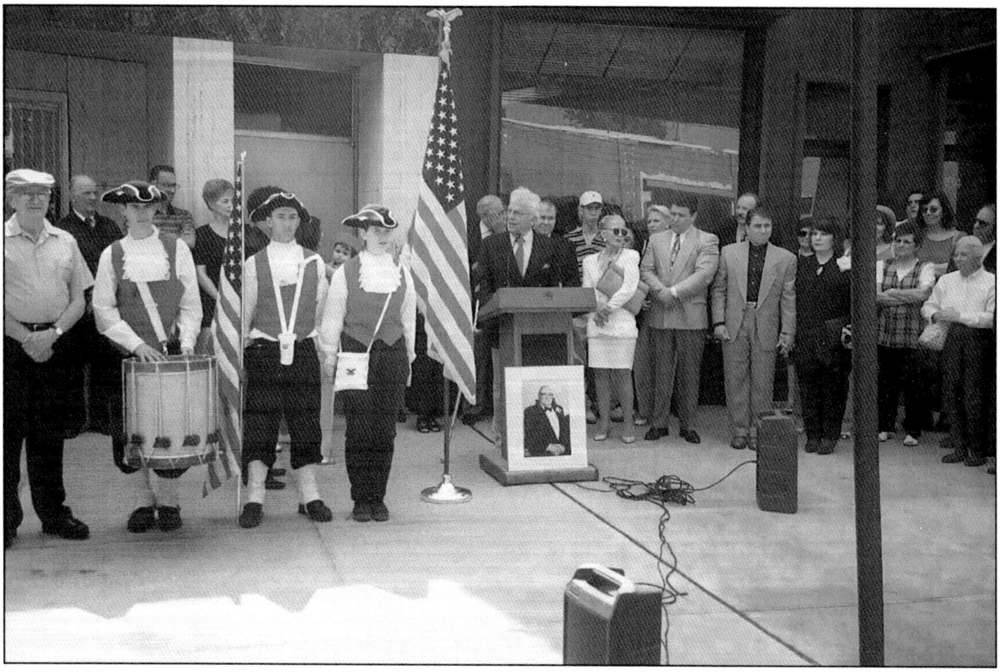

Former Congressman Mario Biaggi speaks at the street sign dedication to Ralph "Dutch" Balsamo at Westchester Avenue and Sands Place. The grand event took place on June 21, 1996.

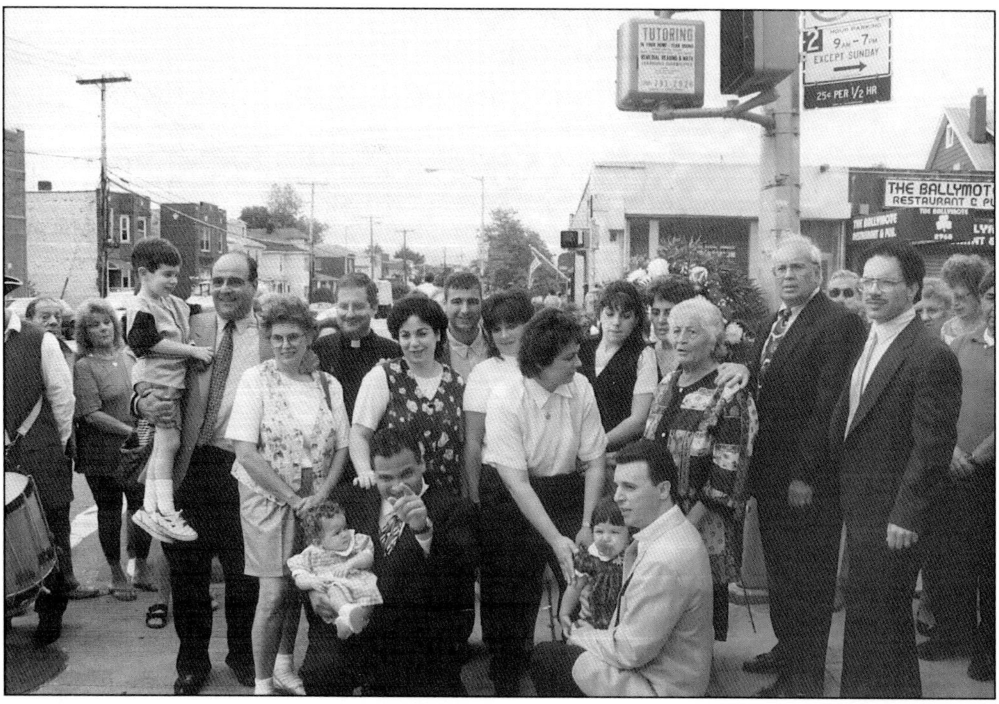

Family, friends, and dignitaries gather for the dedication of Rocco Travaglino Corner on June 10, 1996, at Middletown Road and Crosby Avenue. Councilman Michael DeMarco and planning board 10 chairman Jimmy Vacca can be seen at the right.

Eight

Stormy Weather

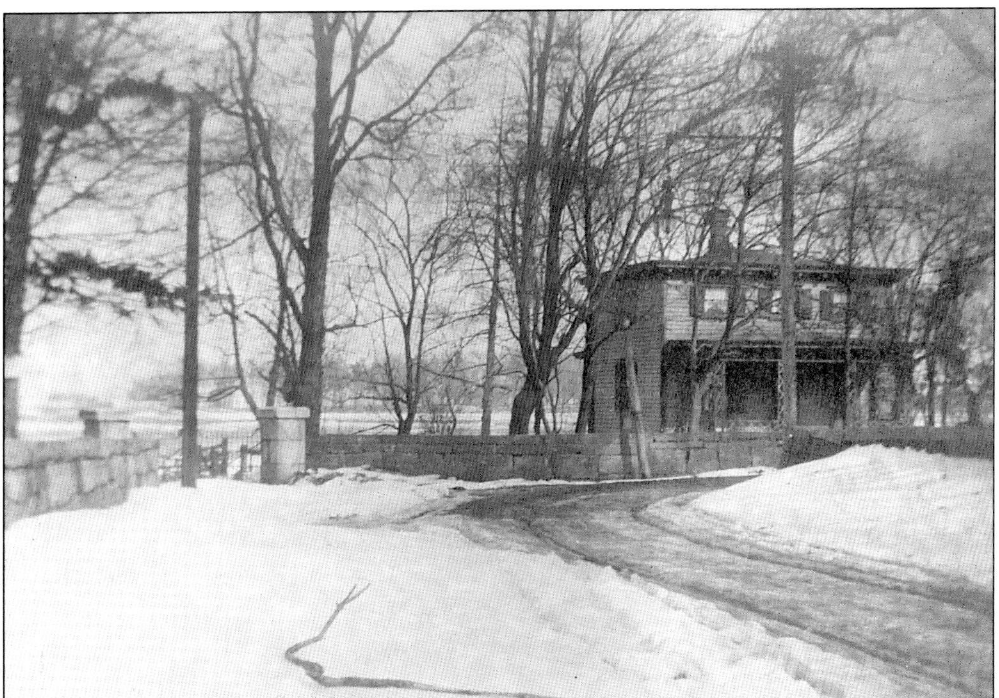

Winds up to 80 miles per hour, heavy rain, and freezing temperatures came upon New York City on March 11, 1888. The following day, the rain changed to snow, and 20.9 inches fell, snarling our streets. The police stopped pedestrians to check for frostbite, and the city came to a standstill. After the blizzard, paymaster Reid of Fort Schuyler photographed what is now Pennyfield and Harding Avenues, with Locust Point (then an island) in the eastern background. The Gallagher farmhouse survived into the 1930s; the building can be seen at the right in this picture supplied by John McNamara.

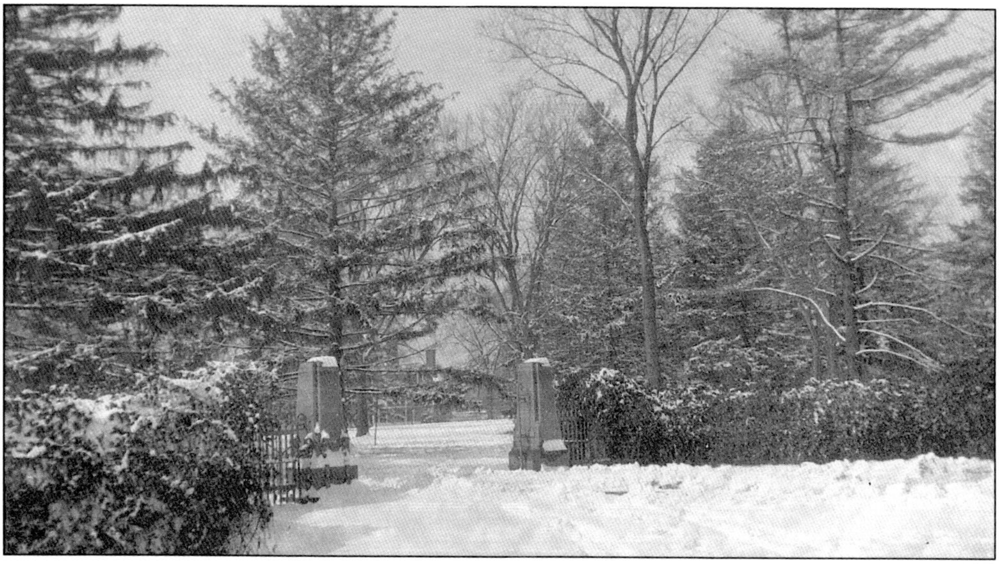

This 1912 photograph from John McNamara shows the entrance to Pleasance, the Archer Milton Huntington Estate, at the foot of Waterbury Lane (now Middletown Road). Note the carriage tracks and hoof marks in the snow. The chimneys can be seen dimly in the background beyond the two gateposts. The last time I looked, the capstones from the posts were just inside the fence, which is now part of Pelham Bay Park. It is interesting to note that Mr. Huntington often commuted to his office by boat. A path from the back of his home led down to his dock on Eastchester Bay.

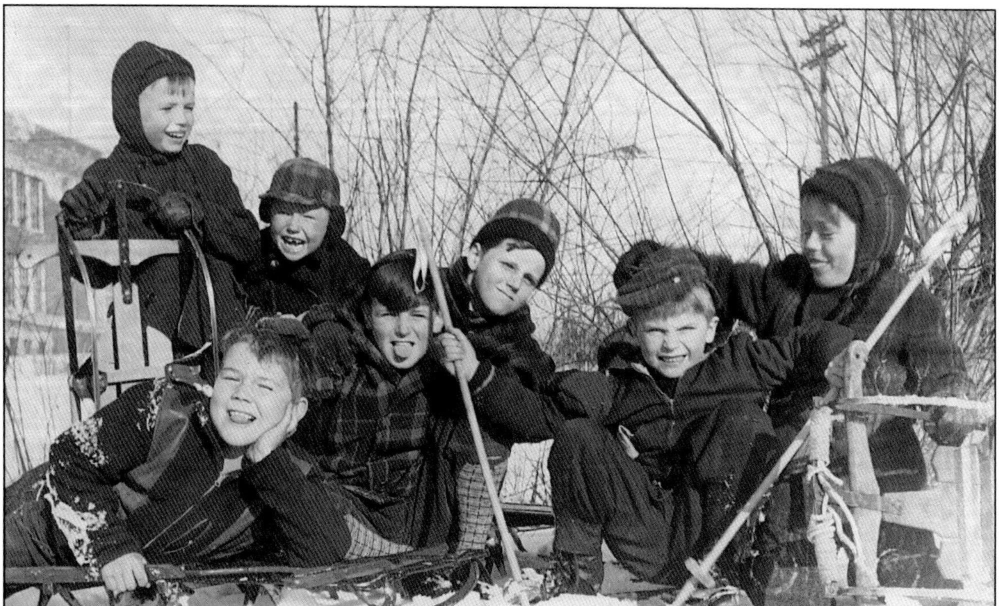

This snow scene was photographed on Clason Point in 1942. Eddie Bausbacher and Bernhardt Seifert are among the youths enjoying sledding. The building at the left background is P.S. 69, located on Theriot Avenue.

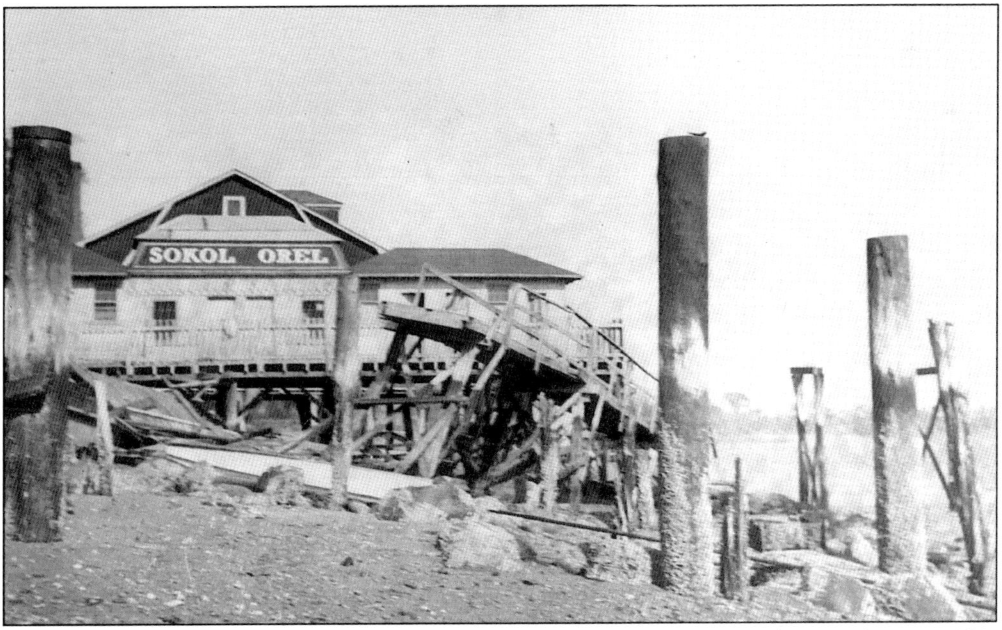

Greta Zarookian supplied this picture, taken the day after the hurricane of September 21, 1938. The house that stood atop the pilings in the foreground was washed away, and the German Stadium dock was dropped at the Sokol Orel Club. The view looks eastward. Schurz Avenue is on the left, and the East River is on the right.

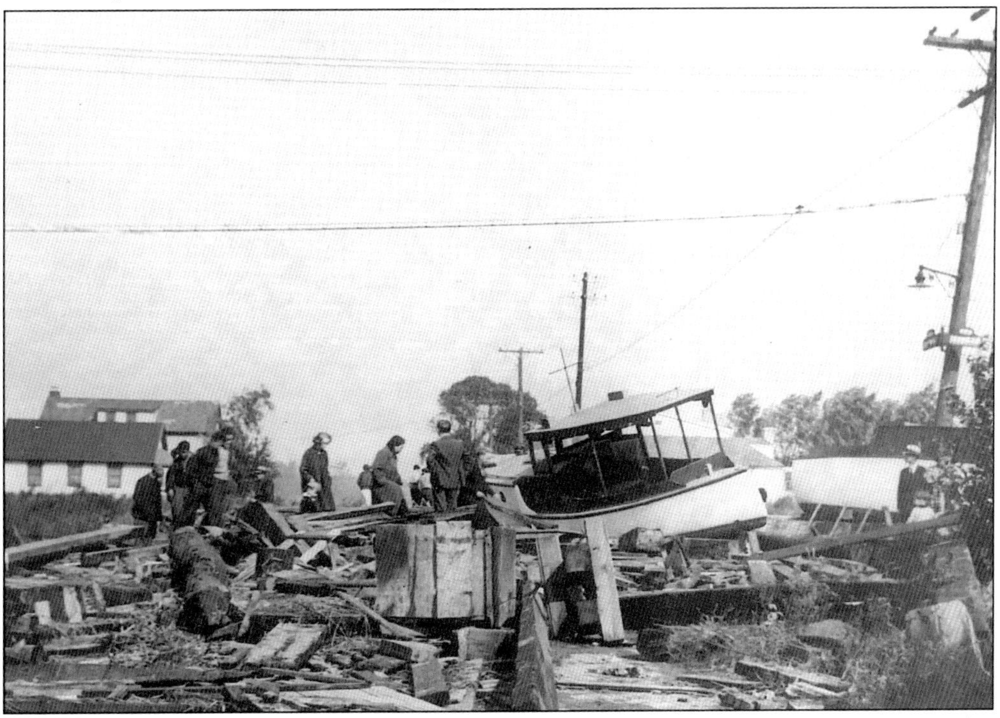

The hurricane of September 21, 1938, created extensive damage throughout coastal areas. This photograph, supplied by Greta Zarookian, was taken at Harding and Emerson Avenues the following day and vividly shows the washed-up boats and debris.

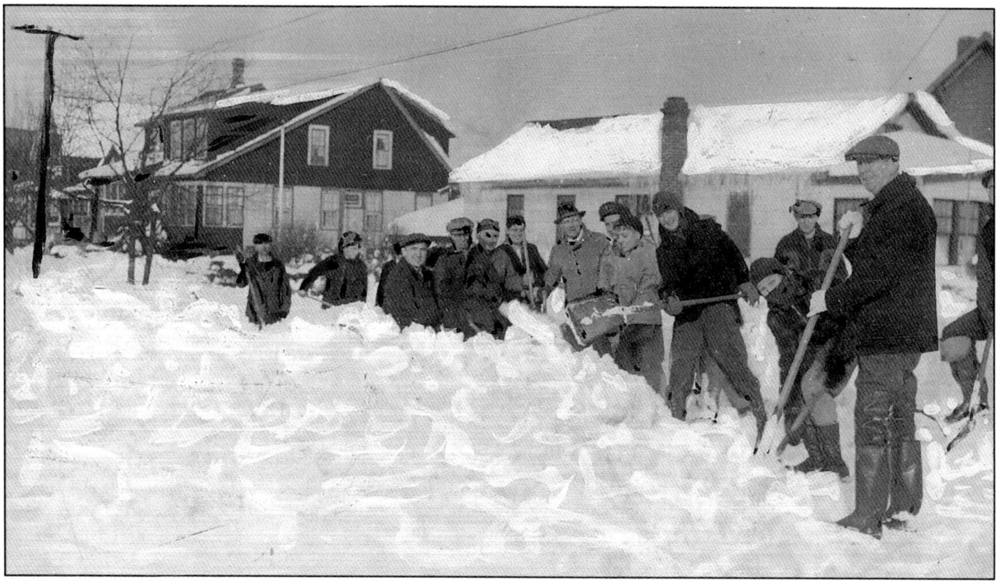

The snowstorm of December 26th and 27th, 1947, dropped 26.1 inches of snow on the Bronx. Neighbors got together on Pugsley Avenue off Gildersleeve Avenue to begin the clearing process in this photograph. (Courtesy of Arthur Seifert.)

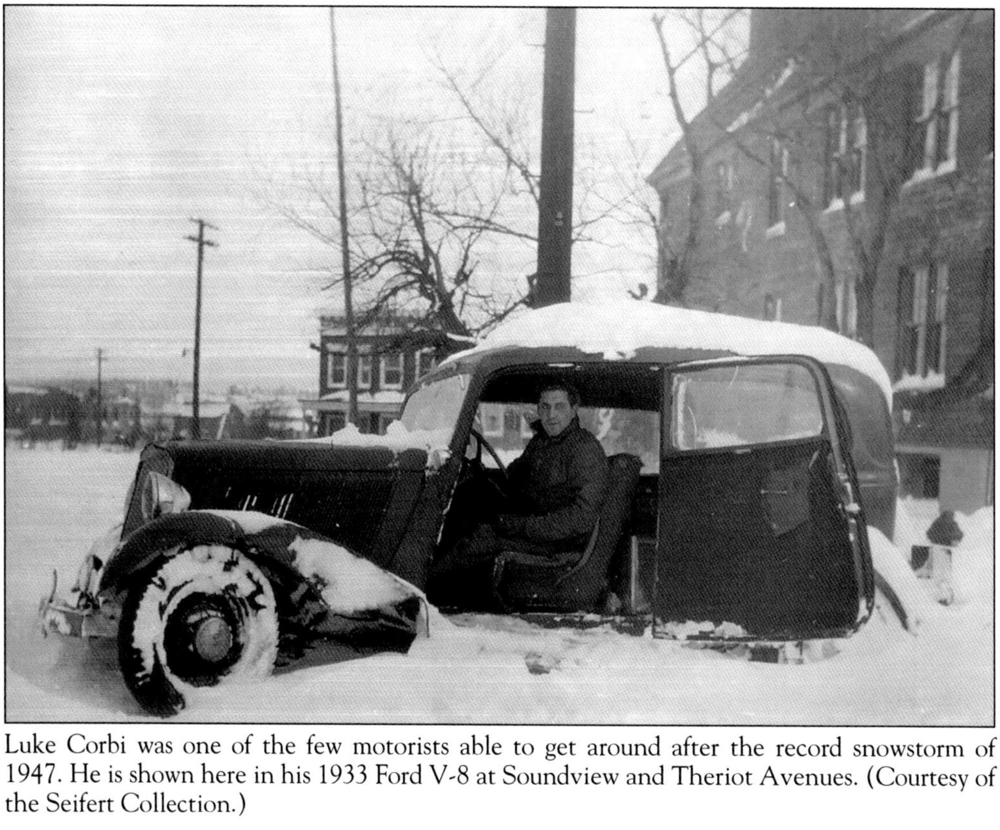

Luke Corbi was one of the few motorists able to get around after the record snowstorm of 1947. He is shown here in his 1933 Ford V-8 at Soundview and Theriot Avenues. (Courtesy of the Seifert Collection.)

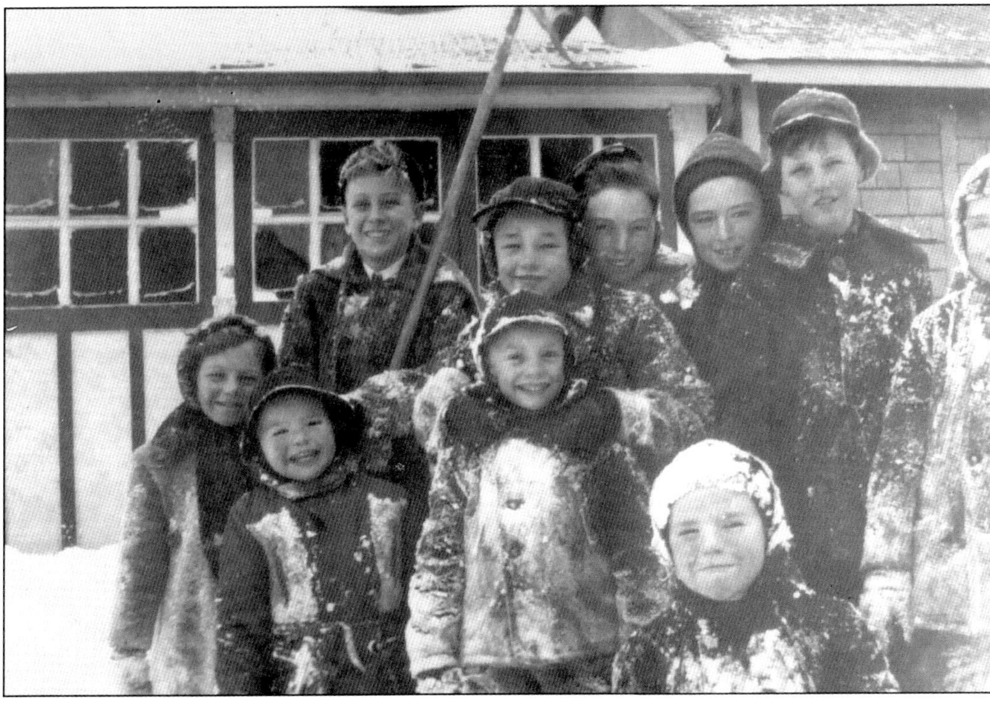

Ken Roberts supplied this snapshot that was taken on Edison Avenue while these children were shoveling out after the 1947 snowstorm. The snow began on Friday, December 26, 1947; by the following day, a massive 26.1 inches had accumulated. The four youngsters in front are, from left to right, as follows: (front row) Judy Gaffney, Jerry Worrell, Bobby Thomma and Fred Worrell; (back row) Jimmy Gaffney, Billy Thomma, Ken Roberts, Bobby Prescott, Gerry Jennings, and George Dempster. Randall Avenue is at the right.

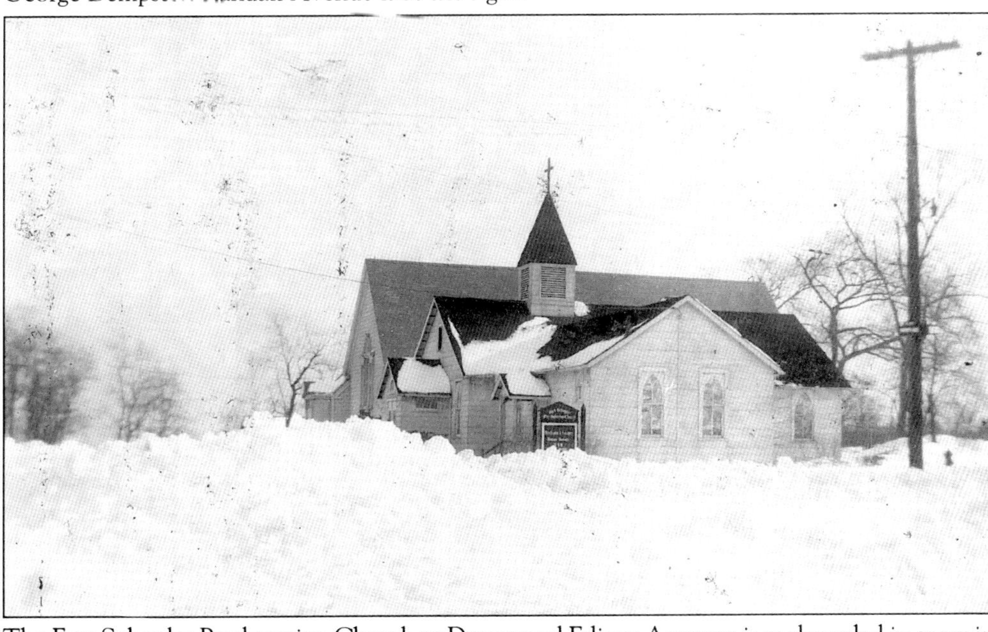

The Fort Schuyler Presbyterian Church at Dewey and Edison Avenues is enshrouded in snow in this 1948 winter scene. John McNamara supplied the photograph.

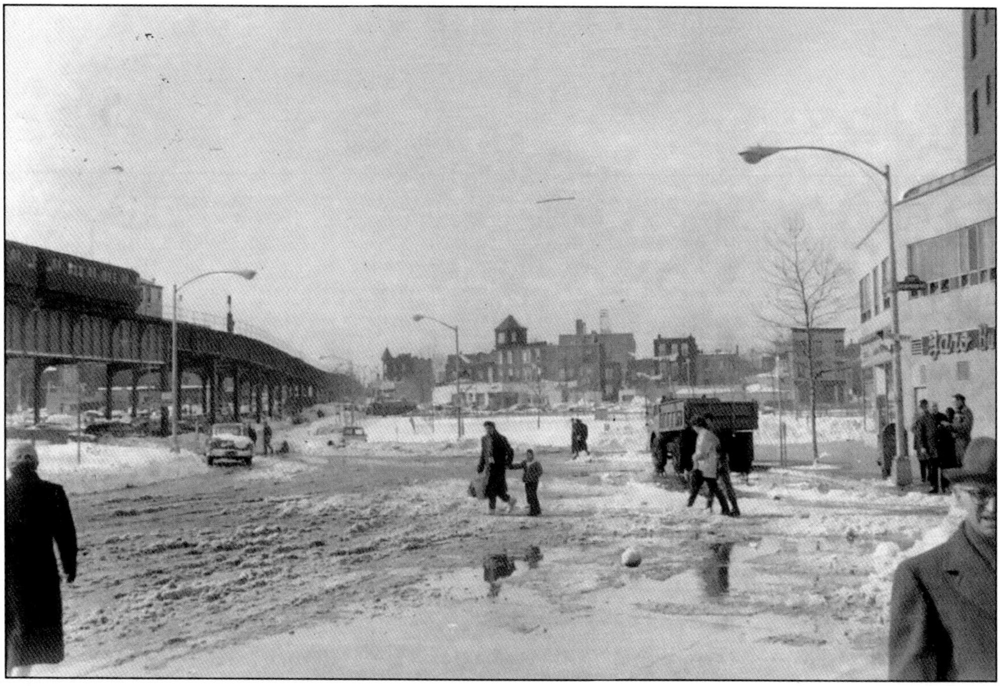

Ed Wolf took this photograph at Hugh Grant Circle after the heavy snowstorm of 1961. He was facing south toward White Plains Road. Note the Westchester Avenue El at the left and Zaro's Bakery at the right. Officially, 17.4 inches of snow fell on February 3rd and 4th, but the drifts presented the usual obstacles.

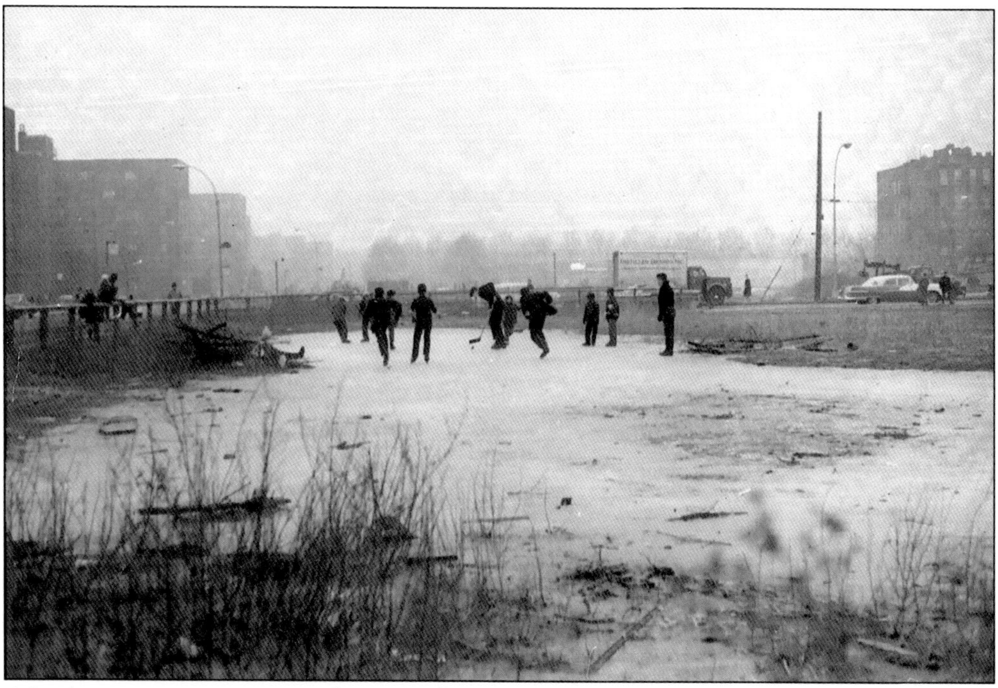

A hockey game is in process in this 1961 photograph by Ed Wolf. The winter scene occurred off St. Lawrence Avenue near the Bronxdale Housing Project.

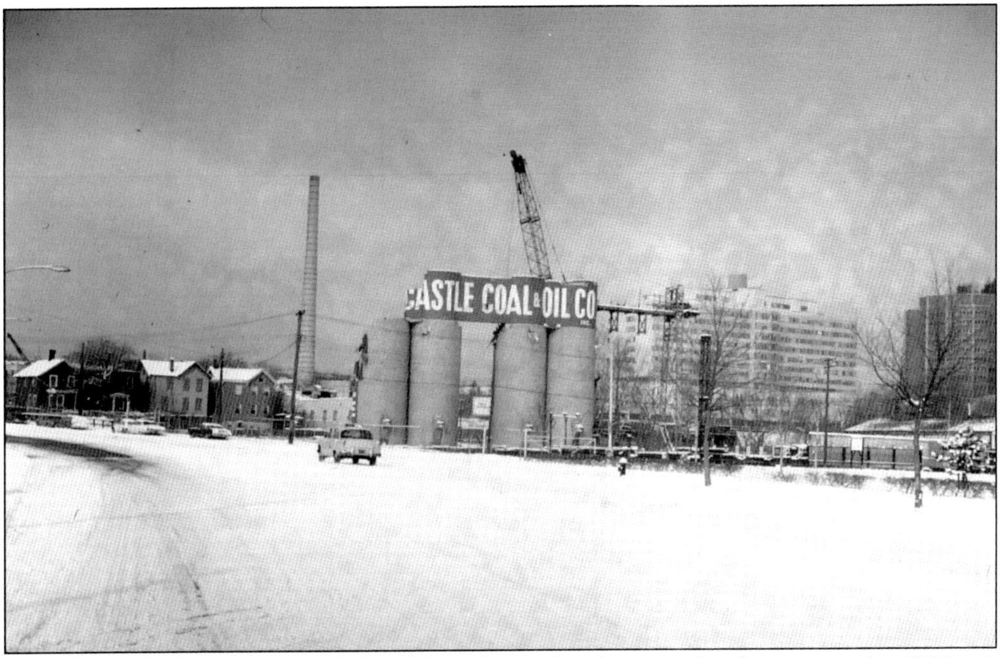

The coal bunkers at Waters Place and Eastchester Road were a familiar site in the 1960s. A lone taxi traverses the road on this snowy day in this northwestward view. Ron Schliessman provided the picture.

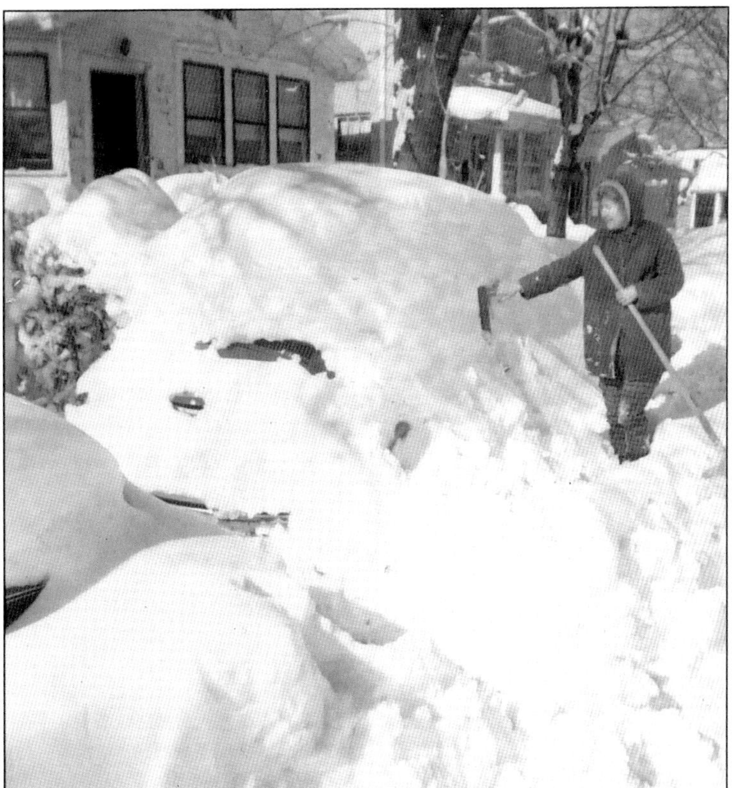

Pauline McNamara of Edgewater Park is shoveling out her new Volkswagon Beetle after the snowstorm of February 9, 1969. Officially 15.3 inches of snow fell, but as you can observe in this picture, the drifts were several feet high.

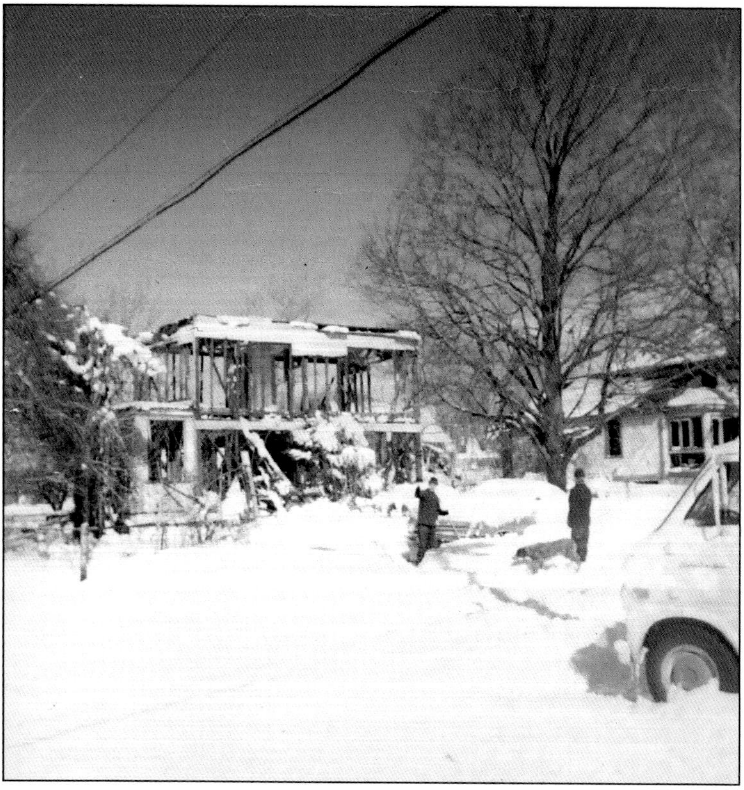

Northeast of the Pennyfield stores on Miles Avenue was the old Cambell farmhouse. The family grazed their cows along the north side of Miles Avenue at Edgewater Park, and this scene shows the demolition of the house by local youngsters after the blizzard of February 1969.

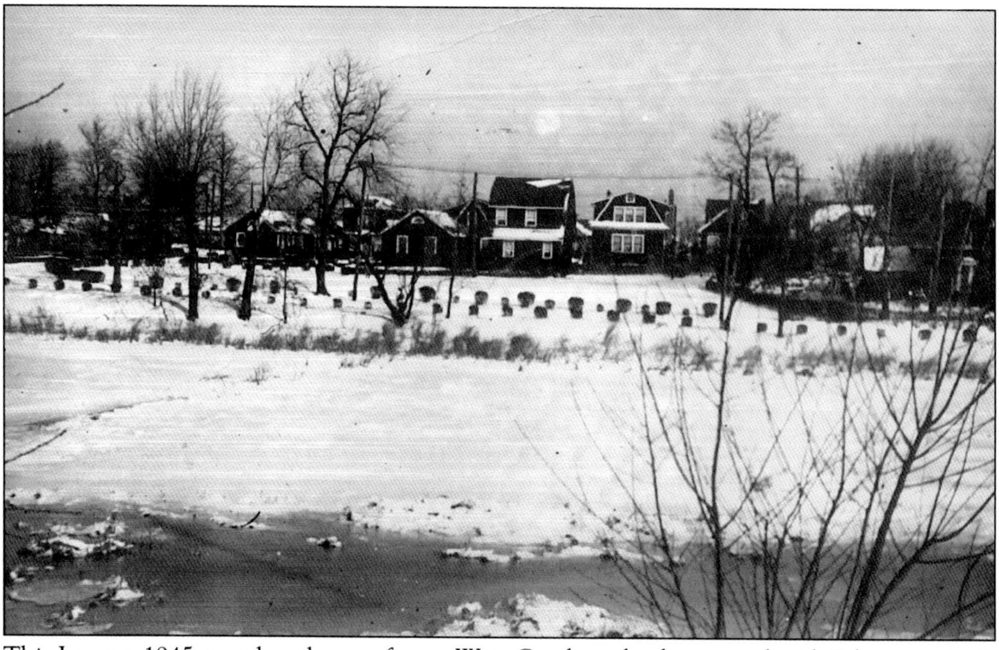

This January 1945 snapshot shows a frozen Weir Creek in the foreground with Edgewater Park in the background. The box-shaped objects are neatly trimmed evergreen bushes, and the houses beyond them are in "E" section in this easterly view. The creek was lost in the construction of the approaches to the Throgs Neck Bridge.

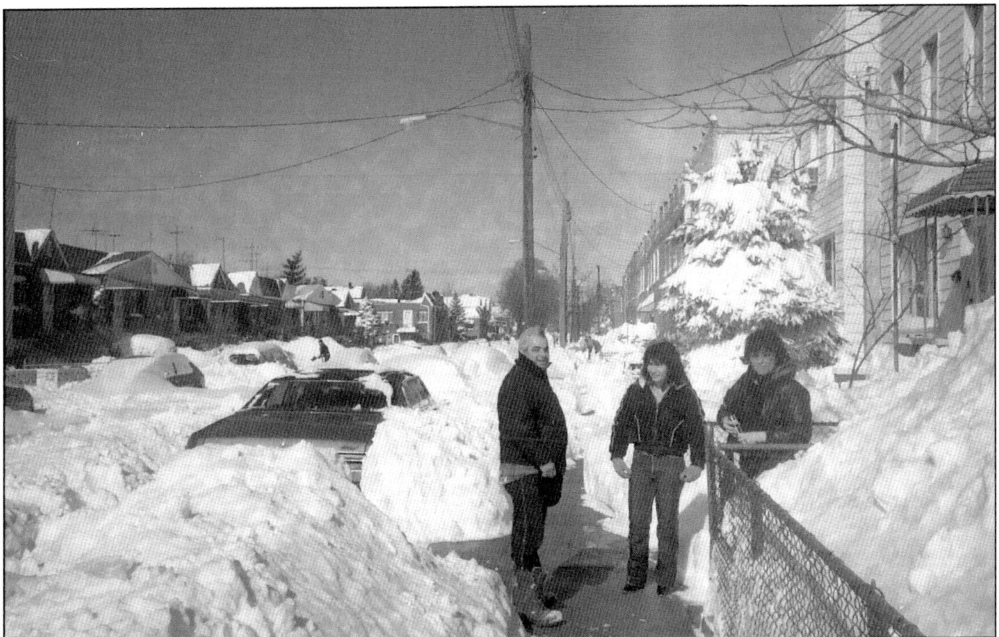

The blizzard of 1983 started on Friday, February 11th and continued through the following day, depositing 21 inches of snow on the area. Ken Roberts took this photograph of Pete Ruggiero, Angela Regina, and Patricia Ruggiero on Revere Avenue just north of Dill Place. The view looks to the north.

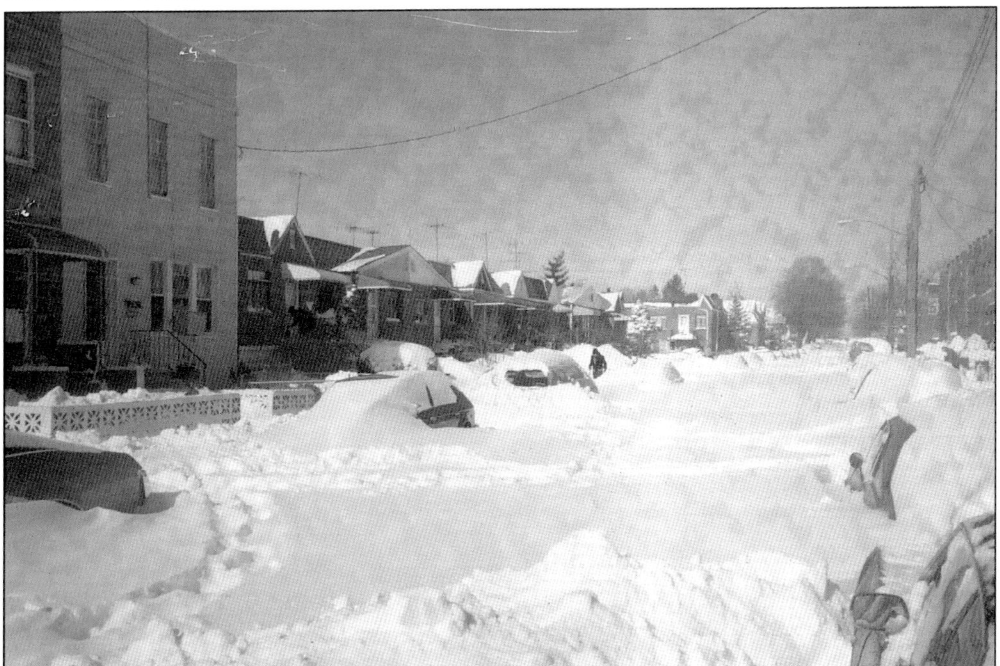

Ken Roberts took this photograph of Revere Avenue, which shows absolutely no vehicular traffic. Residents soon ran out of places to pile the snow that clogged area roadways. The view looks northward from just north of Dill Place. The photograph was taken on February 12, 1983.

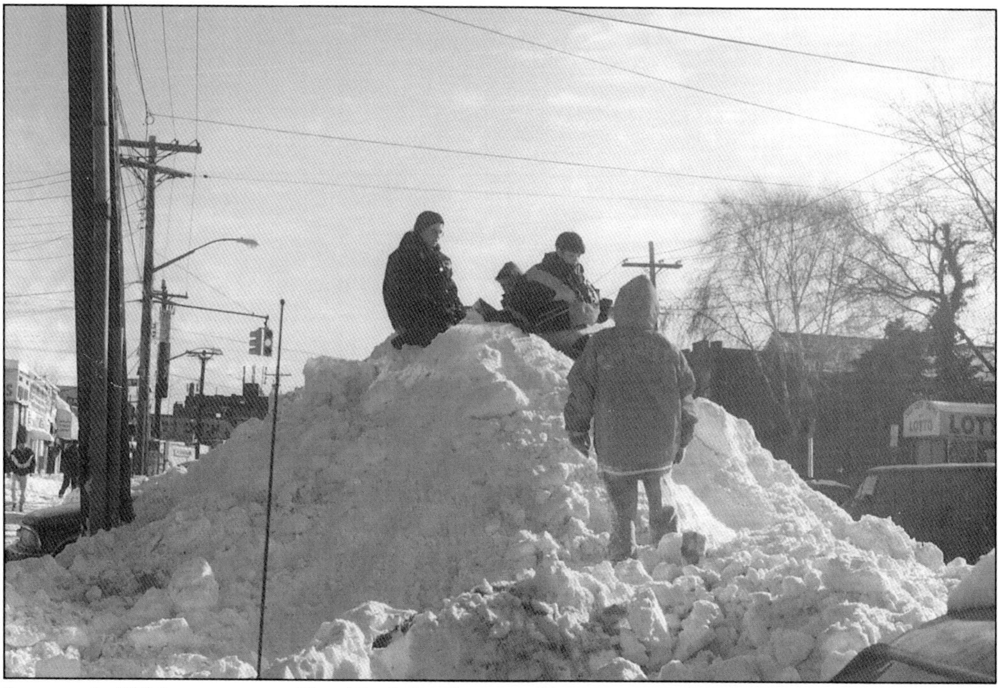

January 8, 1996, was an unofficial holiday for most Bronxites as they began shoveling out after the blizzard that dropped 25 inches of snow on the area. This picture shows East Tremont Avenue just north of Coddington Avenue.

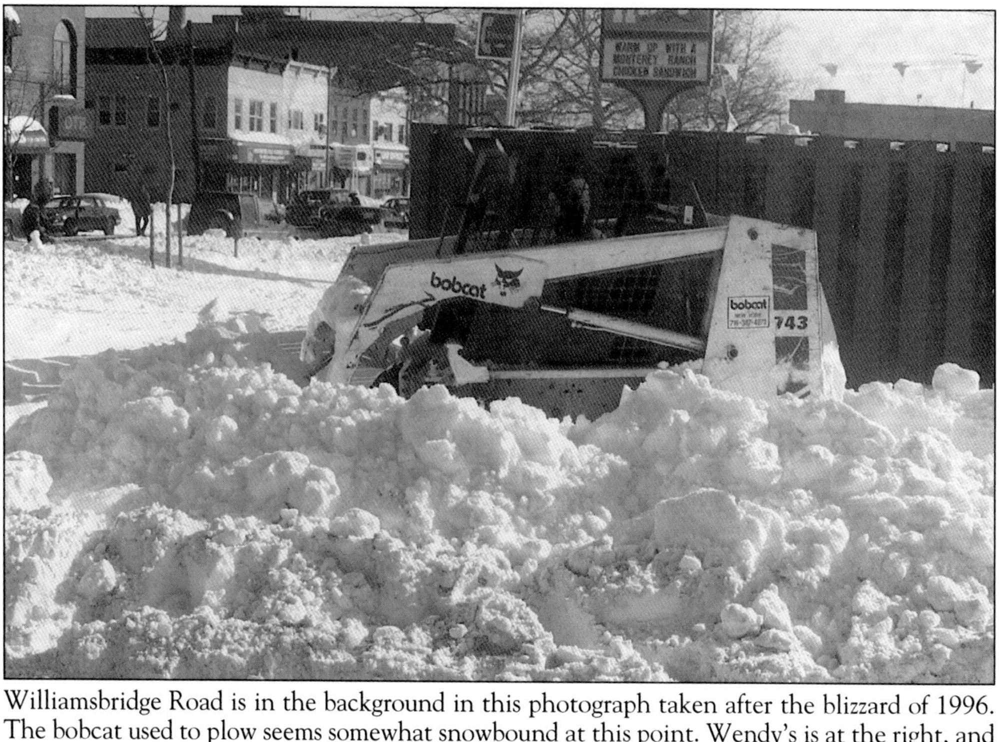

Williamsbridge Road is in the background in this photograph taken after the blizzard of 1996. The bobcat used to plow seems somewhat snowbound at this point. Wendy's is at the right, and the area shown is at St. Raymond Avenue, just west of Westchester Square.

Nine

Sports

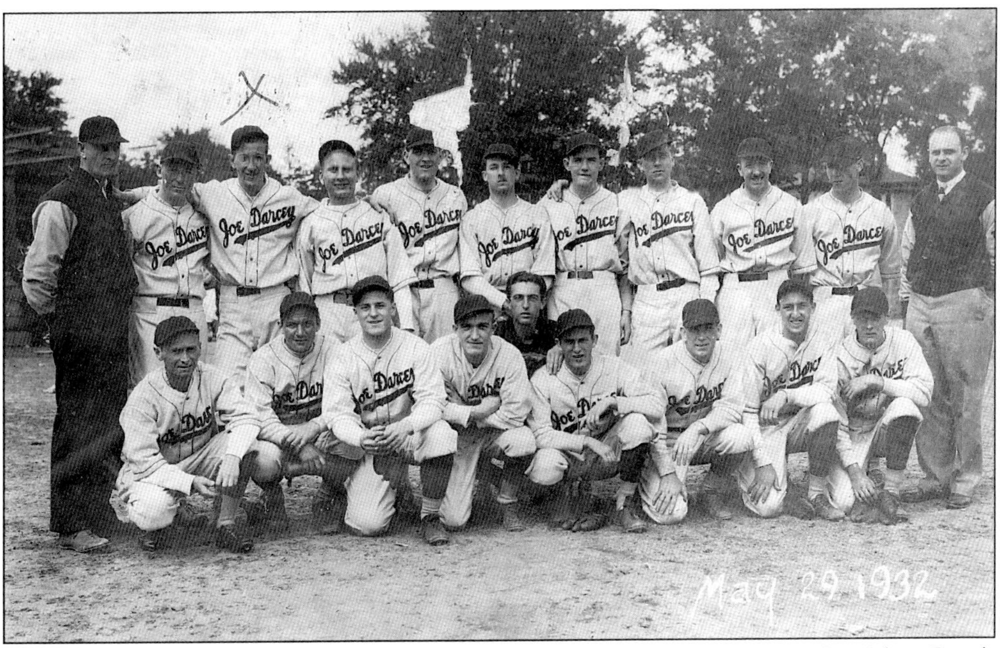

This photograph of the Joe Darcey baseball team was taken on May 29, 1932. Silver Beach resident Joe Darcey was a well-known entertainer of the day who traveled the northeast circuit singing in the Al Jolson style. He later operated the Gate Tavern off Pennyfield Avenue.

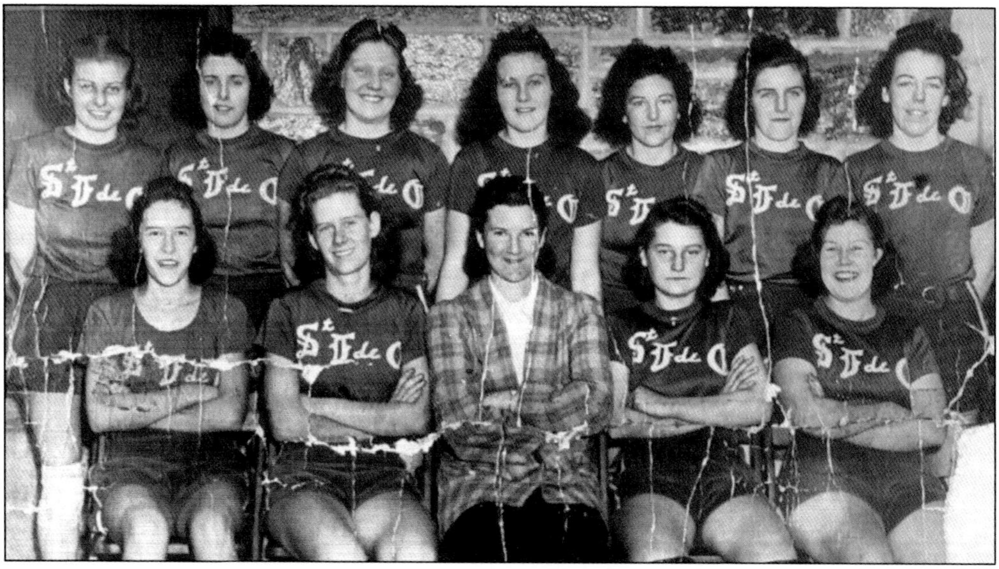

This girls' basketball team of 1938 was sponsored by the St. Frances de Chantal Parish. Featured in this photograph are the following, from left to right: (front row) May Roche, Doris Fanning, Louise McSwigin (the coach), Mildred Davis, and Betty McHugh; (back row) Dot Battersby, Virginia Regan, Madeline McHugh, Catherine Connors, unidentified, Kay Regan, and Rose Campbell. (Photograph courtesy of Jim McSwigin.)

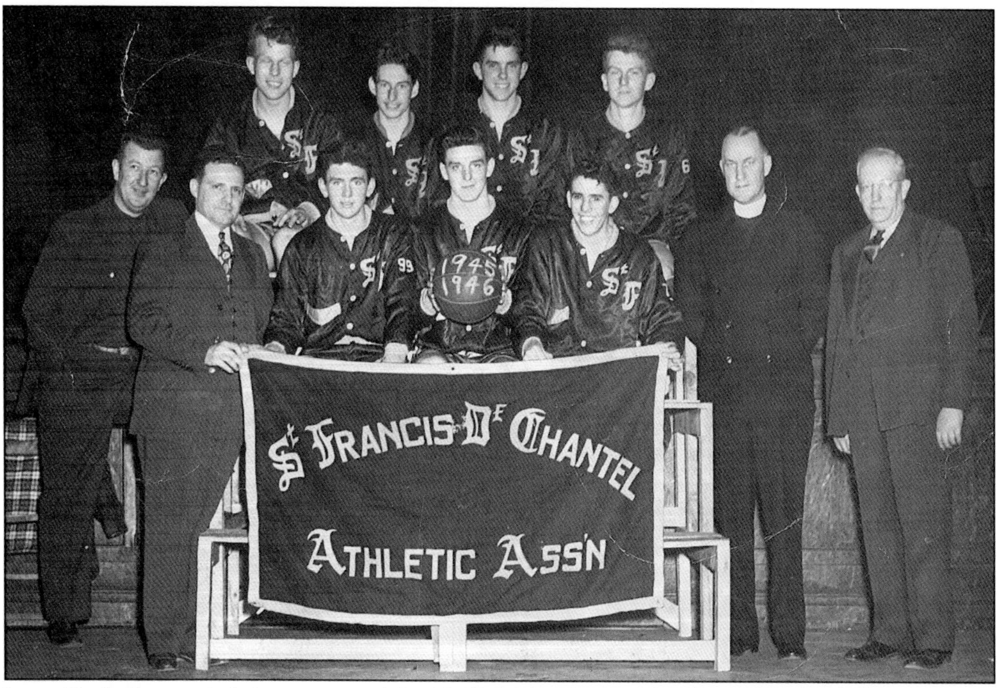

Larry Haskell provided this picture of the 1945–46 St. Frances de Chantal basketball team. Note the two errors in the spelling on the banner. Seen here, from left to right, are as follows: (front row) coach Jim McSigin, Jim Arenholz, Ed Braniff, Albee Lerch, Richie Lacina, the chaplain, and Louis "Doc" Zawar; (back row) Larry Haskell, Ribby Robinson, Walter "Ike" Lorenz, and Richie Borstelmann.

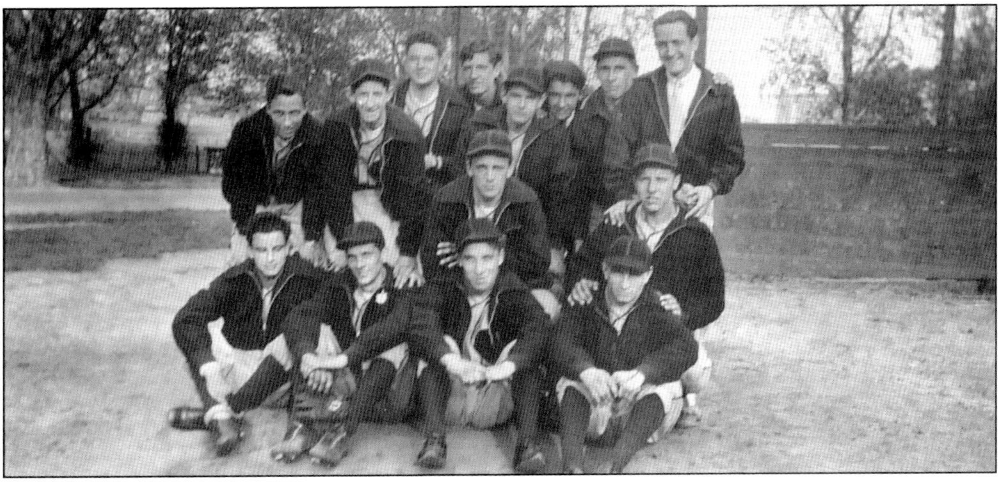

The Gamma Delta Fraternity baseball team was popular throughout the Bronx. This picture was snapped at the Catholic Protectorate field in 1934. Pictured from left to right are as follows: (front row) Pat Cerillo, George Egan, Jack Ryan, and "Lefty" McCauley; (middle row) Eddie Englert and Edgar Siedenzahl; (back row) Ted Goodfleisch, who supplied the photograph; "Doc" Sisca; Charlie Hughes; "Sonny" Brandon; Tommy Fields; Willie Bernitt, who was just visiting; Walter Leve; and the coach, Maurice Olivere.

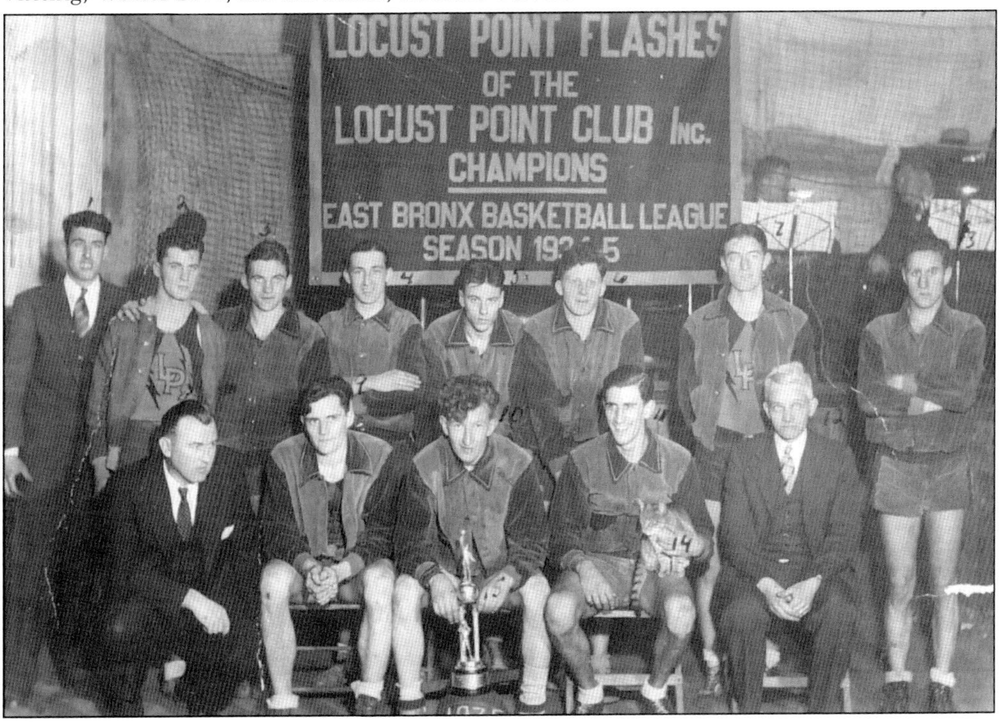

The Locust Point Flashes were the East Bronx Basketball Champions for the 1934–35 season. Jim McSwigin, front and center, holds the coveted trophy. To the right of McSwigin is the team's feline mascot, Flash, on Harry Leith's lap and the manager, Mr. George Dannenfelser. Others pictured are Frank Carson, Buddy Smith, Danny Howard, Brother Matios, Ed Oswald, Red Stolles, Bill Tarpey, Pete Cafferlie, Ray Quinn, Joe Mantz, the coach, and Dr. Frank O'Keefe.

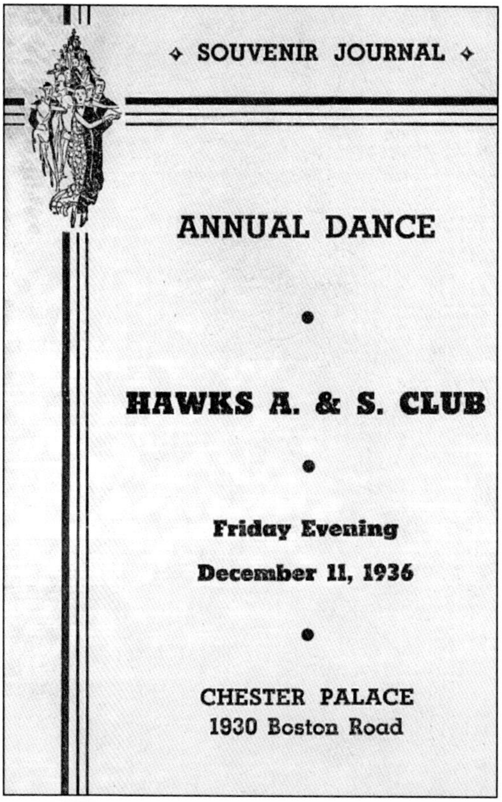
✧ SOUVENIR JOURNAL ✧

ANNUAL DANCE

•

HAWKS A. & S. CLUB

•

Friday Evening

December 11, 1936

•

CHESTER PALACE
1930 Boston Road

The Hawks A.&S. Club was a major attraction in the East Bronx up until World War II. They played baseball on Hawk Field, located on Philip Avenue off Quincy Avenue. This souvenir journal is from their annual dance held at the Chester Palace on December 11, 1936. Walter Birsner provided the program. Alfonso Amabile was the president that year.

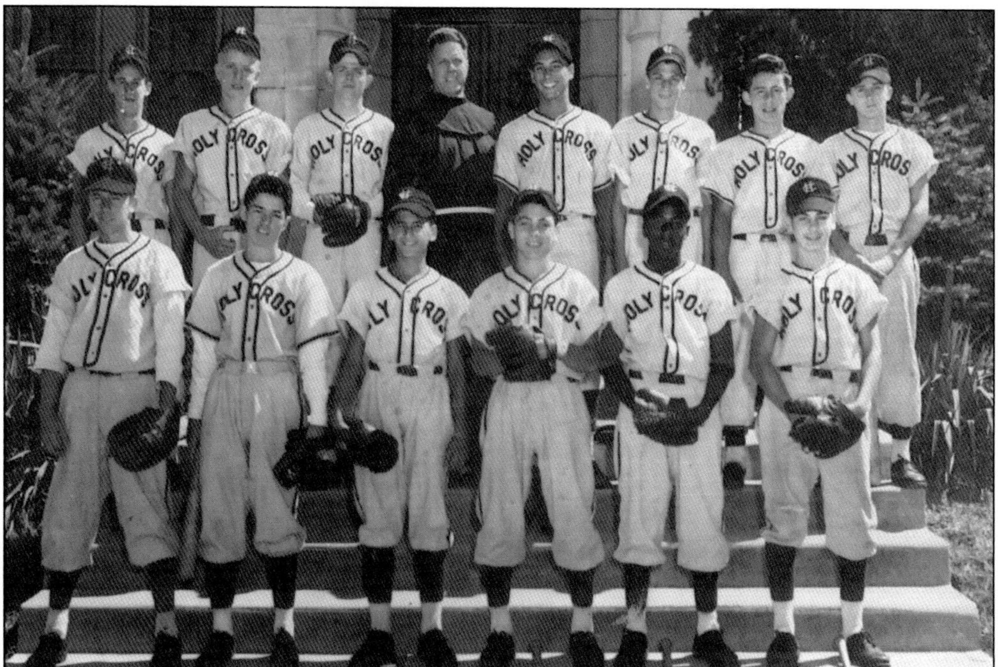

Holy Cross Church and School fielded their own baseball team, shown here on the steps of the Franciscan Friary on Soundview Avenue. Arthur Seifert provided this *c.* 1950 picture.

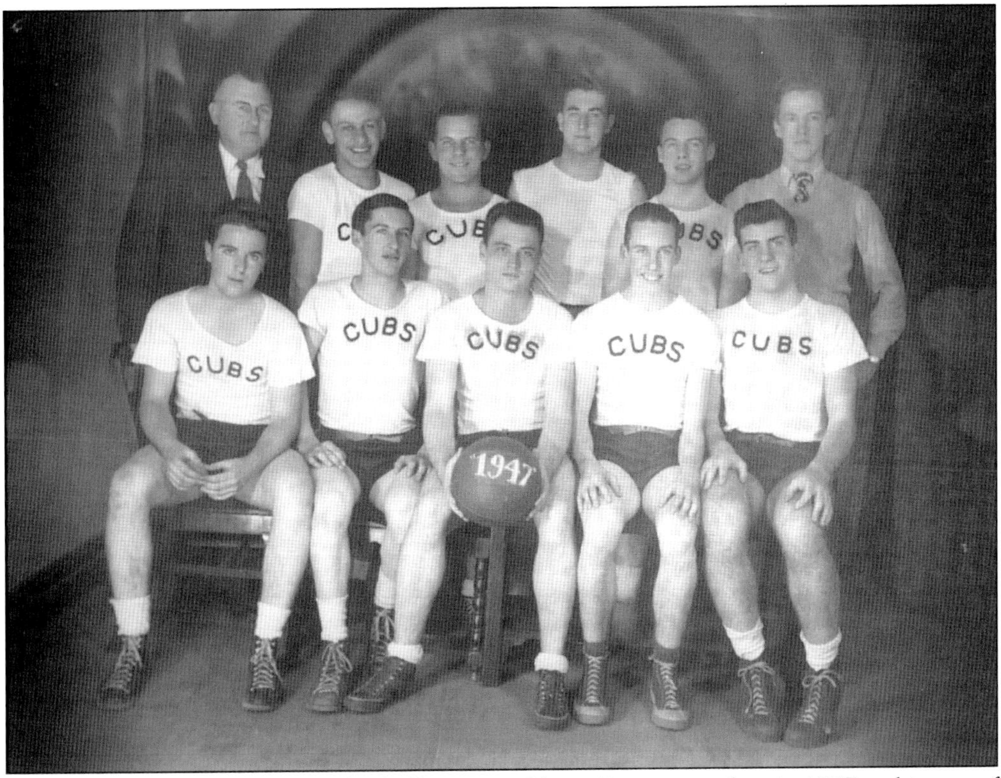

This photograph of the Cubs basketball team on Clason Point was taken in 1947 and is part of the Seifert Collection.

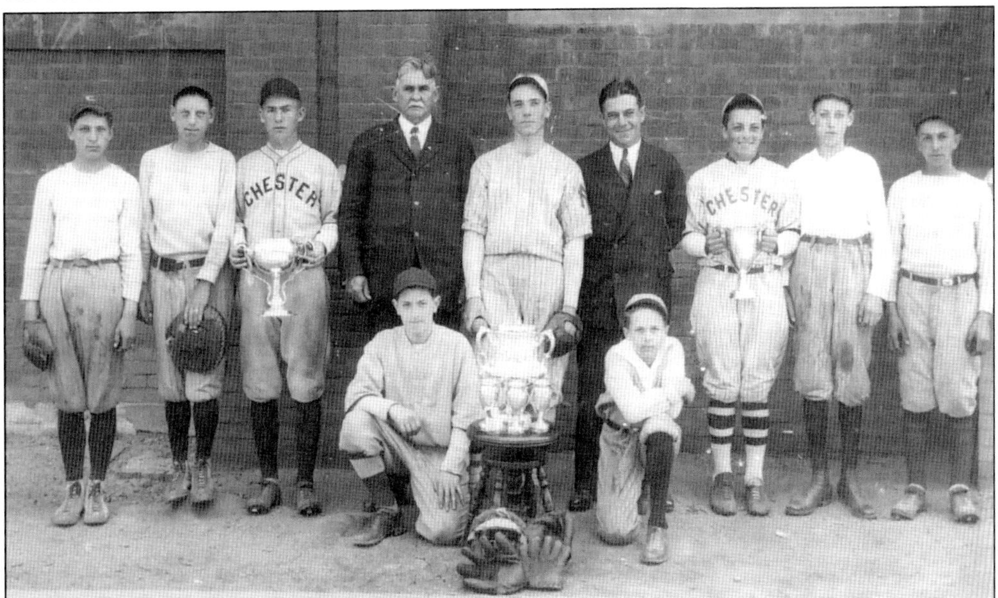

The P.S. 12 baseball team is showing off their trophies outside their Westchester Square School in this 1926 photograph. Dr. John F. Condon, the principal, is the fourth from left, and Frank Fonzo is on the extreme right.

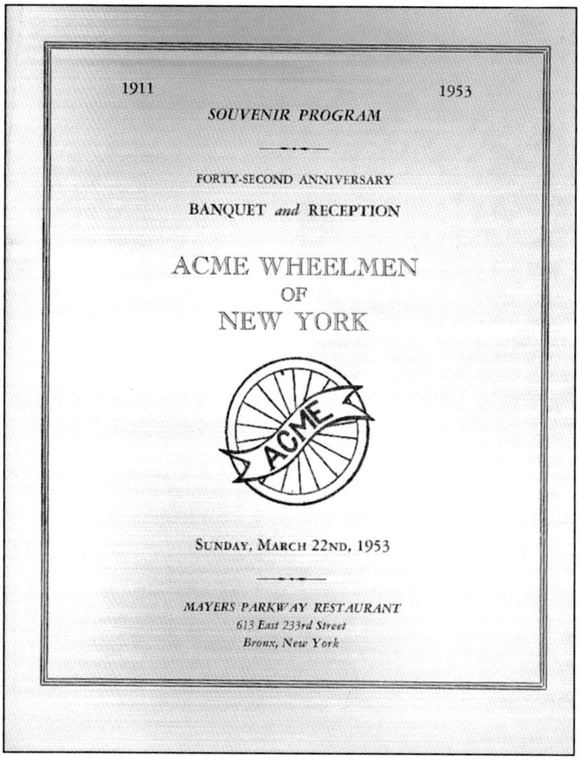

1911 1953

SOUVENIR PROGRAM

FORTY-SECOND ANNIVERSARY

BANQUET *and* RECEPTION

ACME WHEELMEN
OF
NEW YORK

SUNDAY, MARCH 22ND, 1953

MAYERS PARKWAY RESTAURANT
613 East 233rd Street
Bronx, New York

This souvenir program of the Acme Wheelmen, provided by Ron Schliessman, is from their 42nd anniversary banquet and reception, held at Mayers Parkway Restaurant at 613 East 233rd Street in the Bronx. It was held on March 22, 1953. The committee was led by Charles Muller. Thomas Perangelo served as president that year.

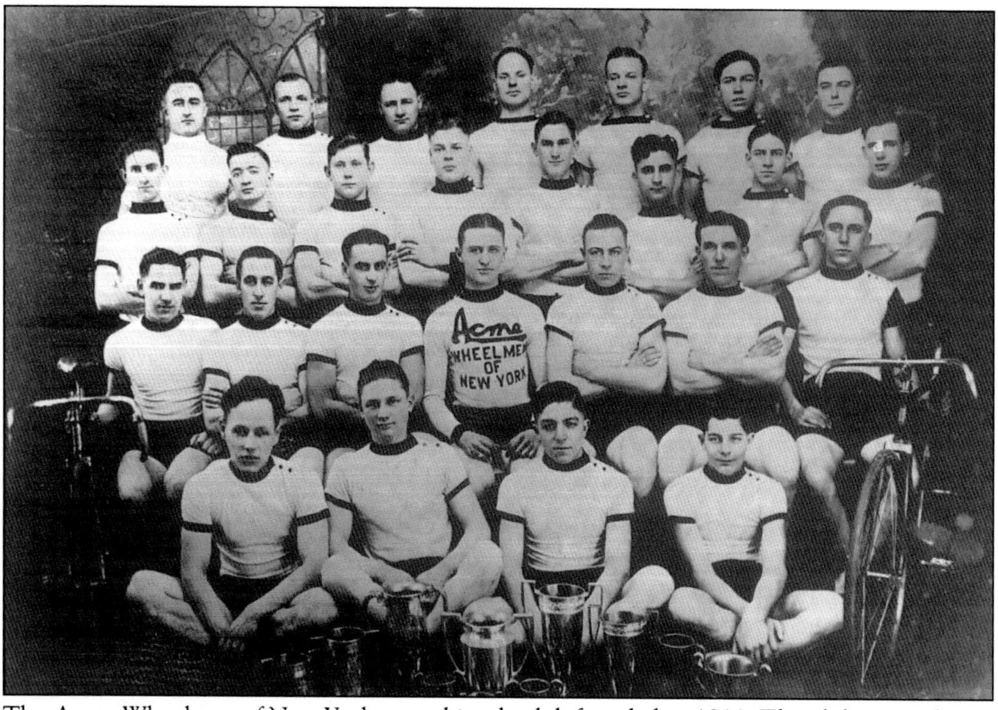

The Acme Wheelmen of New York was a bicycle club founded in 1911. The club was rather elite in that you had to prove your skills at racing before being accepted. (Photograph courtesy of Ronald Schliessman.)

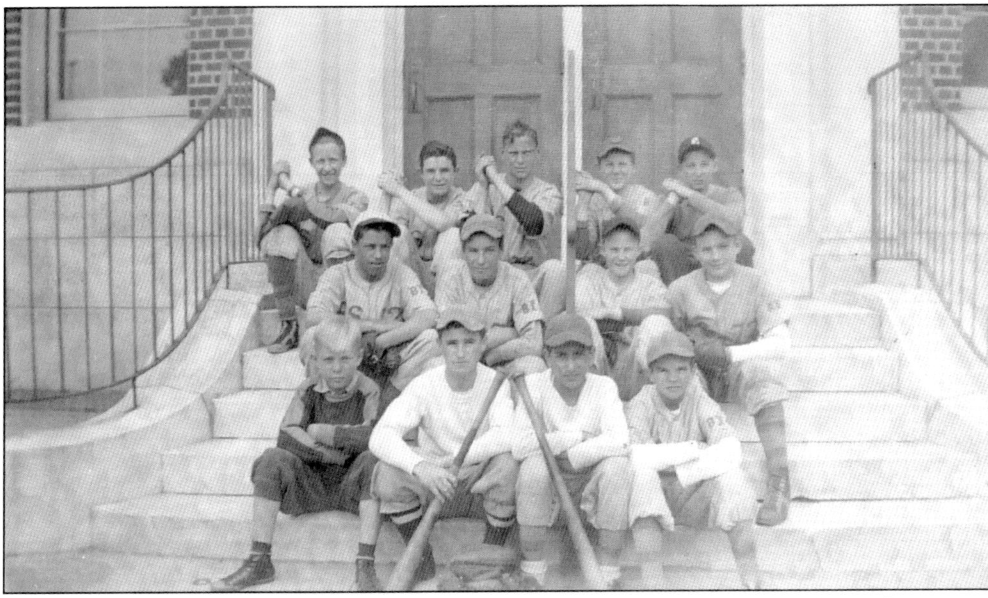

This snapshot of the P.S. 72 baseball team was taken *c.* 1930 at the school, located at Dewey and Edison Avenues. The photographer was facing north.

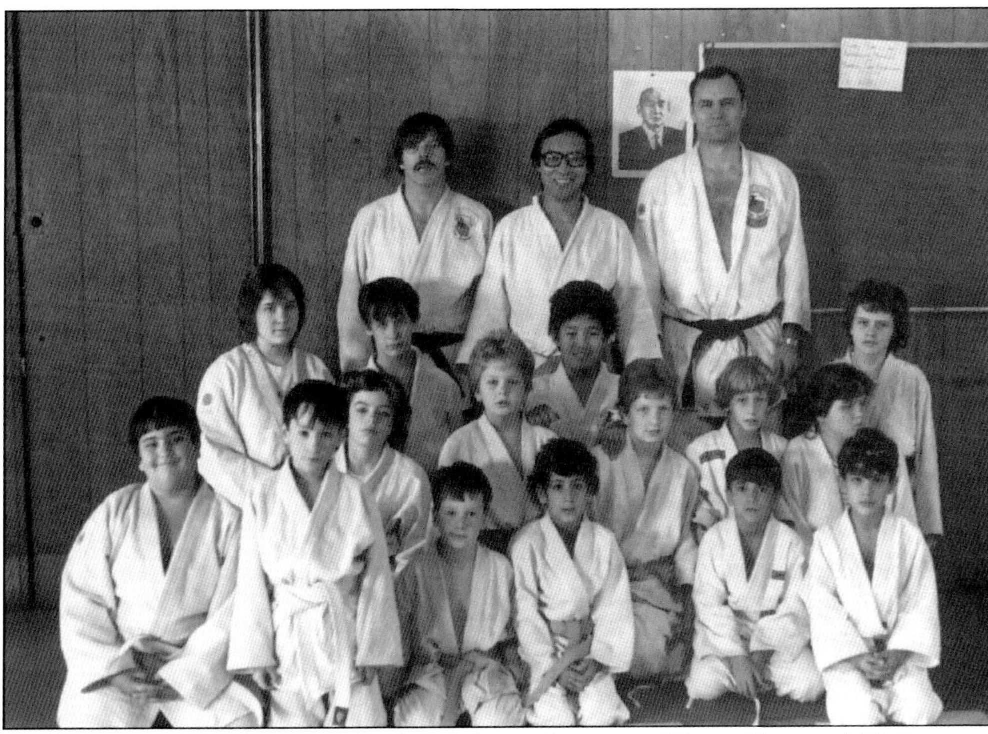

Seen here at the Matsumora Clinic, from left to right, are as follows: (first row) M. Rosiconi, J. Munafo, J. McAleet, R. Garibian, J. Caggiano, and D. Aloisio; (second row) S. Rodriquez, R. Myers, J. Hooks, and R. Heffernan; (third row) J. Nelson, J. Heffernan, M. Tollens, A. Marino, and M. Myers; (fourth row) Senseis J. Mazzariello, Y. Matsumora, and George Pasiuk. The photograph was taken in the mid-1980s.

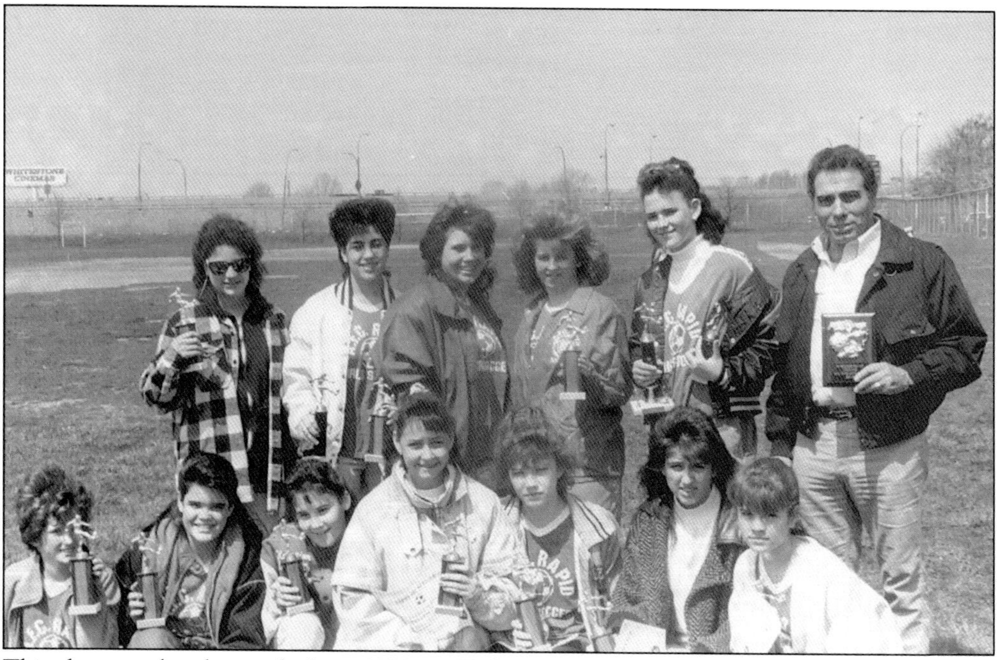

This photograph, taken in the late-1980s on Wil Cintron Field off Balcom Avenue, shows the girl majors of the AFC Rapid soccer team. The view is to the north toward Bruckner Boulevard.

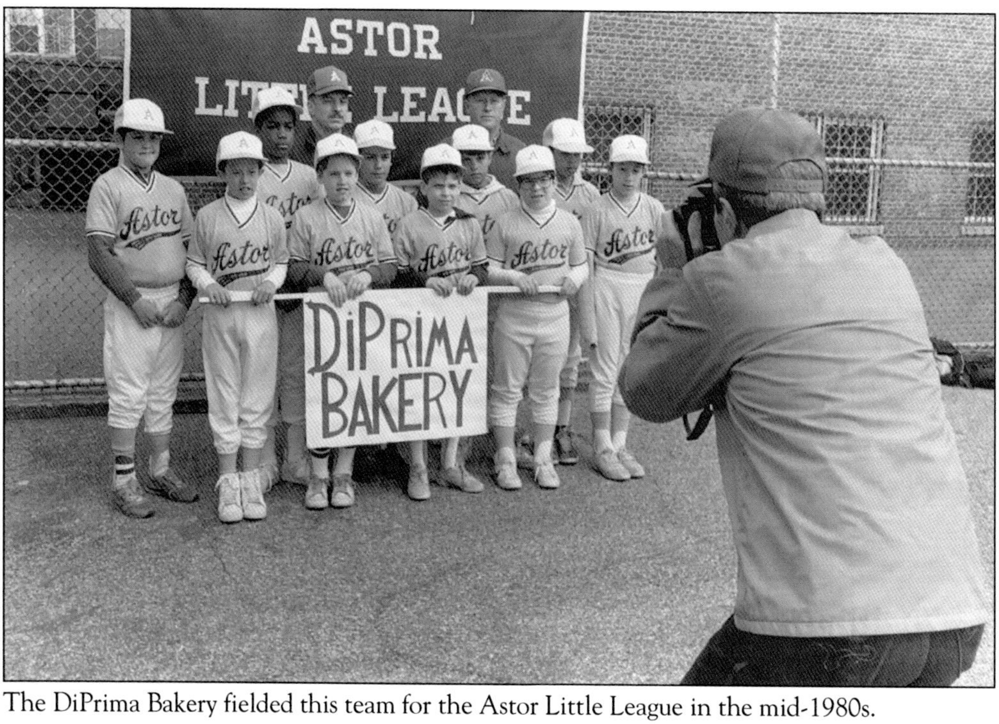

The DiPrima Bakery fielded this team for the Astor Little League in the mid-1980s.

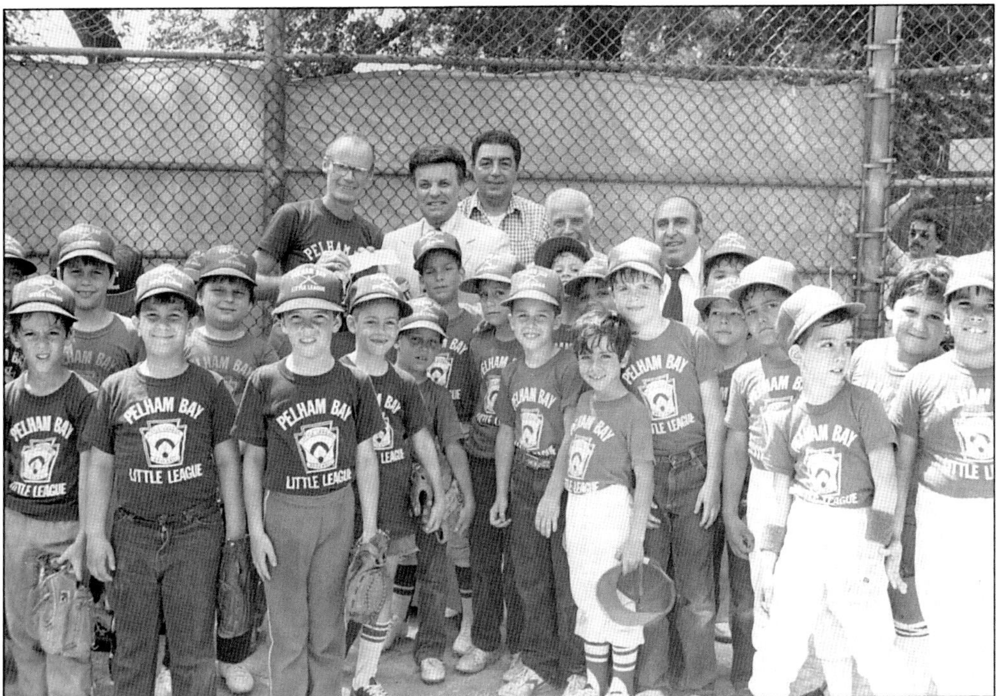

With help from sports columnist Nick Aromando, the Pelham Bay Little League was established on June 12, 1955, by a group of parents that included Louis Vinaccia, Jerry Mazzo, Sam Licata, Phil Tuebl, Lou Cristofaro, and Louis Puccio. Taken in the mid-1980s, this photograph includes Senator John Calandra in the center rear with the while jacket.

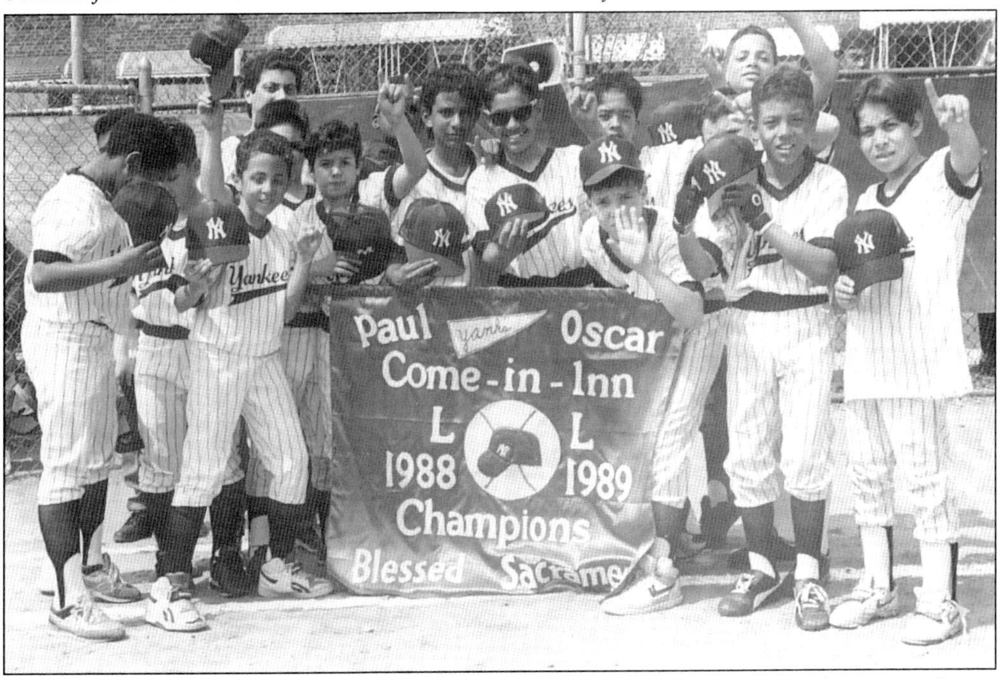

The Little League has fielded some great teams over the years. The 1988–89 champions shown here represented Blessed Sacrament Church.

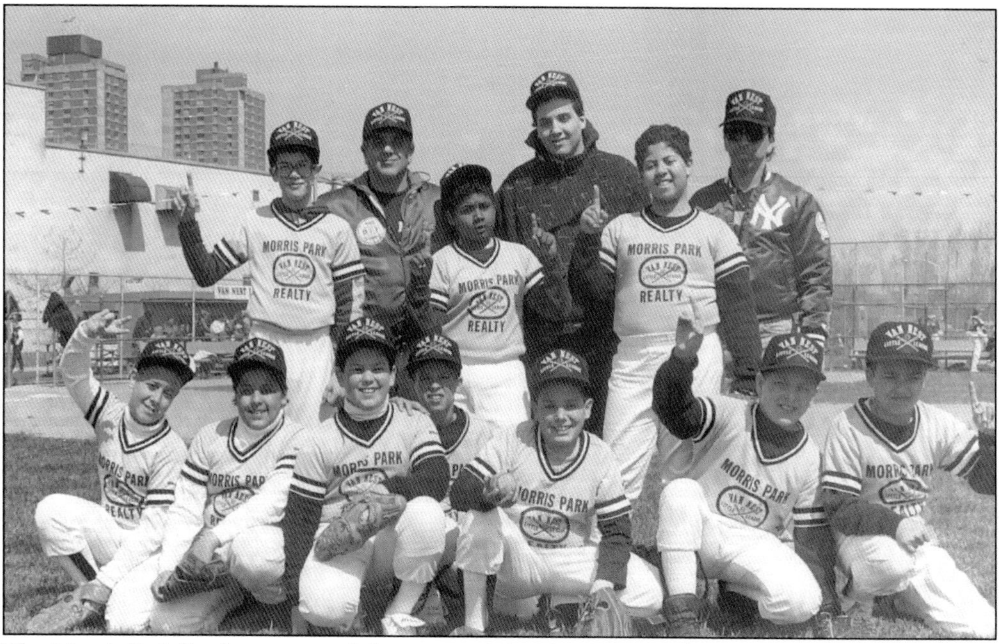

The Morris Park Realty sponsored this team of the Van Nest Little League in the late-1980s.

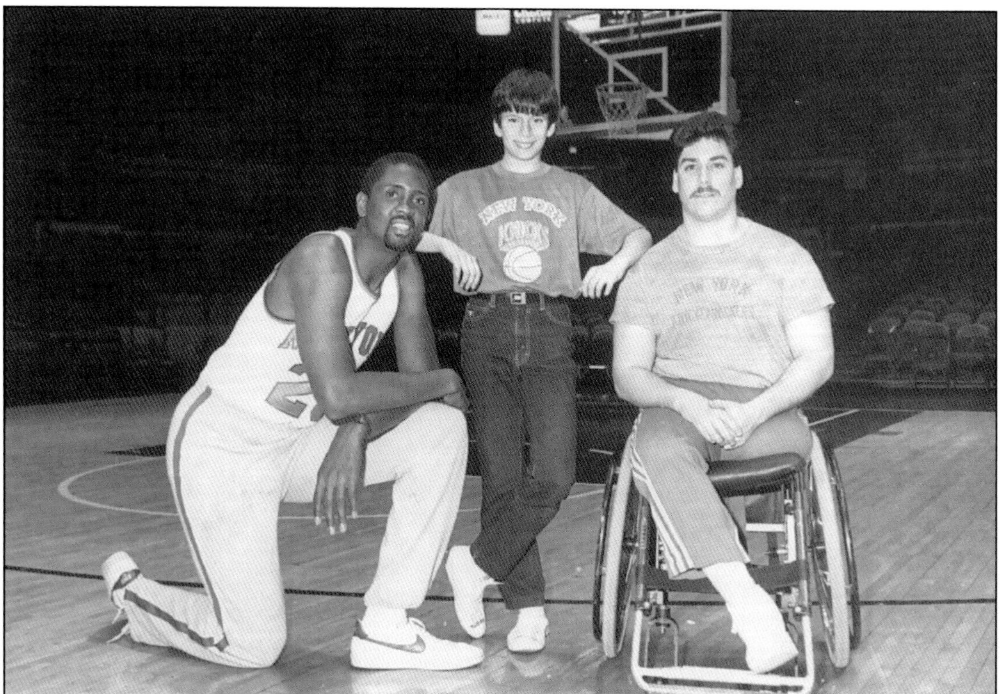

An Easter Seal Shoot-out was held in March of 1985. Seen here, from left to right, are Bill Cartwright of the Knicks, P.S. 71 student Ethan Jeremy Brown, and Bobby Cugini.

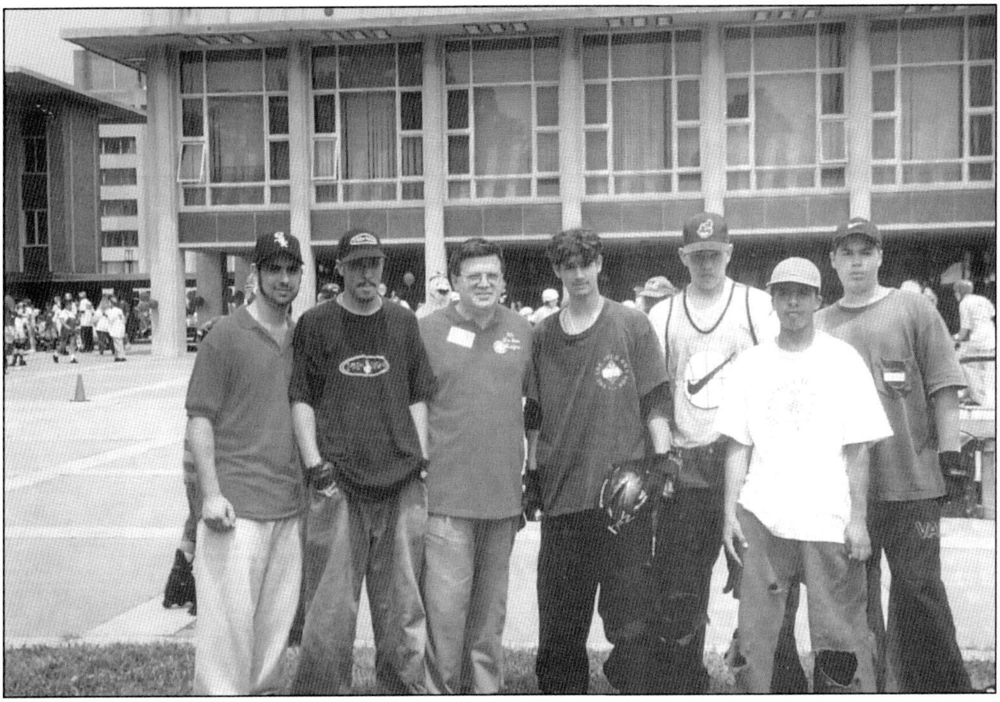

Assemblyman Steve Kaufman sponsored a rollerblading day at Fort Schuyler to teach and support safe skating. The assemblyman is third from left in this photograph taken in July of 1996.

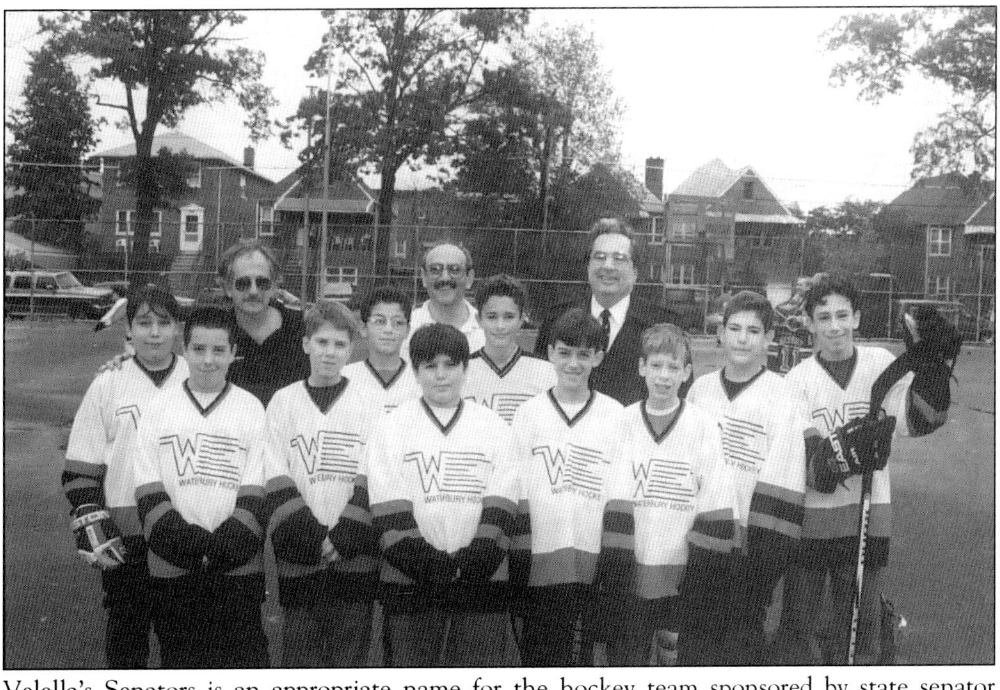

Velella's Senators is an appropriate name for the hockey team sponsored by state senator Guy Velella, shown here in the suit and tie. Waterbury Hockey, appropriately, plays at Bufano Park, also known as Waterbury/LaSalle Park. This photograph was taken in the mid-1990s.

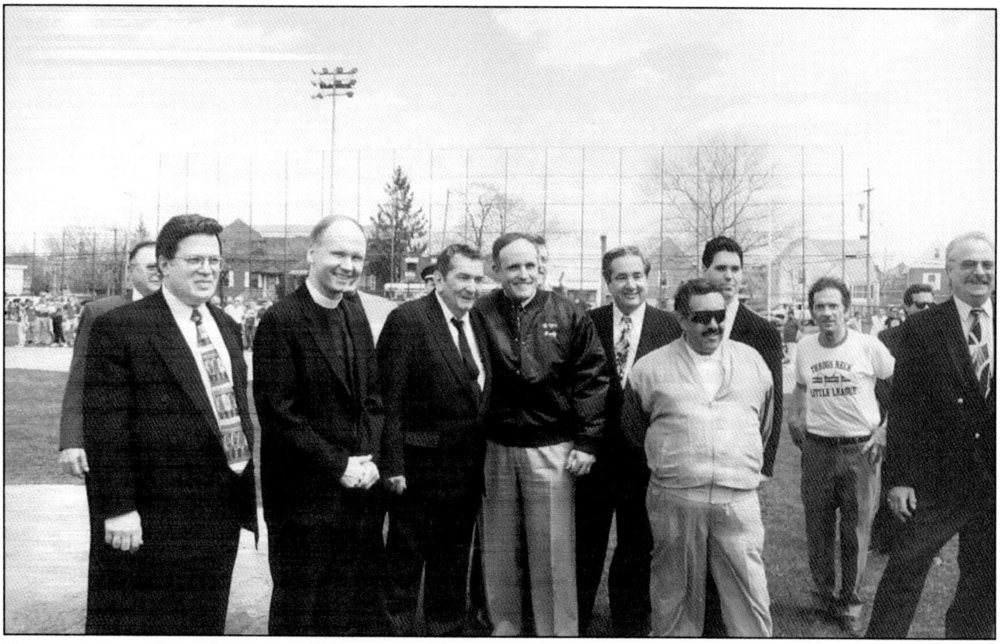

Dignitaries gathered at the Throggs Neck Little League (TNLL) field a couple of years ago. Seen here are, from left to right, assemblyman Steve Kaufman, Father Donald Baker from St. Frances de Chantal Parish, Leo Viti of the TNLL, Mayor Rudolph Giuliani, and state senator Guy Velella.

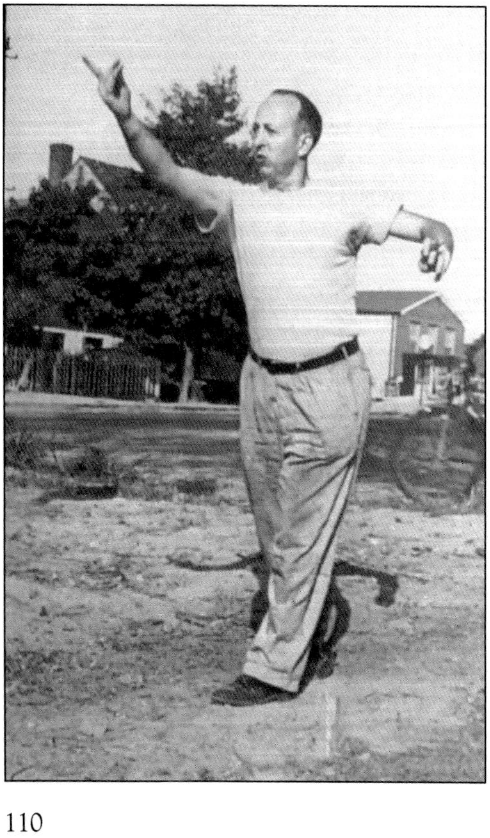

John Rush attempts a ringer at the horseshoe pit located at East 177th Street and Hatting Place in Locust Point. The photograph was taken in 1949.

Ten

THE OLD AND THE NEW

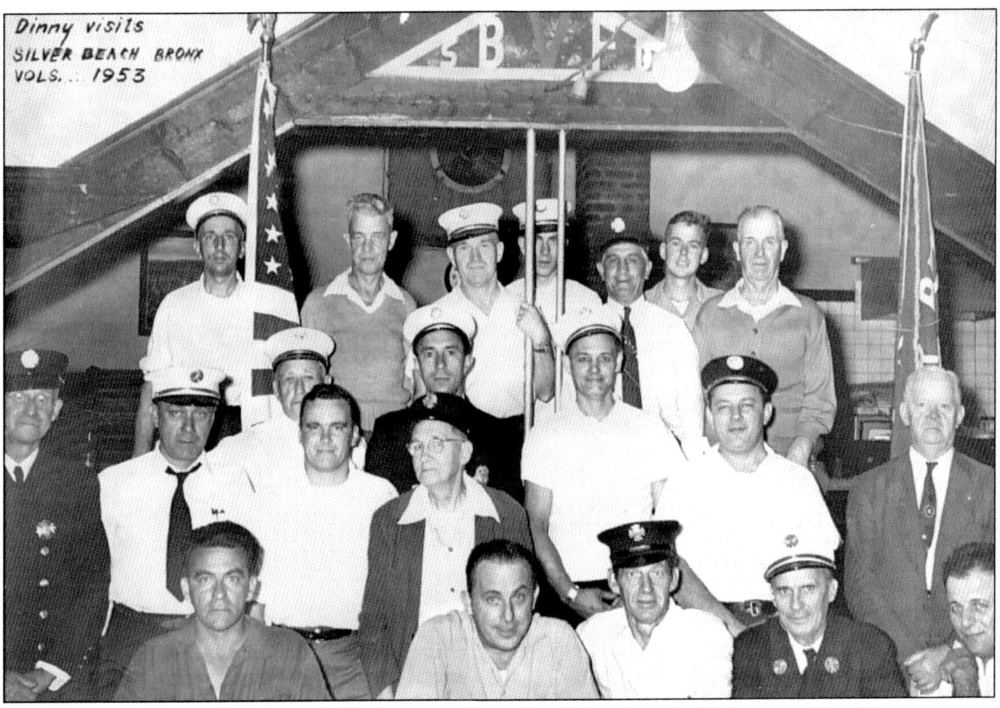

Arthur Seifert provided this 1953 photograph of the Silver Beach Volunteer Fire Department.

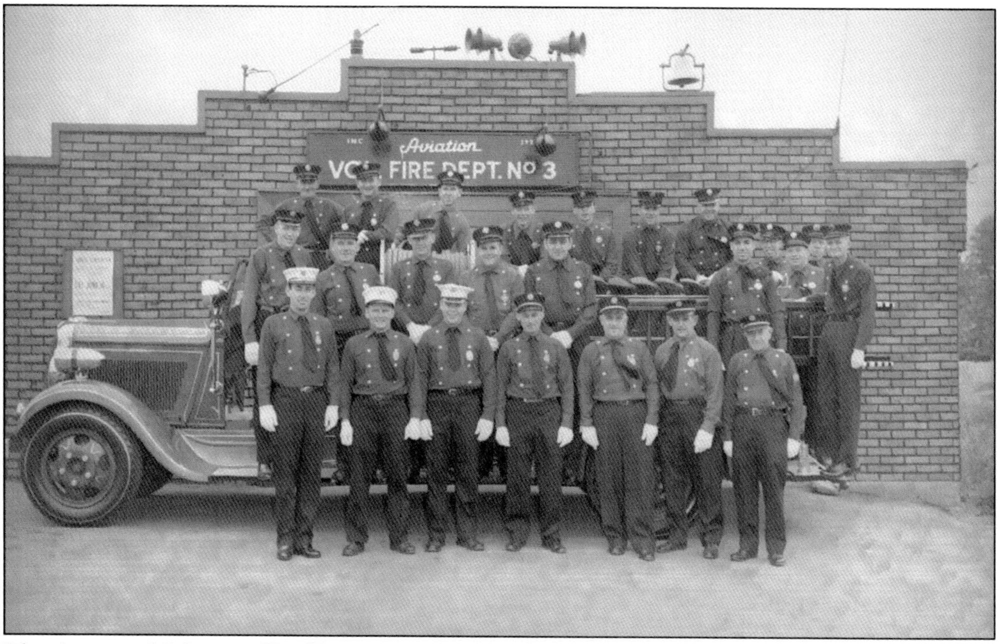

The Aviation Volunteer Fire Department No. 3 of Clason Point poses in this 1952 photograph. The fire truck is a 1936 Dodge, which they acquired in 1949. (Photograph courtesy of the Seifert Collection.)

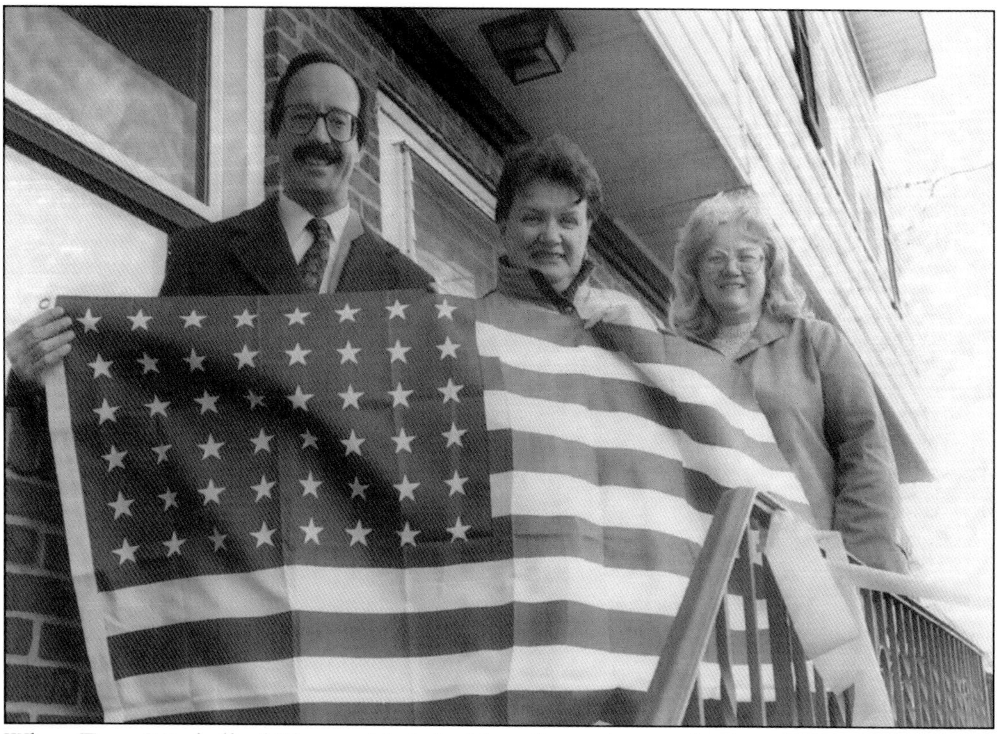

When Terry Mitchell of Throggs Neck had her flag stolen in the late 1980s, Congressman Elliot Engel came to her assistance and provided a new one. Seen here are, from left to right, Elliot Engel, Terry Mitchell, and Peggy Vega of the Throggs Neck Home Owners Association.

City councilwoman June Eisland, at left, had fought for better lighting at the Pelham Bay subway station in 1987. Seen here are, from left to right, June Eisland, Anna Cappel of the Transportation Disabled Committee, Harry Marx, Kim Mazza, Sally Fassler, Philip McGrade (pointing), and Jim Slender. McGrade, a Transit Authority engineer, was pointing out other planned improvements, such as escalators and elevators.

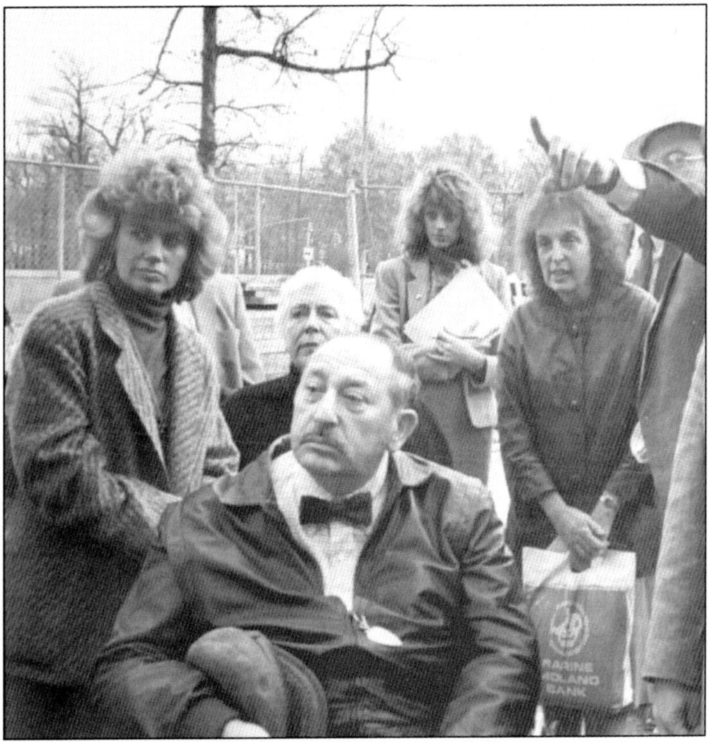

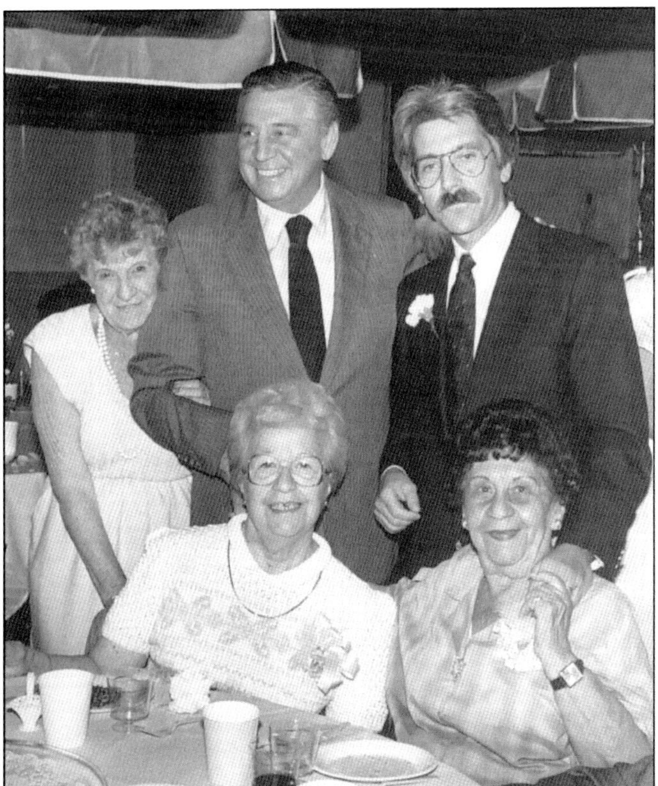

Councilman Jerry Crispino and William Frohlich, president of Beth Abraham Hospital, pose with volunteers Rose Arbeitman, Teresa DeSimone, and Eleanor DeMilta at a volunteer luncheon in the late 1980s.

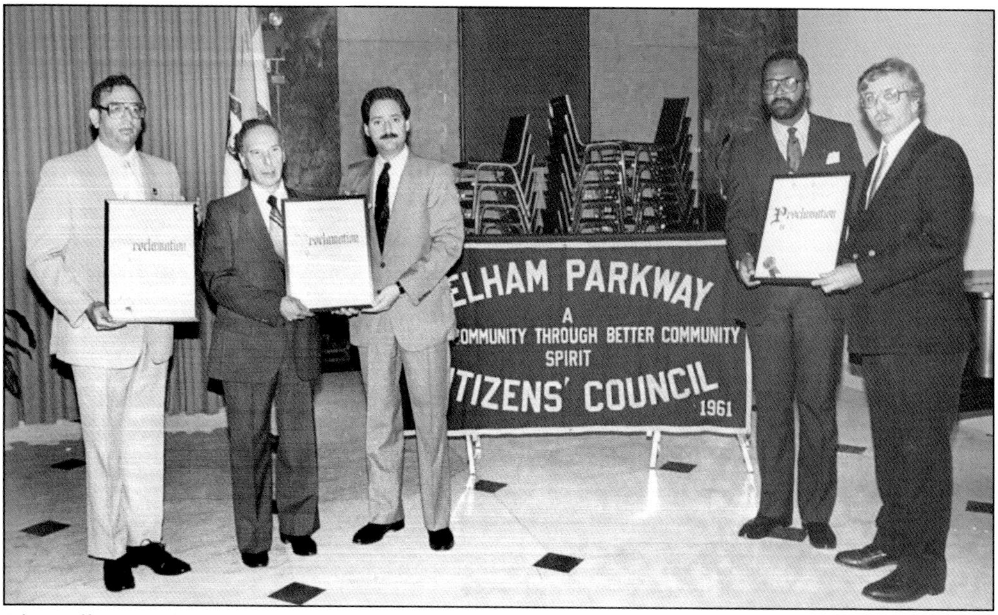

The Pelham Parkway Citizens' Council was established in 1961. This photograph presents the celebration of POW-MIA Day in the late 1980s.

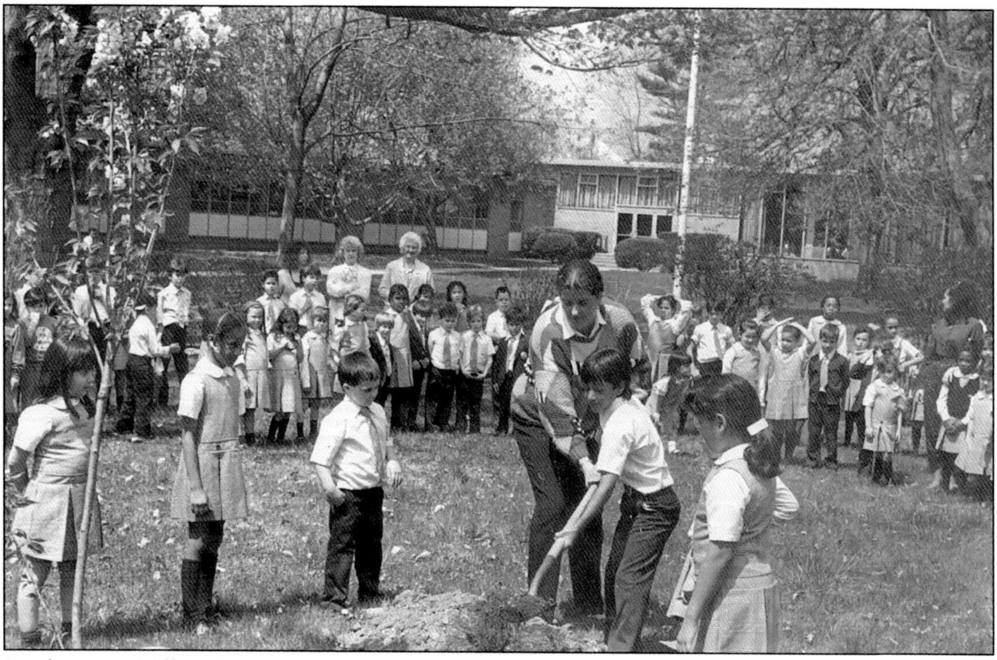

Students at Villa Marie Academy on Country Club Road learn the importance of natural pollution control as they plant a tree on their grounds during the mid-1980s.

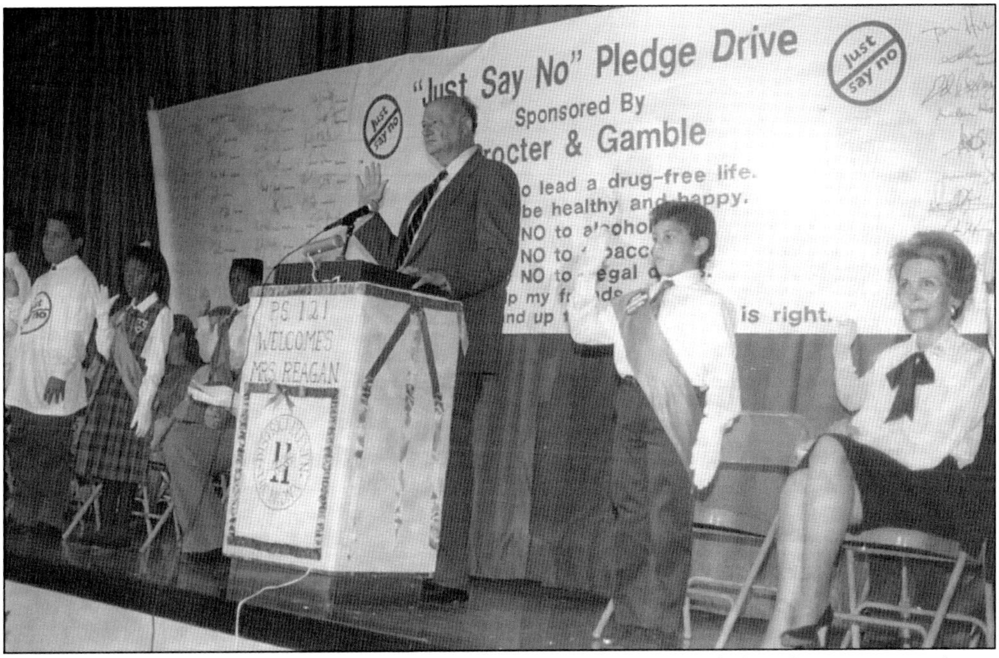

P.S. 121 at 1250 Arnow Avenue presented a "Just Say No" pledge drive against drugs. Mayor Edward Koch is at the podium, and First Lady Nancy Reagan is seated at right.

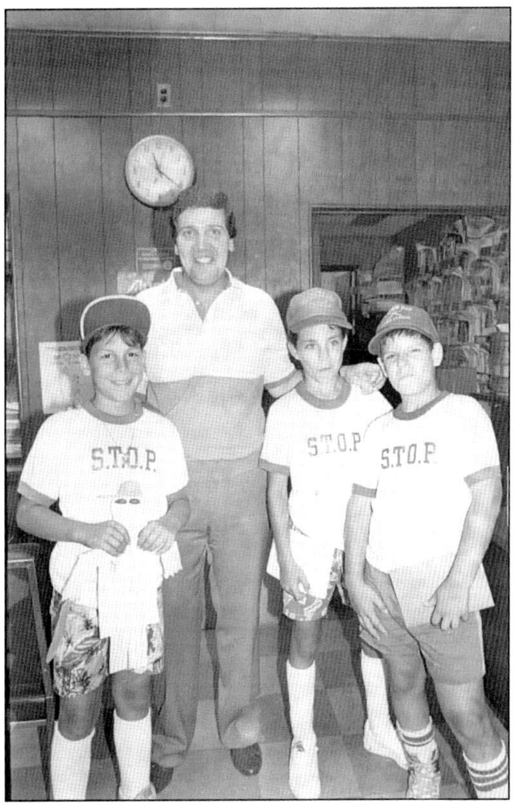

Services Through Organized People (STOP) has sponsored after-school programs at P.S. 14 and P.S. 71, in addition to their numerous other activities over the past 25 years. Seen here are, from left to right, Frank Lattera, Vinny Tolentino, Joseph Coniceloi, and Anthony Ardis.

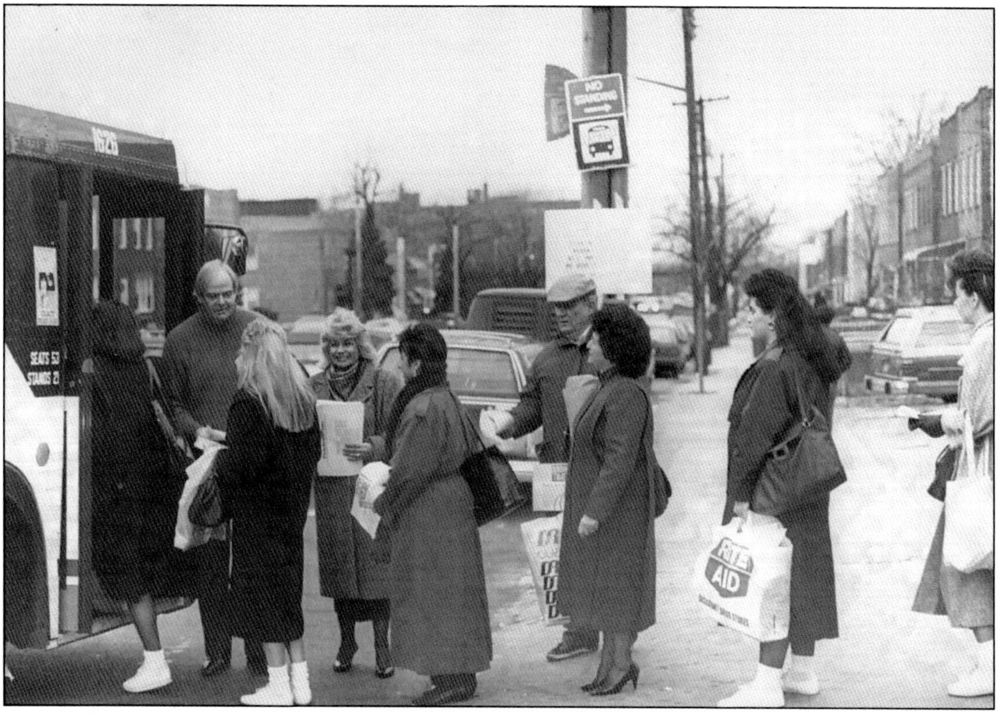

Assemblyman John Dearie fought against a raise in express bus fares in this photograph. He and his two assistants, Fran Mahony and Jim McQuade, are handing our literature at Randall and East Tremont Avenues during the mid-1980s.

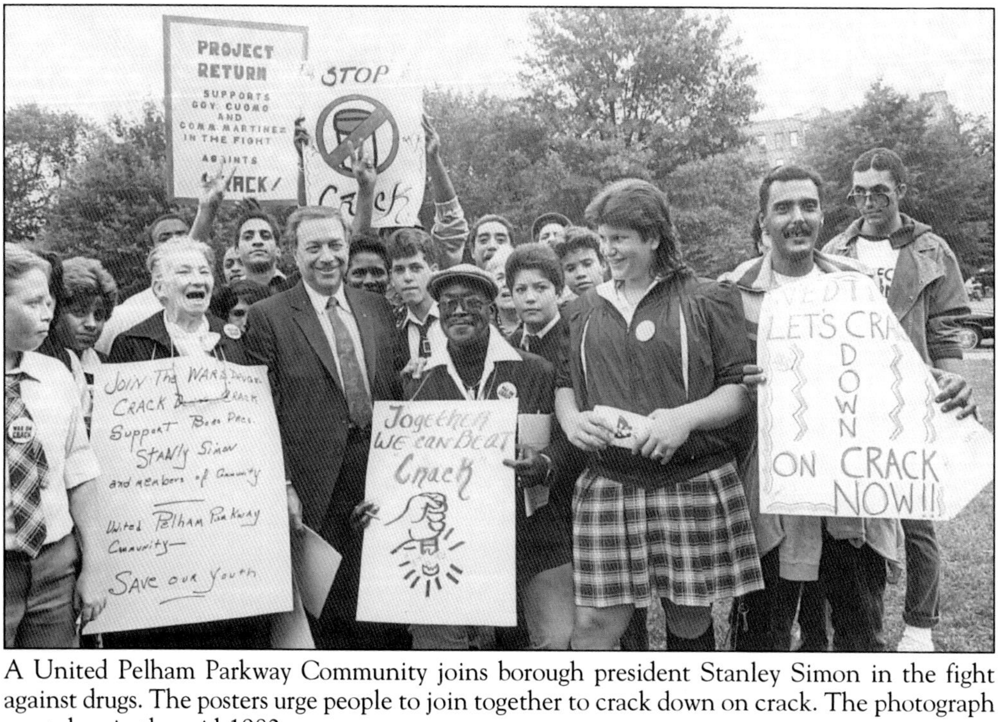

A United Pelham Parkway Community joins borough president Stanley Simon in the fight against drugs. The posters urge people to join together to crack down on crack. The photograph was taken in the mid-1980s.

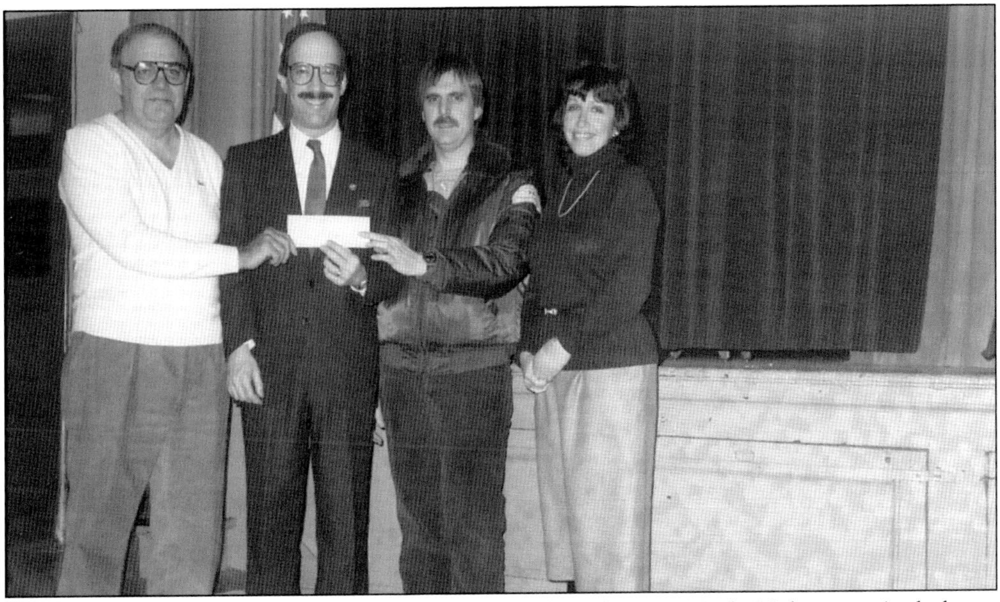

Congressman Elliot Engel presents a check to the Throggs Neck Volunteer Ambulance Corps on behalf of the Northeast Bronx Community Association. Seen here are, from left to right, Neil Cucinello, Engel, Ian Cope, and Debby Linhardt. The photograph was taken in December of 1989.

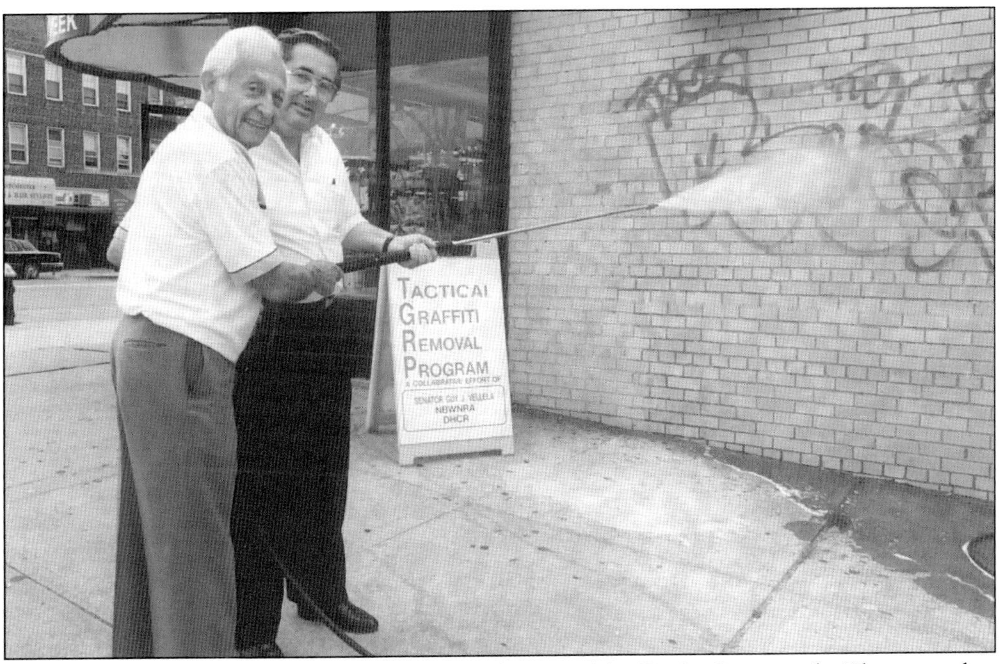

The Eastchester Civic Association was formed in 1925 by Emile Cavanaugh. The name has since been changed to the Chester Civic Improvement Association, Inc. Lou Salvati and Senator Guy Velella join hands in this picture of a graffiti removal program at Eastchester and Mace Avenues. As a historical note, there was an earlier organization called the Chester Taxpayers' Alliance that was presided over by Henry Jarvis, *c.* 1916. This photograph was taken in the late 1990s.

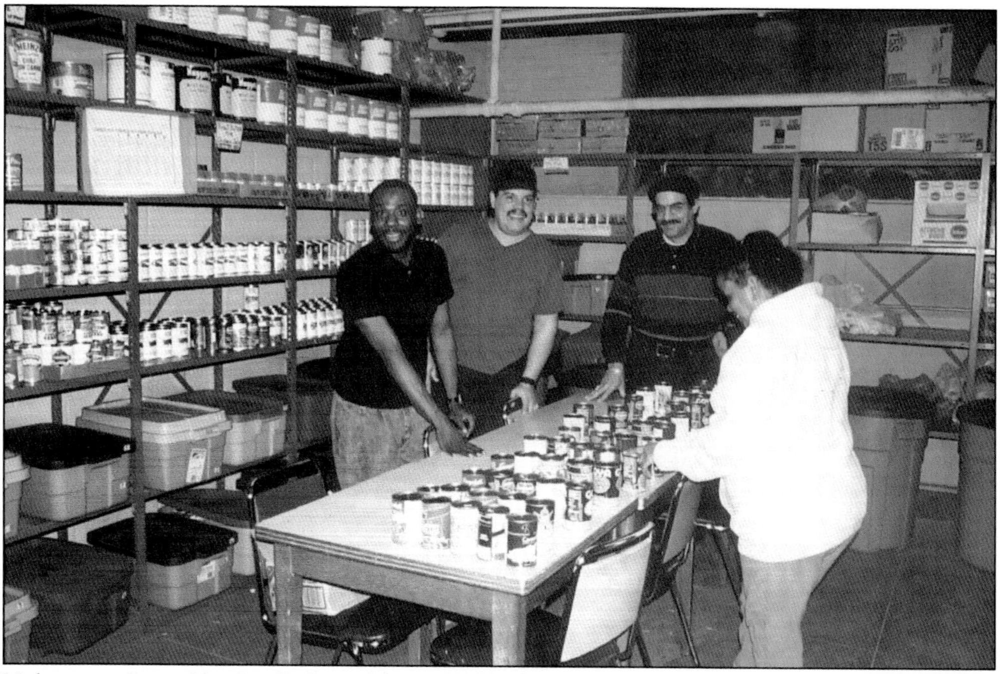

Volunteers Jean Charles, Robert Alicia, Wilfred Cotto, and Sonia Large of the East Bronx Hunger Program received foodstuffs from Rev. Dennis Winslow at Castle Hill Avenue and Unionport Road for Christmas distribution in 1995.

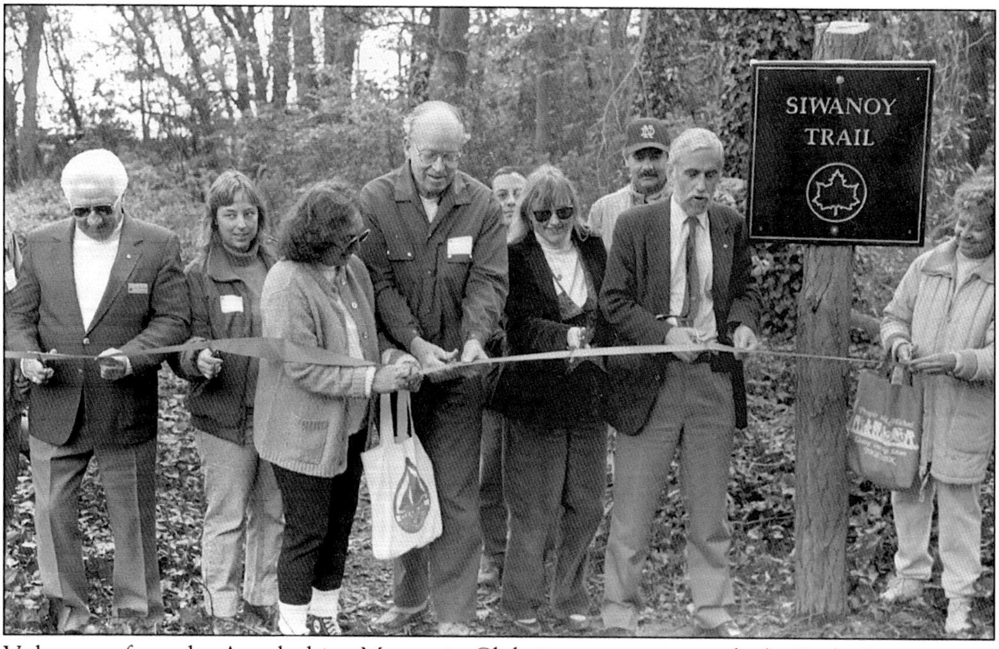

Volunteers from the Appalachian Mountain Club, in cooperation with the Parks Department, helped create the six-mile long Siwanoy Trail near the Bartow-Pell Mansion in Pelham Bay Park. Parks commissioner Henry Stern is shown closest to the sign in this 1989 photograph of the ribbon-cutting ceremony. Bronx parks commissioner James Ryan is at the far left, and community activist Jorge Santiago is among those in the background.

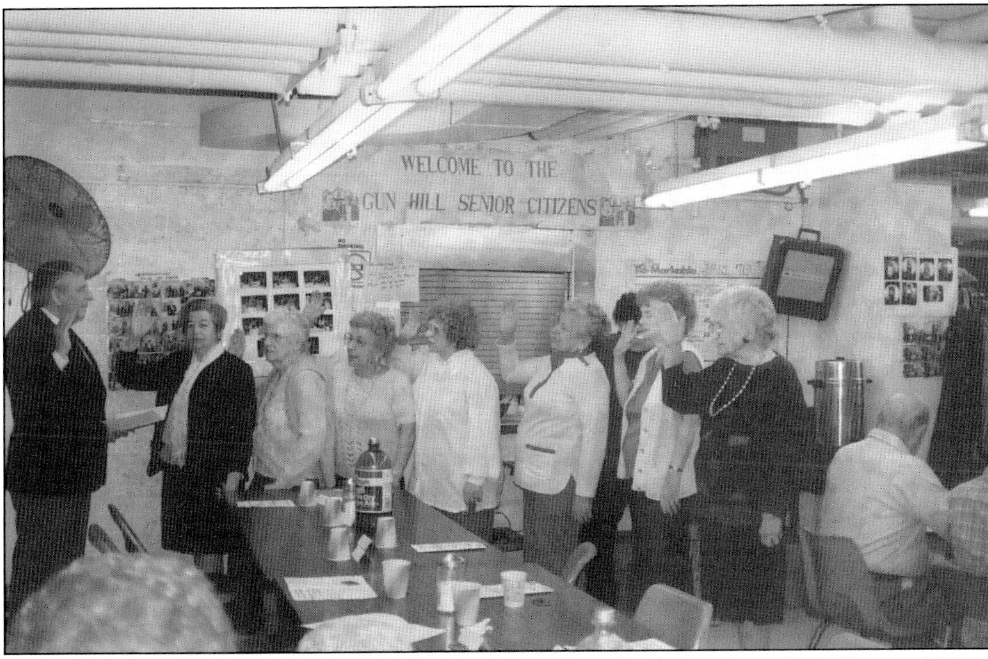

Councilman Jarry Crispino installs the executive board of the Gun Hill Senior Citizen Center on Holland Avenue on January 24, 1990. Seen here are, from left to right, as follows: Jerry Crispino, Bernice Pomilla, Sylvia Steinfield, Rose Carlantone, Ann Colucci, E. Kopf, Mary Petelli, and Ida Meinstein. Not shown in this photograph are F. Adams, Rose Calio, Annette DeLuca, Dorothy Pappas, and Dr. A. Hecht (the director).

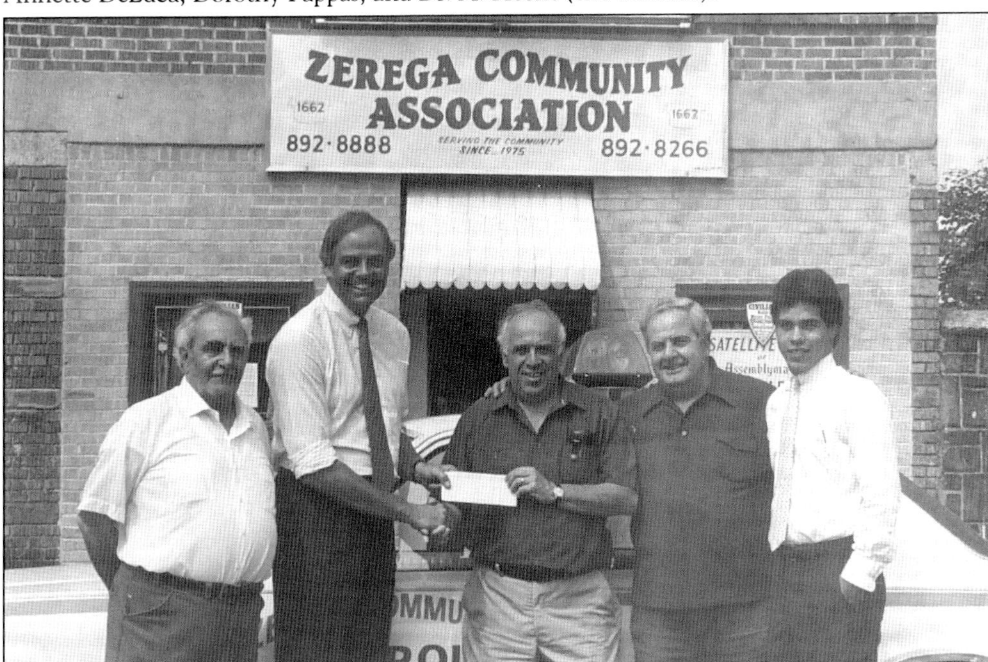

The Zerega Community Association was established in 1975. This photograph was taken in 1982 and shows assemblyman John Dearie presenting a check for their community patrol.

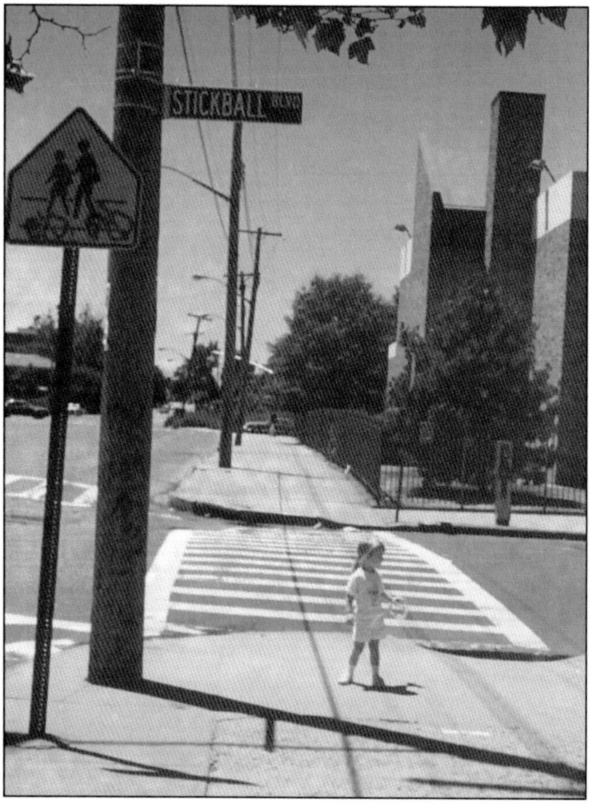

The author took this picture of Stickball Boulevard in 1988, at Randall Avenue next to the Kipps Bay Boys Club. It was named to honor the ball game of that designation. The little girl in the foreground is the author's daughter Erin.

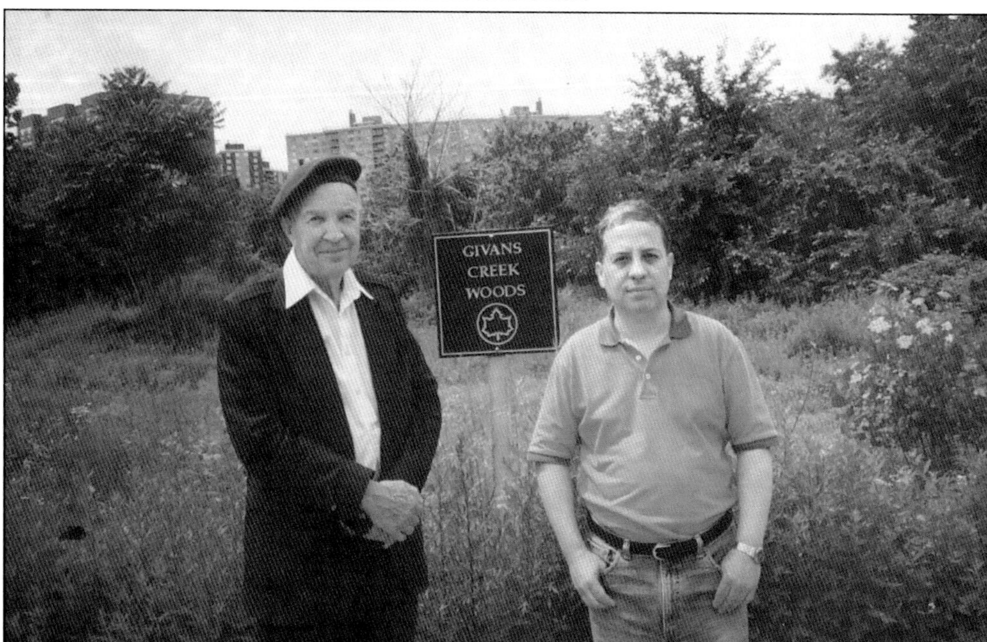

Bronx historian John McNamara, left, is shown with Jorge Santiago, a community activist and environmentalist who worked on the preservation and dedication of Givens Creek Woods. The occasion was recorded on June 22, 1997. The north end of Co-op City is in the background.

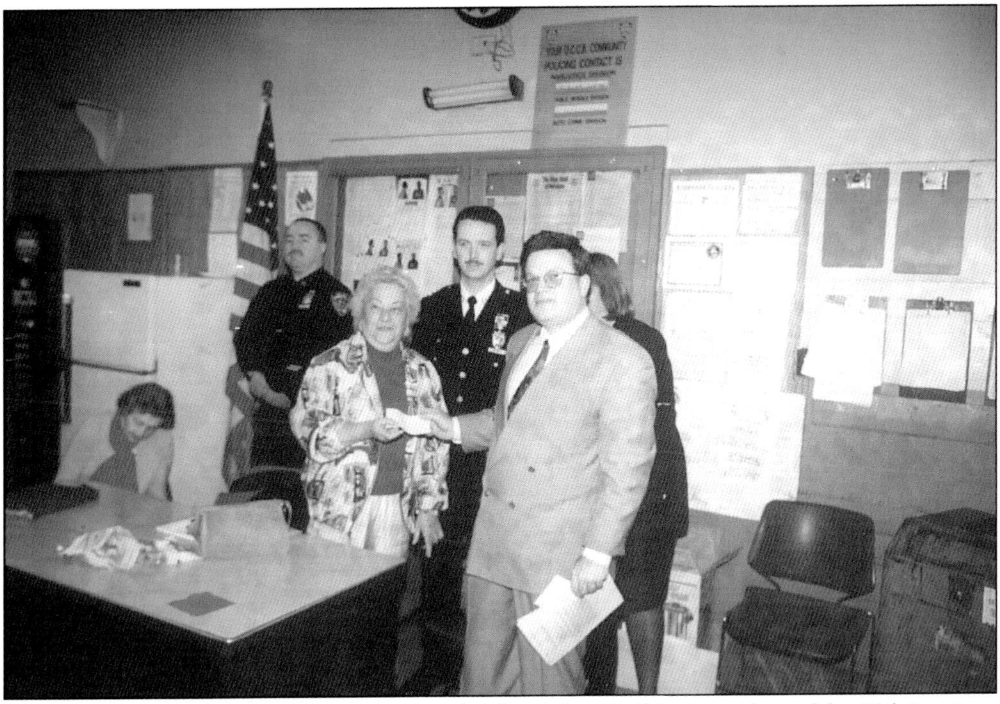

Assemblyman Stephen Kaufman presents a check to Marge Jeffries, president of the 45th Precinct Community Council. Police Officer Dan Cotter and Captain Pfifer look on.

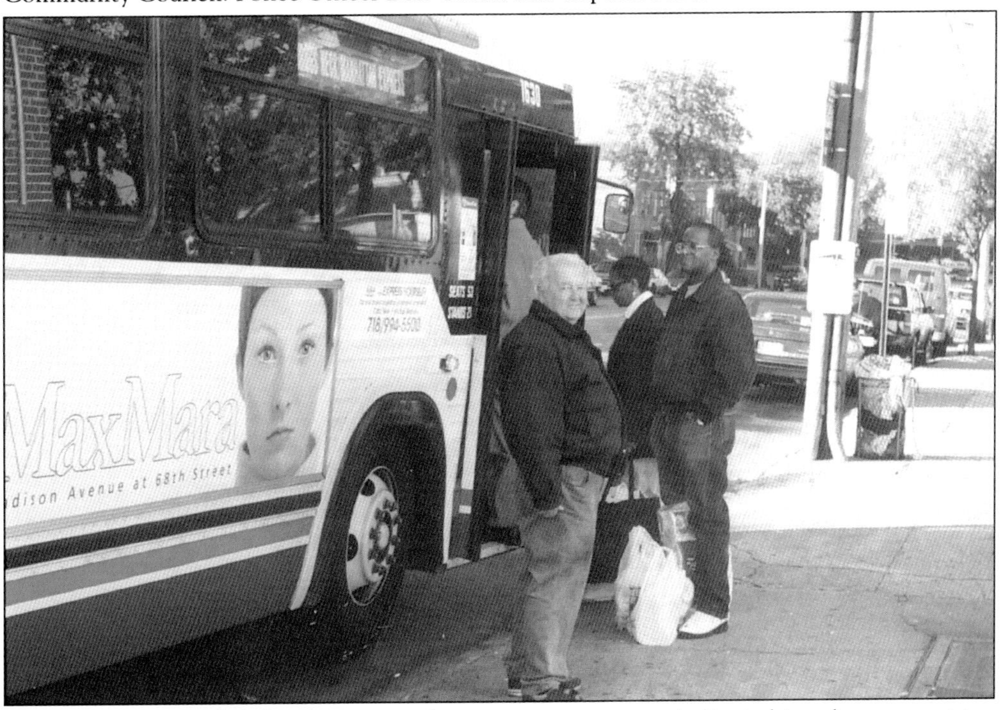

Paul Stewart, at the left, has been a comfort to numerous young ladies in his volunteer position at Randall and East Tremont Avenues, where he meets and greets passengers boarding the express bus to Manhattan. The photograph was taken on October 17, 1998.

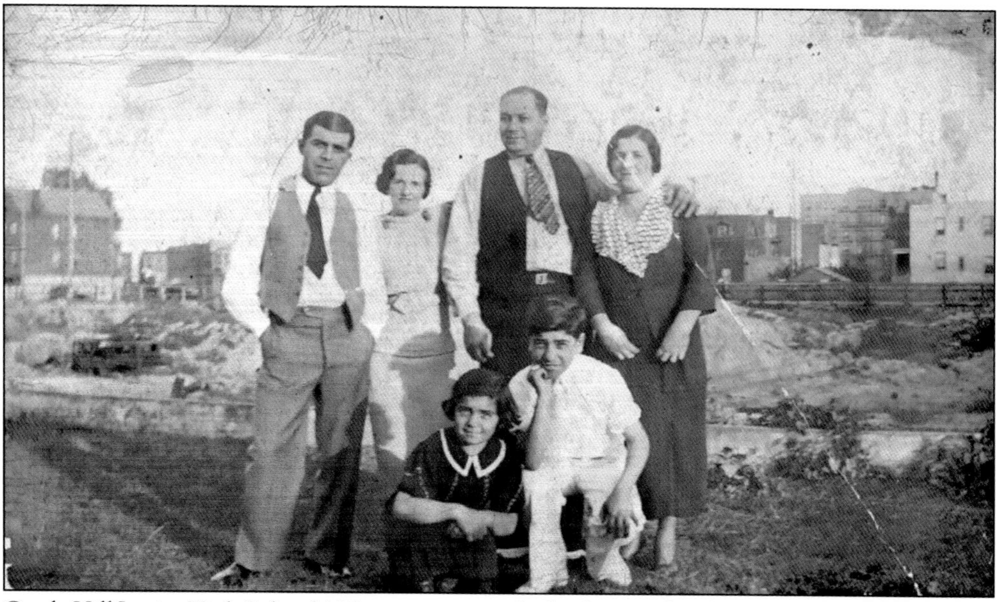

Castle Hill Junior High School 127 now occupies the background in this 1930s photograph taken on Purdy Street looking east. Castle Hill Avenue would be at the left, and St. Raymond Avenue would be at the extreme right. Pictured here are, from left to right, Tony and Charlotte Ferrara, Frank and Jenny Lisanti, and (in front) the two children, May Lisanti and Emil Ferrara.

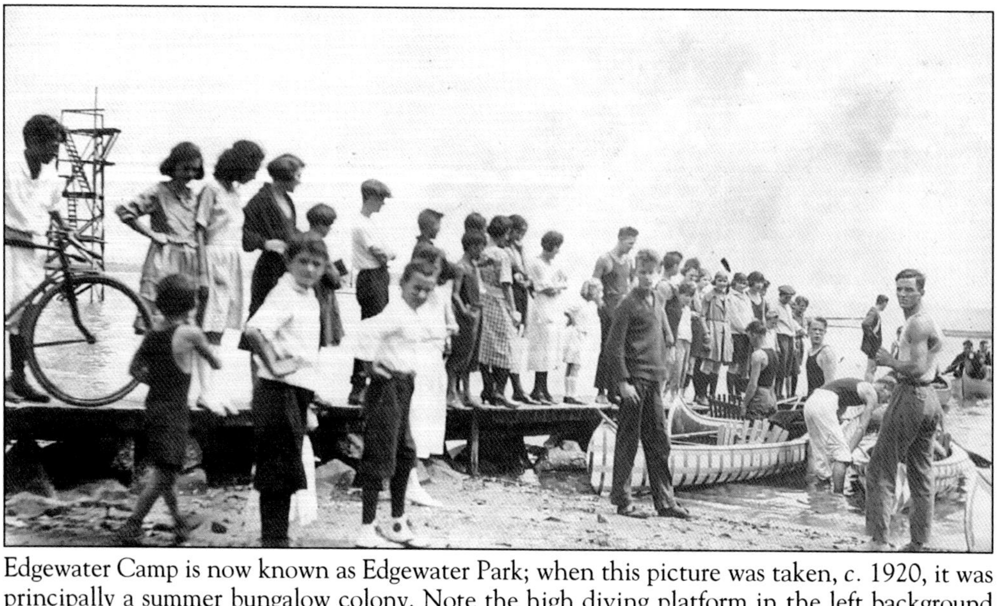

Edgewater Camp is now known as Edgewater Park; when this picture was taken, *c.* 1920, it was principally a summer bungalow colony. Note the high diving platform in the left background and the canoes at right. Some young men are sporting knickers, and all are wearing shirts.

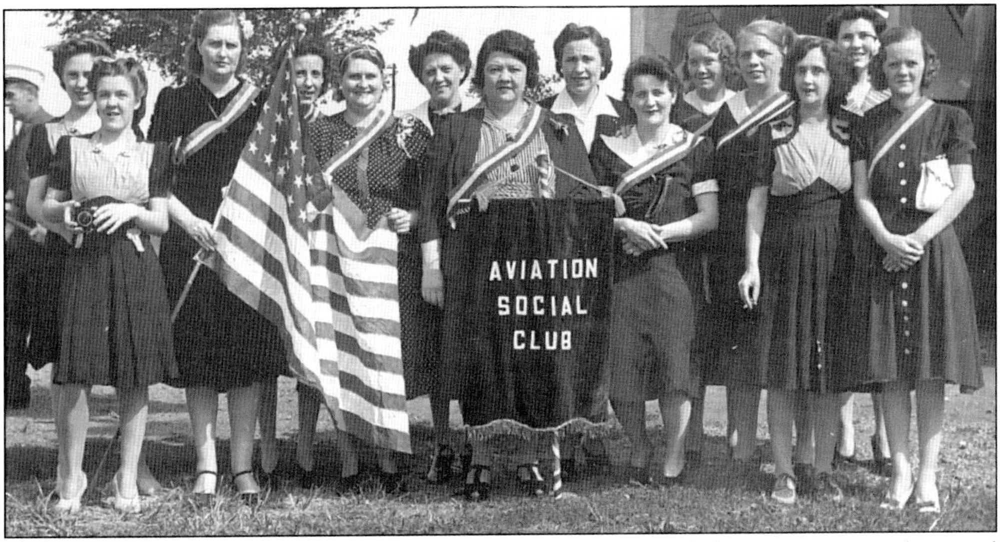

The Aviation Volunteer Fire Co. was established in 1923. The ladies soon organized a social club as an adjunct. This photograph from the Seifert Collection was taken in the mid-1940s in front of their firehouse on Clason Point.

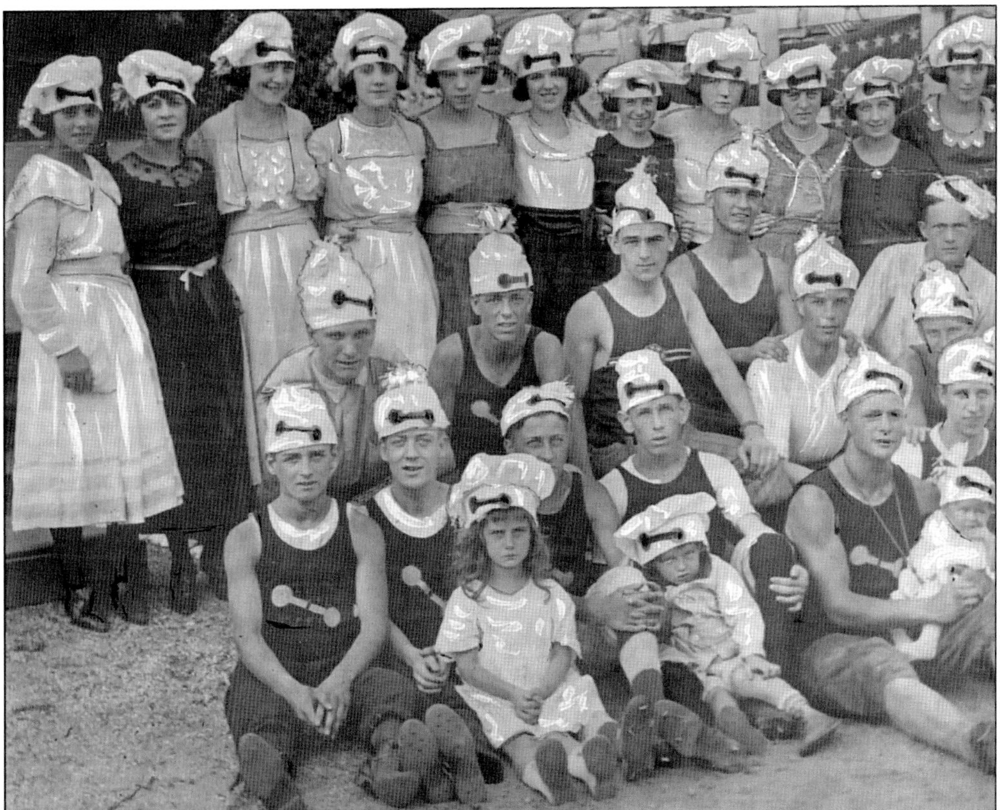

The Dumbells was a social and sport club at Higgs Beach during the 1920s. Among those to be found in this picture from the Seifert Collection are Bernie O'Connell, the Kiesel boys, Wil Reihn, and Frank Crocus. Higgs Beach, by the way, is now known as Harding Park.

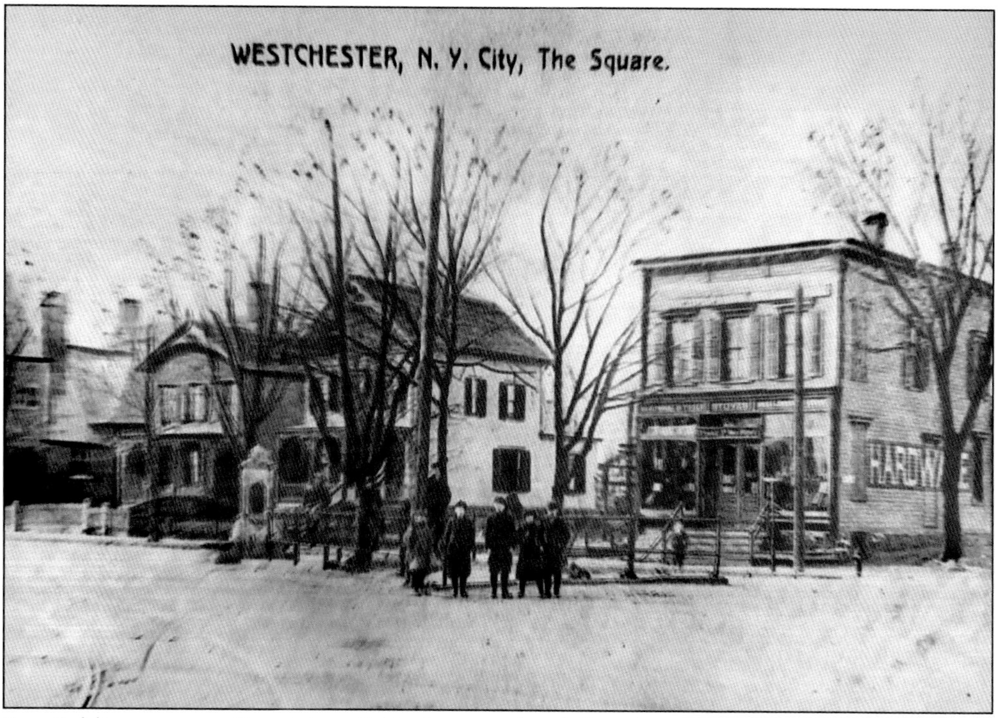

Ron Schliessman supplied this *c.* 1900 photograph of Westchester Square. The hardware store at the right was Van Riper's and was just south of Benson Street. The two houses to the left of the store are private homes, and the next building is the Huntington Free Library. When Lane Avenue was paved, the Cooley Fountain, toward the left, was moved across the street. The fountain was a source of refreshment for horses in these pre-auto days.

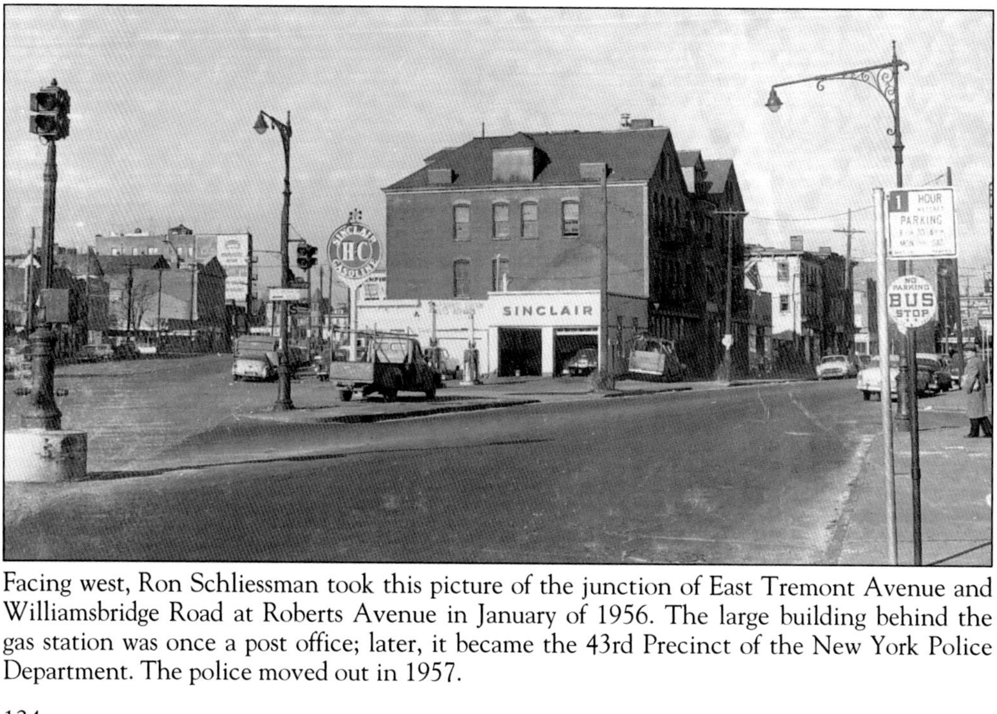

Facing west, Ron Schliessman took this picture of the junction of East Tremont Avenue and Williamsbridge Road at Roberts Avenue in January of 1956. The large building behind the gas station was once a post office; later, it became the 43rd Precinct of the New York Police Department. The police moved out in 1957.

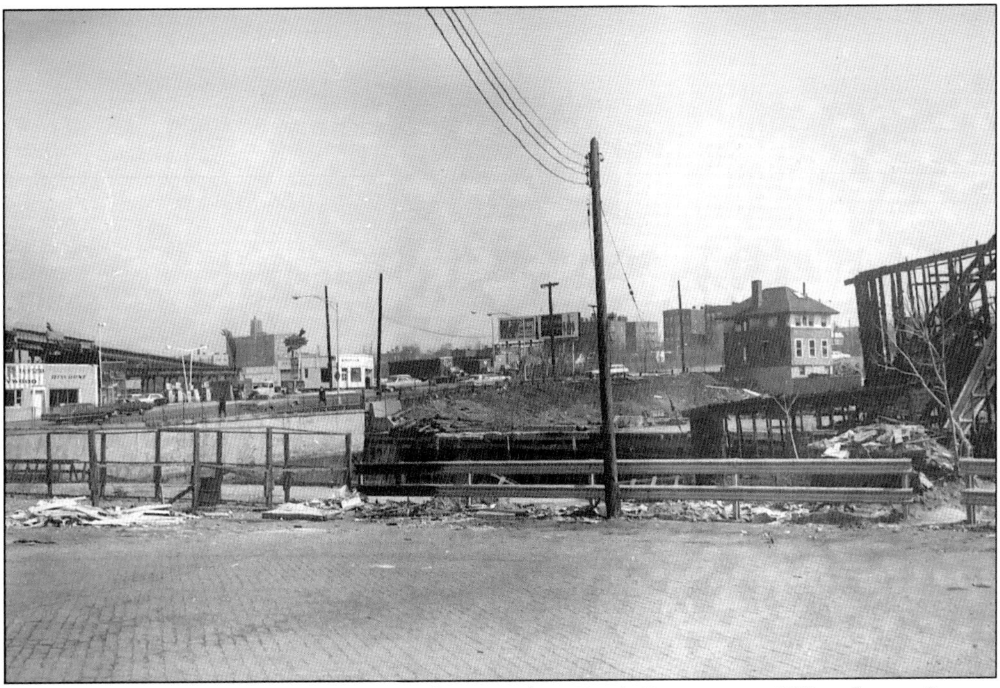

Ron Schliessman snapped this historic photograph at Dock Street east of Westchester Square on April 7, 1968. He was standing at the junction of Dock and Kirk Streets. Tremont Avenue is at the left. Note the el and the Appleton building, both toward the left. Ron was looking east over Westchester Creek toward the old Schildwachter Building on the east side of the creek, which is predominately visible to the right of the utility pole in the foreground.

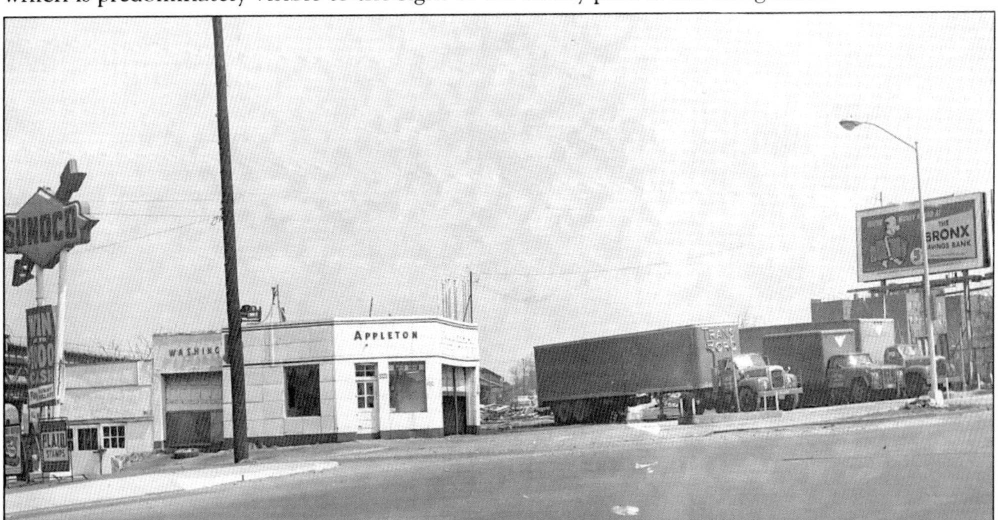

Historical photographer Ron Schliessman took this photograph of the Appleton Building on East Tremont Avenue, east of Westchester Square, on April 7, 1968. Tan Place (now Little League Place) is at the left side of the building; it joins Tremont to Westchester Avenue. The elevated line of the IRT is visible at the extreme left.

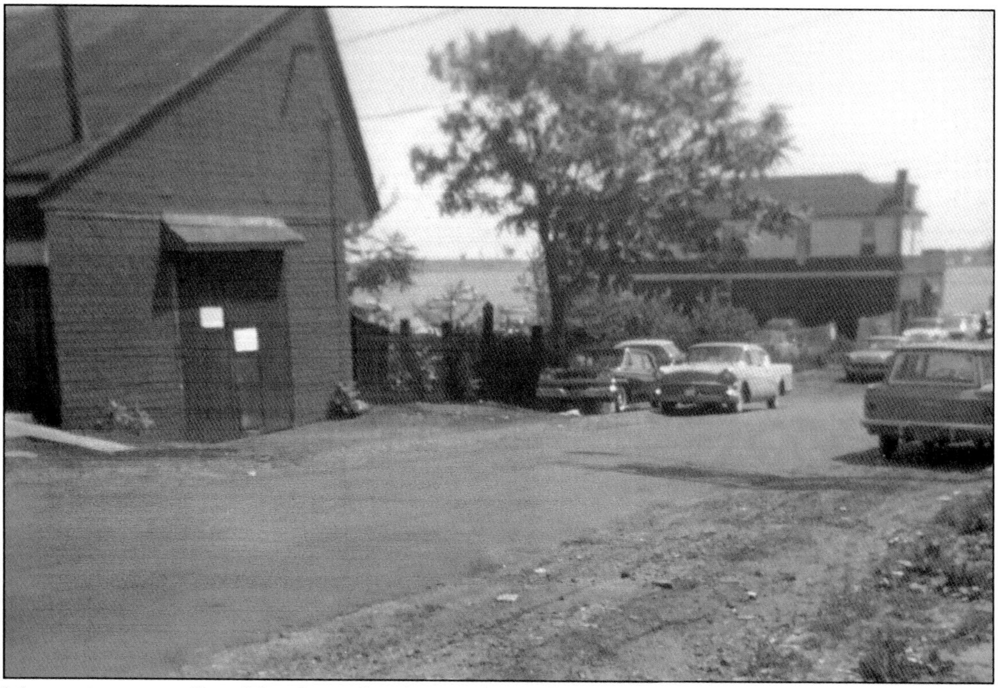

Many visitors to City Island are familiar with Fordham Street because the old schoolhouse, which is now home to the City Island Historical Society, is located there. It also leads to the Hart Island ferry slip. This 1963 photograph was supplied by John McNamara.

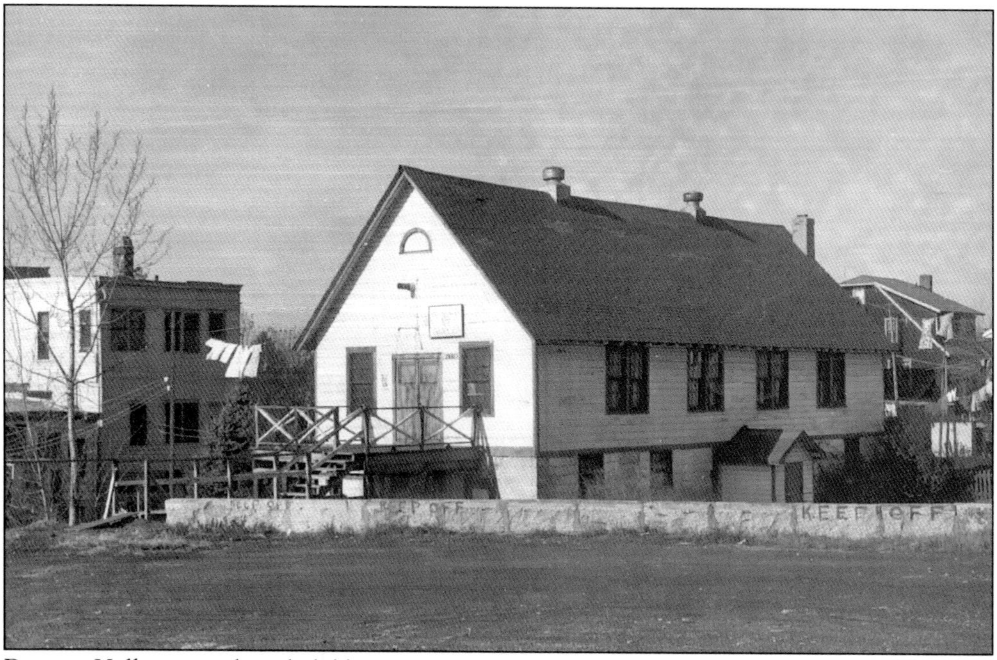

Deering Hall was a political clubhouse prior to World War II; it faces Eastern Boulevard (now Bruckner). Nearby Revere Avenue was still called Harriet Place by oldtimers, who named the hall for Alderman James A. Deering. The building is now home to the Knights of Columbus. The picture was taken by Ron Schliessman on December 10, 1956.

The tepees outside the Indian Museum's storage building at Bruckner Boulevard and Middletown Road outlasted over three decades of winter weather, because they were made of concrete. This photograph was taken on October 23, 1988 by the author.

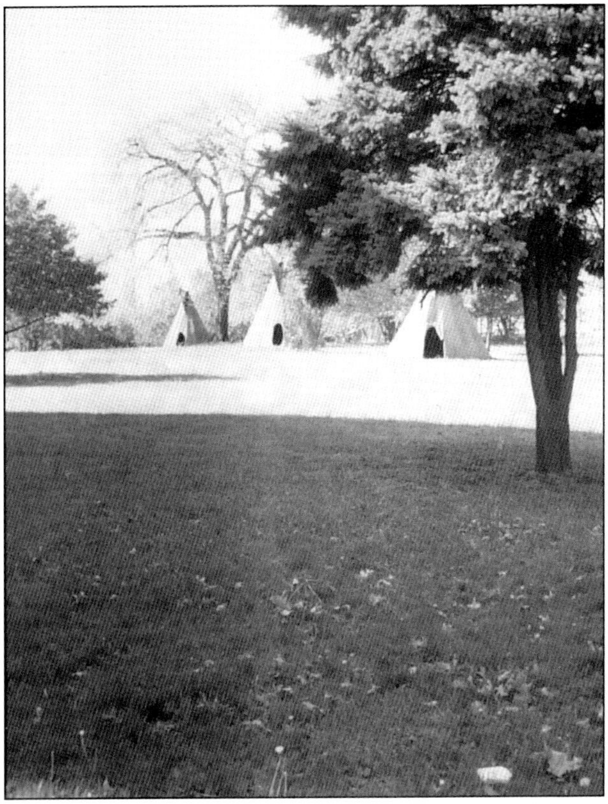

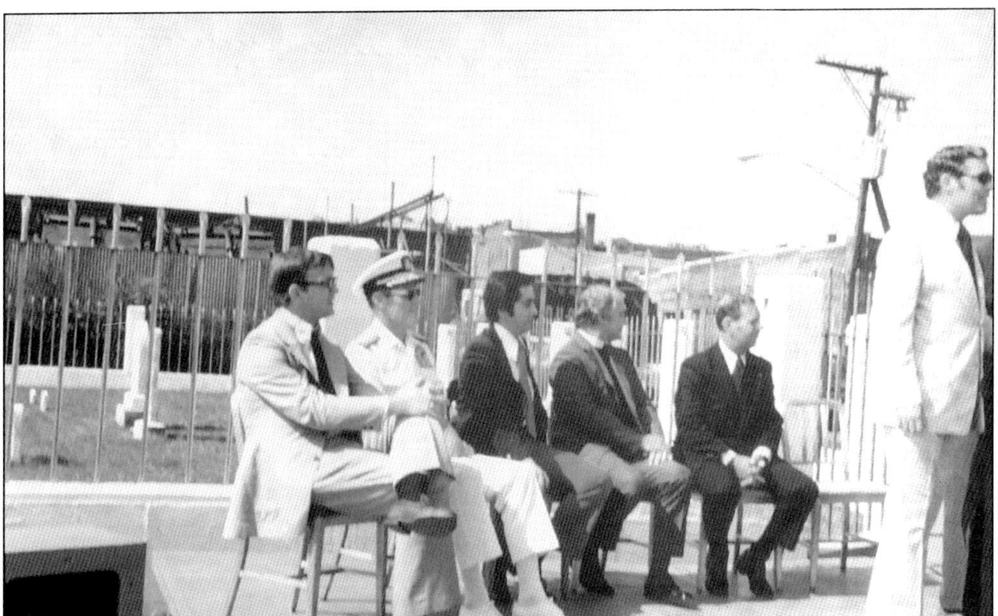

The Ferris Family Cemetery on Commerce Street, east of Westchester Avenue, was re-dedicated on September 10, 1974. Note the granite grave markers in the background. (Photograph courtesy of Ron Schliessman.)

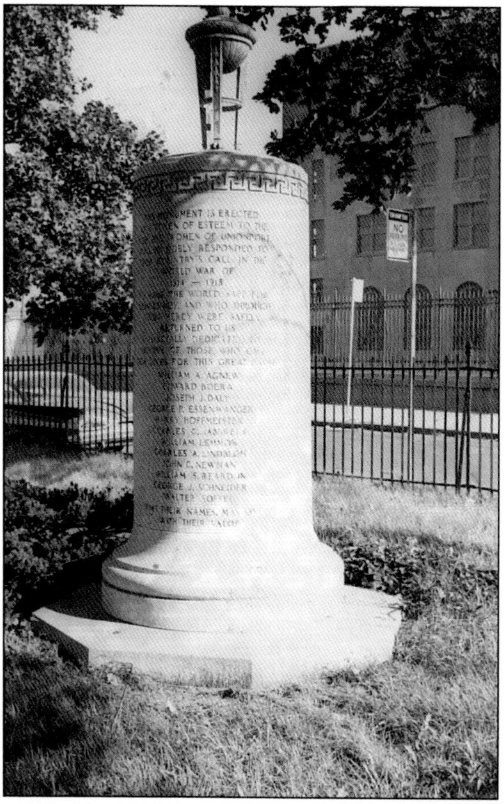

Edward Wolf took this photograph of the World War I monument to veterans of Unionport in 1962. It is located at the Cross Bronx Expressway and Castle Hill Avenue.

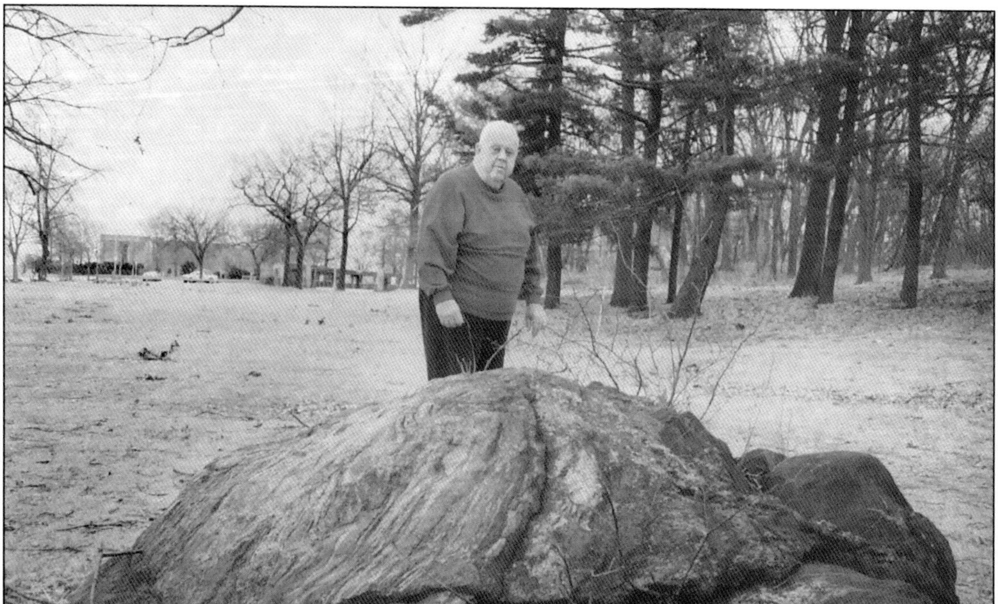

The author took this picture of Skippy Lane of the City Island Historical Society on February 7, 1999. He is standing in front of Jack's Rock. Very little of the rock shows today due to the fill from the creation of Orchard Beach. The Long Island Sound would be in the far background, and the beach parking lot is out of sight at the left.